Jean —

I thought you might
enjoy this. Happy birthday

Roy

April 29, 2002

WEST POINTERS
AND EARLY
WASHINGTON

The Contributions of
U.S. Military Academy Graduates
to the Development of the
Washington Territory,
from the Oregon Trail to the Civil War
1834-1862

Edited by

Major General John A. Hemphill, USA-Ret.

and

Robert C. Cumbow

**The West Point Society
of Puget Sound, Inc.**
Seattle, Washington
1992

Library of Congress Cataloging-in-Publication Data

West Pointers and Early Washington

Includes index.

1. Washington, State of — History
2. Northwest, Pacific — History
3. United States Military Academy (West Point) — History

I. The West Point Society of Puget Sound, Inc.   II. Hemphill, John A., MG, USA-Ret., 1927-
III. Cumbow, Robert C., 1946-

Library of Congress Catalog Card Number and ISBN Pending

CONTENTS

Appendix

ILLUSTRATIONS

WEST POINTERS
AND EARLY
WASHINGTON

Dedication

The West Point Society of Puget Sound
is proud to dedicate this book to two members of the Class of 1931
who have been the prime movers of our society.

Brigadier General Charles Coburn Smith, Jr. (U.S. Army, Retired)

and the late

Colonel Charles North Howze (U.S. Air Force, Retired)

FOREWORD

The history of the state of Washington is filled with stories of frontiersmen, loggers, railroad tycoons, gold-seekers, engineers, and adventurers. In this fascinating mix, graduates of West Point have played a major role in shaping what Washington has become, beginning in its territorial period and continuing throughout its 100-plus years of statehood. We focus here on the early years.

The West Point Society of Puget Sound, inspired by the celebration of Washington's centennial, prepared the historical and biographical sketches collected here to memorialize and honor the role that West Point graduates have played in the early history of our state. The reader will discover a surprising breadth in the roles played by these men. The earliest was B. L. E. Bonneville, whose name remains familiar throughout the state. Another was the first Territorial Governor, Isaac Ingalls Stevens. The reader will see how the values of "Duty, Honor and Country" exemplified by these and other USMA graduates influenced their actions and molded their contributions to Washington state.

It is not surprising that many of the great engineering projects in our frontier territory and state were strongly influenced by USMA graduates. West Point was our nation's first engineering school, and its great early leader Sylvanus Thayer (USMA Class of 1808) went on to influence a generation of engineering teaching and to have a hand in establishing other engineering programs.

The superb quality of life we enjoy here has balanced a growing economy with a magnificent physical environment worth preserving. We're proud that West Pointers have played an important role in this achievement.

Richard R. Sonstelie
USMA Class of 1966
President
Puget Sound Power & Light Company
February 1992

PREFACE

This book was written by volunteers from the West Point Society of Puget Sound, a group of graduates of the United States Military Academy residing in the Pacific Northwest.

We are proud to have worn cadet grey uniforms and to be graduates of the United States Military Academy, the great national university located at West Point, New York. West Pointers have served our country since the first cadet, Joseph Gardner Swift of Maine, graduated in 1802, to serve with distinction as an engineer, both as an Army officer and in civilian life. In the War of 1812, Swift was recognized by a brevet promotion to brigadier general. At graduation, each cadet is assigned a distinctive "Cullum Number," designating a permanent place in the "Long Grey Line" that began with General Swift and extends through the latest class to graduate. The "Long Grey Line" is the symbol of bonding gained through sharing the regimen of cadet life in preparation for service to the nation.

In the spring of 1989, Richard R. Sonstelie (USMA Class of 1966), then President of the West Point Society of Puget Sound, initiated a study of West Pointer contributions to The Territory and State of Washington as the Society's project for the State's Centennial. That study resulted in this book. Many members of the Society knew that two West Pointers who became Presidents of the United States — Ulysses Simpson Grant (USMA Class of 1843) and Dwight David Eisenhower (USMA Class of 1915) — had served here in Washington. Initial research revealed that the first Governor, Isaac Ingalls Stevens, was the brilliant first graduate of the Class of 1839. The last graduate of the Class of 1846, George Edward Pickett, whose famous attack at the Battle of Gettysburg is studied by all cadets, received the "thanks" of the Territory of Washington Legislature before the Civil War began. But these turned out to be only the "tip of the iceberg." The first West Pointers came along with the first settlers, before the Territory of Washington existed. And they never stopped coming. West Pointers have contributed importantly to Washington through its territorial years and up to the present day, pursuing military careers; participating as businessmen and professionals in the state's economy; and living in retirement after military and civilian careers. The names, the lives, the contributions were too immense to cover in a single publication. The book that was to survey West Pointers' role in nearly 150 years of Washington history became the smaller volume you now hold, focusing on those first West Pointers who set the tone for the growth of Washington in the ten years following congressional creation of the Territory of Washington in 1853.

This first decade — 1853 through 1862 — was a traumatic time. A growing number of settlers and the implementation of governmental policies conflicted with the traditional ways of the Indians. West Pointers were prominent participants in the clashes resulting from this conflict of cultures. Of the West Pointers serving in the Territory during this ten-year period, nine were chosen to be the subjects of monographs in this book, to honor their prominence in

Territorial history.

The monographs by themselves are limited in scope, and present only segments of the events of this troubled decade. To provide the reader with the setting, the book begins with a historical story titled "A Decade In Washington Territory, 1853-1862," which serves as the backdrop against which the monograph subjects appear as the major characters of the drama. After a brief introduction, the historical story introduces the reader to the Indian tribes and selected Indian leaders who were also key players in the unfolding drama. The historical story continues with a look at the Pacific Northwest before there was a Territory of Washington and ends as both the Territory and West Pointers are touched by the Civil War. The book is intended as both reference and narrative. The armchair reader will profit most by reading the historical story first, as a background to the monographs.

The efforts of many people made this book possible. The monograph authors devoted many hours to research and writing. I sincerely appreciate the valuable contributions of Dianna Salsbury and Lorri Anne Hochhaus of Puget Sound Power & Light Co., who provided word processing and copying services; and Sandy Cottrell of Shannon & Wilson, Inc., who performed the drafting and other work necessary for the preparation of maps and charts.

My personal thanks go to editor Robert C. Cumbow of Puget Power for accepting my idiosyncrasies amplified by the pressures to down-size the original effort. Without his talents, determination, and devotion, this book would not have been completed. Also, I wish to thank Colonel Robert L. Bradley, Class of 1949, a former United States Military Academy Associate Professor of English, for reviewing my work.

Recognition goes to a former instructor at both the United States Military and Air Force Academies, Colonel John J. Neuer (USMA Class of June, 1943), for his advice and assistance in reviewing the book.

All of my efforts in the preparation of this book are in gratitude to the United States Military Academy for providing my education and foundation for service to our country. May West Point's "Long Grey Line" continue. The place just before mine is now in "ghostly assemblage": Cullum Number 18228, John Wendell Buckstead of South Dakota, died July 18, 1987, in a single-car accident on a wet State of Washington road while looking for a home to purchase. John had just arrived to take an important position with PACCAR, Inc. of Bellevue, Washington, but departed before he had the opportunity to join the West Point Society of Puget Sound.

John A. Hemphill
Major General, US Army, Ret.
USMA Class of 1951

THE SETTING

A DECADE OF WASHINGTON TERRITORY
1853-1862

In the fall of 1852, independent-minded people from north of the Columbia River in Oregon Territory became disenchanted with their Territorial Government in its new capital of Salem. Their representatives — 48 delegates from the Puget Sound and lower Columbia River areas — met on October 22, 1852, at Monticello, near the mouth of the Cowlitz River. A memorial was drawn up asking Congress to create a new territory named Columbia. This request was approved by Congress on March 2, 1853, with the name changed to Washington to honor the nation's first President and foremost hero.

Founded some 51 years earlier on March 16, 1802, the United States Military Academy at West Point, New York, had graduated 1,578 cadets when the Territory of Washington was created. About 700 West Pointers were serving in the Army in 1853.

From its inception, the purpose of the Military Academy has been to educate and qualify cadets for the Army officer corps. Beginning with the Class of 1818, the Military Academy initiated the first technically-oriented college education in the United States. Basically educated as civil engineers, West Pointers were to figure prominently in the nation's "Manifest Destiny," not only in military duties, but in economic development, business, and politics. Many made significant accomplishments that are forever etched in the history of the nation. The achievements of a number of West Pointers are an integral part of the history of the Territory and State of Washington.

This new Territory of Washington stretched all the way from the Pacific Ocean east to the Continental Divide between the 49th parallel on the north and the Territory of Oregon on the south. In 1859 (see map, "Boundaries of Washington Territory," page 10) a large area was added and then taken away in 1863, as Congress continued creating territories as precursors to states.

Immigrants to this new Territory started to arrive in 1844. Most came overland, a 2,000-mile journey across the continent. A few came by sea. In 1853, there were about 4,000 non-Indians, with fewer than 1,700 considered eligible to vote. Except for scattered mission and trading post settlements, the population was located in the region from the lower Columbia River north through Puget Sound. The weather was mild, comfortable even in the extremes of summer and winter, and plenty of rain fostered the growth of thick forests of tall trees, and promised sufficient moisture for good crops each year, drawing the immigrants to this area.

Fewer than two and a half times as many aboriginal "Indians" competed with the immigrants for space in this region. Most of the Indians lived east of the Cascade Range. Its ridge runs north and south, parallel to the Pacific Ocean shoreline, a few miles east of Puget Sound (see "Map of Places and Events,"

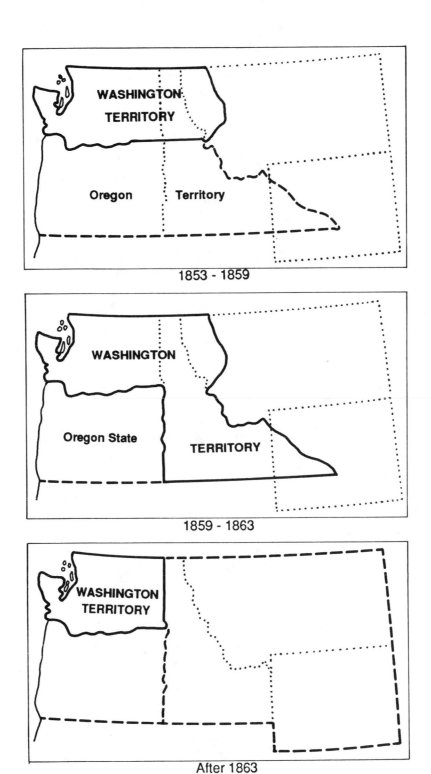

1853 - 1859

1859 - 1863

After 1863

BOUNDARIES OF WASHINGTON TERRITORY

endpages). With peaks towering above 10,000 feet, these mountains are a distinct dividing line between western and eastern Washington, serving as a barrier between inhabitants and weather systems. The Cascades cut off ocean moisture from going inland, creating semi-dry weather on their east side. This causes hot summers, cold winters, and sparse vegetation — less hospitable living conditions than on the mild west side. But in the 1850s, "blood was spilled" as the whites began to compete with the Indian for space in the vast eastern interior of the Territory of Washington.

West Pointers were already in the Territory of Washington when it was created. The first to arrive came as an adventurer in 1834; he returned some 18 years later to command all of the U.S. Army troops and forts in the Pacific Northwest. West Pointers led the first contingent of Army troops sent by the Government to ensure United States sovereignty over the land that became the Territory of Washington. They arrived on May 13, 1849.

By 1862, about 140 West Pointers had served in the Territory of Washington. Of these, nine are memorialized by monographs in this book: an adventurer, a political leader, a protector of Indian rights, a road builder, and several military commanders. Six of the nine became general officers in the Civil War; one was a territorial governor in addition to gaining general officer rank; two died before fulfilling their potential; all commanded men in battle. When in the Territory of Washington, these men ranged in age from recent West Point graduates just beginning their careers to those with years of leadership experience and American frontier service already behind them. These are the West Pointers whose monographs appear in this book:

WEST POINTER	UNITED STATES MILITARY ACADEMY CLASS
Benjamin Louis Eulalie Bonneville	1815
Issac Ingalls Stevens	1839
William Alloway Slaughter	1848
August Valentine Kautz	1852
Silas Casey	1826
George Wright	1822
Edward Jevnor Steptoe	1837
George Edward Pickett	1846
John Mullan, Jr.	1852

These men were but nine individual pieces in the puzzle of historical events. The following introductory story provides other pieces to help the reader understand the episodes of the monographs in historical context. The story begins with the aborigines or Indians, and then covers the United States claim to sovereignty over the Pacific Northwest, and the arrival of West Pointers to implement this sovereignty. Building on that foundation, the story covers political, economic, military, and other events and activities from the creation of Washington Territory in 1853 until the end of 1862, when only three West Pointers remained in the territory. The others had left — most of them to see action in the Civil War. Together, this story and the monographs that follow it explain why these nine West Pointers are etched indelibly into the history of Washington.

Indians of Washington Territory

The Territory of Washington in 1853 was a vast land, but it was not an empty land. The West Pointers found about 28-30,000 Indians of nine language families living in the Territory — and another major language family was added with the boundary change in 1859. These language families were divided into tribes. A few had large populations, such as the Nez Perce with 6,000 or the 3,000-member Yakima Tribe; but most consisted of 500 or fewer — especially after the white man's diseases ravaged bands, villages, sometimes an entire tribe. (The map "Language Families and Tribes," page 13, portrays the general location of the various language groups and tribes, and identifies the tribes belonging to each language group.) Today, after years of research and study, we know much about these tribes. But in the 1850s, finding and identifying tribes, bands and villages was a formidable task for the Indian agents. One identifying feature was provided by the linguistic characteristics of spoken dialects.

Residing in the estuary area of the Columbia River, the Chinook Tribe was the first to trade with sailing ships as these arrived in the late 1700s and early 1800s. Other Chinookan-speaking people lived in the estuary region and up the Columbia to the villages of the Wishram and Wasco Tribes near Celilo Falls some 160 miles inland. The Chinooks took advantage of their location and became primary traders between the ships and their language cousins, funneling goods to different tribes further inland in exchange for furs and other goods sent down to the estuary. Chinook jargon, about 500 words of the Chinookan tongue, became the language of trade among the Indians of various tribes and was used extensively for communication by the West Pointers and other whites to communicate with the Indians, including at formal councils.

Indian habits, living style, dress, and subsistence depended primarily upon the area of residence, and not upon language group. There was a common thread: Great runs of salmon went from the ocean into Puget Sound and rivers for spawning, creating a dependable food supply. These fish runs extended throughout the Columbia and Snake River system, with the fish traveling as far as the Continental Divide runoff streams to spawn. Berries and roots were also primary ingredients of the diet. None of the tribes was agrarian, though by the time the Territory was formed, Hudson's Bay employees, missionaries, and friendly whites had started some Indians growing potatoes and other vegetables.

Although horses were owned by some Indians west of the Cascades, canoes were the primary mode of transportation, facilitated — indeed, necessitated — by Puget Sound, the numerous rivers, and the coastal waters. The thick forests made

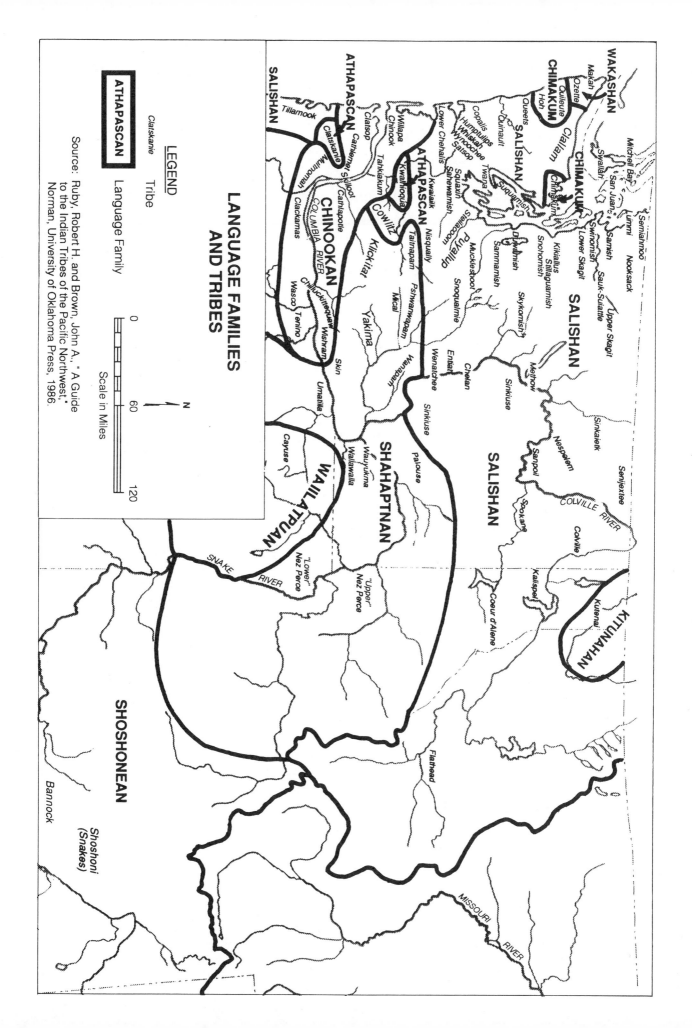

LANGUAGE FAMILIES
AND TRIBES

LEGEND

ATHAPASCAN   Language Family

Clatskanie   Tribe

Source: Ruby, Robert H. and Brown, John A., "A Guide
to the Indian Tribes of the Pacific Northwest."
Norman, University of Oklahoma Press, 1986.

Scale in Miles

0   60   120

N

WAKASHAN

CHIMAKUM
Makah
Ozette
Quileute
Hoh

SALISHAN
Tillamook
Clatsop
Clackamas

ATHAPASCAN
Clatskanie
Kwalhioqua

Clallam
Chimakum

Mitchell Bay
San Juan
Lummi
Semiahmoo
Nooksack
Swallah
Samish
Sauk-Suiattle
Upper Skagit

CHIMAKUM

Queets
Quinault
Copalis
Humptulips
Wishkah
Wynoochee
Satsop
Lower Chehalis
Twana
Squaxin
Sahewamish
Nisqually
Puyallup
Muckleshoot
Snoqualmie
Entiat
Wenatchee
Chelan

SALISHAN

Swinomish
Kikiallus
Stillaguamish
Snohomish
Duwamish
Sammamish
Skykomish
Methow
Sinkiuse
Sanpoil
Nespelem
Sinkaietk
Semijexiqe

SALISHAN

Spokane
Colville
Kalispel
Coeur d'Alene
Flathead

COLVILLE RIVER

KITUNAHAN
Kutenai

CHINOOKAN
Cathlamet
Skilloot
Cathlapotle
Wasco
Tenino
Chilluckittequaw
Wishram

COLUMBIA RIVER

Multnomah
Cascades
Cowlitz
Klickitat
Yakima
Taitnapam
Mical
Pshwanwapam
Wanapam
Palouse
Sinkiuse

ATHAPASCAN

SHAHAPTIAN
Wauyukma
Walla walla
"Lower" Nez Perce
"Upper" Nez Perce

SNAKE RIVER

WAIILATPUAN
Cayuse
Umatilla

Skin

SHOSHONEAN
Bannock
Shoshoni
(Snakes)

MISSOURI RIVER

horse travel difficult. Villages were generally permanently located along waterways and accessible to canoe traffic. Canoe making was an art characterized by processes that followed religious rituals. Some canoes carried parties of 20 or more. Great war canoes made by the Indians of the Queen Charlotte Islands north of Vancouver Island appeared in Puget Sound propelled by the paddles of up to 60 warriors.

By contrast, the tribes of the Columbia Plateau, regardless of language family, were part of the horse culture associated with the American Indian throughout the Great Plains and western United States. Hunting parties made long treks by horseback across the Continental Divide to hunt buffalo in competition with the plains Indians, while the majority of the tribe remained behind, gathering food from its normal area of domicile. Children learned riding skills at an early age, and by their teens were excellent equestrians, appearing to be glued to their mounts.

War was conducted primarily on horseback, using tactics learned from the tribes of the Great Plains. Although proficient in warfare as individuals and small groups riding together, these Indians (and the others in the western part of Washington Territory) never developed the concept or capability of using their numbers in mass. Warriors did what they wanted to do during the battle, in contrast to the discipline of white military units. Consequently, Army and volunteer Militia units were able to match the Indians on the battlefield with much fewer numbers than their opposition.

Indian Leadership

Capability was the essential qualification for becoming chief of a band or village and the head chief or a principal chief of a tribe. Separate war chiefs gathered warriors from throughout the tribe and associated tribes when such forces were needed. A chief's authority depended upon his persuasion of others to follow him, and it was a council of chiefs, not just a head chief, which made decisions. This unstructured leadership confused the whites in determining which chiefs to meet with for decision making. Often lesser-ranking chiefs and others without chief status were chosen to conduct councils and business because of their ability to communicate with the whites.

The chiefs of the various villages, bands and tribes met and held councils with one another. They preferred to ponder and consider issues, not to be rushed into decisions. Oratory was an essential ingredient of their councils, each participant spreading his views for consideration.

The chiefs were prominent men in their societies, and many were great men of their day. Some of their names are etched forever in the history of the Territory of Washington, and many of these appear in the monographs and later in this story. The next few paragraphs introduce the reader to most of these leaders, who will be encountered later in this book.

One of the great chiefs of the time was Garry, a Spokane chief. In 1829, he returned to his tribe after being educated in the English language at the Anglican Mission in Red River (Winnepeg), Canada, and became a tribal spokesman. He fostered Christianity among his people. Before the tribe was threatened with the loss of its lands, the Spokanes were friendly to the whites, and Chief Garry regularly entertained whites passing through tribal lands.

Fully conversant in English, Chief Garry understood what the treaties meant and refused to enter into treaties giving up tribal lands. Chief Garry and some other tribe members did not move to the Spokane Reservations established in the 1870s and '80s. When Chief Garry had grown elderly, the land he had farmed for years was claimed by whites. The chief lost his farm and died in poverty.

Chief Pewpewmaxmax of the Walla Wallas was a wealthy man owning about 2,000 horses and many head of cattle, which were pastured in the Walla Walla Valley. He was generous and shared with his people. An entrepreneur, he sold beef to settlers passing through the Walla Walla area.

Chief Pewpewmaxmax went with Chief Garry and others to California for horse trading. There his eldest son was killed by an American. When the American was not brought to justice, he went back for revenge, but instead of getting even, he fought for the Americans in the Bear Flag Revolt.

Probably the most prominent chief was Kamiakin, a Palouse married to a Yakima woman, who resided with the Yakimas and was looked upon as a chief by both tribes. Chief Kamiakin by nature was reserved and often pushed others forward in councils with the whites. Although suspicious, he was not originally antagonistic towards whites. In 1853, near the present city of Yakima, influenced by Roman Catholic missionaries, he had a garden and sold produce to settlers who passed that way. He complained at the First Walla Walla Council in May, 1855, about being away from his gardens. Treaties to take away lands caused Chief Kamiakin's hatred, distrust, and charismatic rise to leadership against the white intrusion.

Chief Kamiakin's brother-in-law was Owhi, a major Yakima chief. Chief Owhi's son, Qualchan, was a young and active Yakima war chief. These relatives joined Chief Kamiakin in leading the opposition to treaties and stopping whites, settlers and soldiers from going onto the Columbia Plateau.

Among the many leaders of the Nez Perce, Chief Lawyer stands out for his role in keeping both factions of the tribe friendly with the whites even during difficult situations. As a young man allied with a group of trappers, he was wounded in a skirmish with Blackfeet and Gros Vertes, causing a permanent injury that bothered him for the rest of his life. Named "Lawyer" by the trappers for his eloquent oratory, he rose from commoner status to head chief through his skills and ability to interact with the whites. Chief Lawyer understood the power of the whites and always negotiated a compromise, retaining as much as possible for his people.

Another senior spokesman for the powerful Nez Perce, Chief Looking Glass, never eclipsed Lawyer as head chief, but pungently faced down the West Pointer Governor and Superintendent of Indian Affairs for the Territory of Washington, Isaac I. Stevens, with piercing questions about the integrity of the land reserved by treaty for his tribe. Promises of integrity were not kept; the Nez Perce Reservation was severely reduced in size after a few years.

The Nez Perce were divided into two groups. The Upper Nez Perce resided in the Lapwai area near the juncture of the Clearwater and Snake Rivers, while the homeland of the Lower Nez Perce was the Wallowa Lake area southeast of the Walla Walla Valley. Head Chief Lawyer was recognized as the leader of the Upper Nez Perce; Chief Joseph was the leader of the lower group. Each group consisted of many bands headed by lesser chiefs. Although the whites believed that Chief Lawyer spoke for all, agreements to include formal treaties were binding only on the bands whose chiefs approved.

During the 1850s, the Nez Perce provided warriors under War Chief Spotted Eagle as part of Volunteer Militia and Regular Army forces. Spotted Eagle's warriors performed well; however, in one major operation, the West Pointer in charge of the unit gave up trying to force them to employ unit integrity and discipline on the battlefield.

Christian missionaries were some of the first whites to live among the Indian tribes. Upon returning from his schooling in 1829, Chief Garry began preaching among his people and others, causing great interest in Christianity by many. The Nez Perce sent a delegation to St. Louis in search of white men to teach them more about Christianity, causing Catholic and Protestant organizations to send missionaries to the Pacific Northwest. Over 20 missions were established in the area that became the Territory of Washington. Many of the chiefs and their followers accepted Christianity — at least to the extent of their understanding and acceptance of the doctrine; polygamy and promiscuity were customs missionaries found difficult to change.

Chief Joseph was one of the first Nez Perce to accept Christianity. He followed his religion devotedly until the Nez Perce lost additional land in 1863. This caused the chief to believe that the whites used Christianity as a tool to rob his people of their land. Chief Joseph destroyed the Gospel of Matthew given at his baptism and turned his back on Christianity and whites.

A prominent Nez Perce village chief, Tee-ma-tee or Timothy, was an early Presbyterian convert. At the First Walla Walla Council in the spring of 1855, he preached a sermon on the Ten Commandments during a service attended by many of the whites. Later, he was credited with leading a beleaguered Army force away from annihilation by a vastly superior number of Indians. Later in life, Timothy was living off of the Nez Perce Reservation as a white, following his faith.

United States Sovereignty In The Pacific Northwest

In the 18th century, explorers searched along the Pacific Coast for the outlet of the great "Oregon River," which was known to rise somewhere beyond the headwaters of the Missouri River and flow into the Pacific. But it was a seaborne fur trader from Boston searching for new sources of furs who is credited with the discovery. On May 11, 1792, Captain Robert Gray and his crew sailed the 220-ton ship *Columbia Rediviva* into the estuary of the great "Oregon" River. This was during President George Washington's first Administration, when the frontier of the fledgling United States had not yet passed the Mississippi River.

Twelve years after Captain Gray discovered the "Oregon" River, the expedition led by Captains Meriwether Lewis and William Clark[1] spent the winter of 1805-06 at Fort Clatsop[2] on the south bank of the "Oregon" River estuary after traveling down this river and some of its major tributaries. When the expedition leaders reported to President Thomas Jefferson in 1806, settlers were pouring into the Mississippi River Valley and were not prepared to go further west.

Following the Lewis and Clark expedition came fur trading companies organized for operations in the interior beyond coastal areas which had been easily reached by sailing ships. First to come was John Jacob Astor's Pacific Company, sending parties by sea and overland to found Fort Astoria in 1811, on the south side of the "Oregon" River estuary. The next year, fur trading operations were pushed inland to the Okanogan, Spokane, Snake and Walla Walla River areas.

Coming overland from eastern Canada were the British North West and Hudson's Bay Companies, moving into the Pacific Northwest in competition with the American company. British naval dominance during the War of 1812 caused the Pacific Fur Company to sell out to the North West Company rather than lose all as war booty. Fort Astoria was renamed Fort George by the British.

Attempting to retain peaceful relations after the War of 1812, the United States and Great Britain agreed in 1818 on the 49th parallel as the boundary from the Great Lakes to the Continental Divide and entered into an agreement for 10 years of joint occupancy of the Pacific Northwest. This vast area consisted of lands from the southern border of Russian Alaska at 54 degrees and 40 minutes north latitude, south to Spanish California, and east to the Continental Divide. Fort George was returned to the United States, and the North West Company moved its primary site to the north side of the "Oregon" River, founding Fort Vancouver. This signalled that the British Government had de facto abandoned claim to lands south of the "Oregon" River. Neither government maintained military forces in what was then called the "Oregon Country."

The British position was strengthened by requiring the Hudson's Bay Company to absorb the North West Company, giving Hudson's Bay sole responsibility to represent British interests in the Pacific Northwest. Hudson's Bay used this power to monopolize trade with the Indians. Its headquarters and main depot were at Fort Vancouver; the company also operated a trading post and farming company on Puget Sound. Operations went as far south as the Umpqua River. There were numerous trading posts between the Cascade and Rocky Mountains. By 1836, Hudson's Bay was doing business as far east as its Fort Hall, located about 150 miles north of the Great Salt Lake.

But Hudson's Bay was never successful at colonizing, although the British Government expected the company to do so. Except for retired company employees, most of whom married Indian women, there were only a handful of British settlers. All American settlers were directed into the Willamette Valley to

[1]In addition to the two officers, the expedition consisted of 26 enlisted men, two Army civilian employees, a civilian employee's wife and her child, and a Negro slave. This was the first U.S. Army contingent to enter the lands that became the Territory of Washington.
[2]Fort Clatsop was the first U.S. Army installation in the Pacific Northwest.

British settlers. All American settlers were directed into the Willamette Valley to keep them from disturbing the Indian customers north of the "Oregon" River.

By 1824, American fur trading companies, moving west through the Rocky Mountains, came into competition with Hudson's Bay, raising United States Government interest in the country's claim of sovereignty over the Pacific Northwest. President Andrew Jackson sounded out the British in 1831 on reopening negotiations, but was rebuffed; the British were not ready for further discussions. Based on the 1792 discovery of the "Oregon" River by Captain Gray, the United States then laid claim to all lands drained by the great river system, changing the river's name to "Columbia" after the discoverer's ship, to further support the claim of sovereignty over the lands drained by the river system.

Fur trading brought the first West Pointer to the land that became the Territory of Washington in 1853. This was Brevet Brigadier General Benjamin L.E. Bonneville, a United States Military Academy graduate of 1815. As a captain on leave from the Army in 1834, he went to the Hudson's Bay Company's Fort Walla Walla, spent some days with Chief Joseph, and discussed Christianity with Nez Perce Indians. The first monograph tells the story.

The following year, Captain Bonneville reported on his exploits in person to President Jackson, presenting a map of the Pacific Northwest, Great Salt Lake Basin, and Northern California. This report spurred the President to send naval Lieutenant William A. Slacum to secure firsthand information on the coastal areas of California and Oregon. Spending about a month in Oregon Country, Lieutenant Slacum found fewer than 100 United States citizens permanently residing in the coastal areas, primarily in the Willamette River Valley. Also, he observed the Hudson's Bay Company and its control of Indians through trade.

But the Hudson's Bay Company treated the Indians fairly, and the Company's "King George Men" were generally liked and trusted by the Indians. New England sea captains and their crews, by contrast, treated the Indians harshly, giving the Indians' nickname for Americans — "Bostons" — a connotation of dislike and distrust.

Lieutenant Slacum reported to President Martin Van Buren and the Congress in 1837, recommending that the 49th parallel be the minimum United States northern border demand, to place Puget Sound in the United States. His report also included observations covering Hudson's Bay enterprises: large surpluses of wheat and great quantities of oats, peas, and potatoes were being grown on Company lands; flour ground in the two mills at Fort Vancouver was being shipped to the Russians in Alaska; two sawmills at Fort Vancouver were providing lumber for profitable trade with the Sandwich (Hawaiian) Islands; and stock grazing consisted of over a thousand head of cattle and large numbers of hogs, sheep, horses and oxen. Business in agricultural products led to the organization of the Puget Sound Agricultural Company in 1836, a subsidiary headquartered at Fort Nisqually.

Following Lieutenant Slacum's report, Congress began to debate joint occupancy and the United States claim to the Oregon Country. In 1838, at the Senate's request, the War Department prepared the map that became known as the "Ultimate Map" — showing the boundary at the 49th parallel. This map was distributed in various governmental documents.

That same year, the government sent naval Lieutenant Charles Wilkes with five ships on a four-year expedition of the Pacific. Expedition parties explored Gray's Harbor, the lower Columbia River, Willamette Valley, and Puget Sound. Lieutenant Wilkes lost one of his ships trying to pass through the mouth of the Columbia, and never entered the Columbia with a ship. Other members of the expedition crossed the Cascade Range and went east as far as the Okanogan and Spokane Rivers, Lake Coeur d'Alene, and the Walla Walla River Valley, returning through Yakima country to Fort Nisqually. An artist traveled with a Hudson's Bay fur-trading brigade into the Blue Mountains. There were no Indian problems, and relations with Hudson's Bay were cordial.

Because of ongoing negotiations with Britain over the northeastern boundary with Canada, President John Tyler sent the report of the Wilkes Expedition to Congress in 1842 as a confidential communication. It included a recommendation that the United States claim include the Frazer River, placing the boundary at the 54 degrees and 40 minutes north latitude border with Russian Alaska. The boundary also included the entire Columbia River drainage.

Two years later, James K. Polk was elected President in a campaign that included the famous "Fifty-four forty or fight" slogan. His inaugural address contained belligerent statements on the issue. This address and the obvious public interest brought the British to serious negotiation. At the same time they sent a naval reconnaissance to the Pacific Northwest to assess the military requirements to defend their claim.

Congress followed through, authorizing on May 19, 1846, the establishment of military posts along the route to the Oregon Country and a new regiment, the Mounted Rifles, to garrison these posts, patrol the route and establish a United States military presence in the Oregon Country. However, war had been declared against Mexico six days earlier, and the Mounted Rifles were sent to fight in that conflict.

Less than a month after the declaration of war, the British Government formally proposed to the United States Secretary of State, James Buchanan, that the 49th parallel be extended as the boundary from the Continental Divide to the Pacific Ocean except for Vancouver Island which was to remain British. This proposal included stipulations requiring the United States Government to protect Hudson's Bay Company property rights. British tariff policies had been changed to favor the United States, allowing the die-hard "Fifty-four forty" opposition in Congress to be overcome. The Senate ratified the "Treaty of Washington" on June 18, 1846, less than ten days after it was formally proposed. This established the northern boundary of the Territory of Washington — though a disagreement over ownership of the San Juan Islands would arise in 1859.

The small United States Army, swollen by wartime expansion and volunteer units, went off to fight the Mexican War. When the War of 1812 had broken out, the Military Academy had graduated 89 cadets. West Pointers had served in the War of 1812 and in the Indian conflicts that followed. But the Mexican War was the first real test of the country's Military Academy. Its graduates were primarily lieutenants through majors, with a few in higher ranks. The West Pointers did

The Regulars came home from the Mexican War in high spirits, with soaring morale born of solid achievement. ... The youthful West Pointers had fully vindicated the national military school that had so recently been assailed — and almost abolished — as an aristocratic parasite on a democratic society.[1]

Brevet Rank

At this time, military medals had not yet been conceived in the United States Army; instead brevet promotions were awarded for "gallant and meritorious" service in war. Basically, an officer's rank was determined by the position that he held in a Congressionally-authorized regiment — infantry, artillery, or dragoon — or on the Army Staff.[2] Brevet rank became effective for both authority and pay when an officer was ordered to an assignment in a command or staff position outside of the regiment, on court-martial duty, and in commands consisting of different corps. For example, a regimental major with brevets to both lieutenant colonel and colonel, served as a district commander in his brevet lieutenant colonel rank, the grade authorized for that position. When reassigned, he reverted to his regimental major rank, but could be assigned in the future to another position calling for a lieutenant colonel or a colonel. Often, officers were detached from their regiments, spending many years at higher echelons serving in brevet ranks.

Another use of the brevet system was to provide a method to bring West Pointers into the Army upon graduation when there was no vacancy in a regiment (or Army staff for Ordnance and Engineer officers). Generally, the newly commissioned West Pointer served a few months to a year in a regiment as a brevet second lieutenant before an authorized vacancy occurred. Most often, this required the West Pointer to make two long-distance moves to separate regiments in the first year of service, while a second lieutenant appointed from civil life went directly to a regimental vacancy.

West Pointers received a great share of the brevet promotions given for valorous action during combat in the Mexican War. Almost all received at least one, and a few three. Many were wounded on the battlefield — not a prerequisite to brevet promotion, but another sign of combat service. Six of the nine West Pointers covered in the monographs served as officers in the Mexican War; four were wounded. For "gallant and meritorious conduct" in battle, one received one brevet promotion, and five were awarded two brevet promotions.

---

[1]R. H. Utley, *Frontiersmen in Blue: The United States Army and the Indian, 1848-1865* (New York: Macmillan Publishing Company, Inc., 1973), p. 28.

[2]Army Staff departments were adjutant general, quartermaster, commissary, paymaster, inspector general, surgeon, engineer, topographical engineer and ordnance.

Settlement of the Territory of Washington Begins

Emigration to the Oregon Country did not wait for agreement on border issues or for a war to be won. Settlers came overland and by sea. The Hudson's Bay Company still funneled American settlers into the Willamette Valley, increasing its population from the less than 100 Lieutenant Slacum found in 1836 to over 2,000 in 1844. Among various Indian tribes, missionaries were spreading their message to gain converts. Hudson's Bay's trading posts and the Puget Sound Agricultural Company were flourishing. In the Willamette Valley, citizens had formed a Provisional Government in 1843 to perform governmental functions until the United States Government could establish an appropriate body. Although there was distrust between whites and Indians, conditions were generally tranquil.

Oregon Trail immigration in 1844 brought the first group to settle north of the Columbia River. This party was led by Michael T. Simmons and George W. Bush, both from Kentucky. George Bush, a mulatto, was barred from going south of the Columbia River by the Provisional Government's Negro exclusion law of 1844, designed to prevent slavery. After a year on the north side near Fort Vancouver, Michael Simmons scouted out the south Puget Sound area and led a group of 32 men, women and children in late September, 1845, to found Newmarket at the head of Puget Sound. Still, it would be more than five years before the white population exceeded 3,000.

The increasing number of immigrants brought new challenges and pressures to the Indian. They came to his lands, demanding right of passage and ownership of the land. Indians were dying from white men's diseases, while white settlers and missionaries survived. To make matters worse, the extreme winter of 1846-47 wrought unusual hardships on the Columbia Plateau Indian, causing uncommonly high losses of horses and cattle. Immigration increased to well over 4,000 in 1847 from about 1,350 the year before — giving the Indian reason enough to associate difficulties with the coming of white men. Articulate Indian spokesmen began to warn of dire consequences from the white intrusion.

An immediate result was the murder of 14 white Whitman Mission residents in the Walla Walla Valley by Cayuse warriors in November of 1847. Hudson's Bay, with the help of Nez Perce Indians, rescued the survivors. The Provisional Government sent Volunteers to punish the Cayuse, resulting in the first war between the whites and Indians in the Pacific Northwest. After some encounters, the Cayuse retreated into the mountains with all of their livestock and other belongings, screened by about 400 Palouse warriors. It took until May, 1848, for news of the Whitman Massacre to reach Washington, D.C., but the incident served to accelerate Congressional approval of the Territory of Oregon, which occurred on August 13, 1848.

War with Mexico had ended in February, 1848, but the Mounted Rifles would not be ready until the next spring to start for the Oregon Territory. To expedite getting troops to the new territory, Companies L and M of the First U.S. Artillery were brought up to strength. The contingent left Governors Island, New York Harbor, on November 10, 1848, aboard the War Department's 700-ton transport

Massachusetts, a full-rigged ship with auxiliary steam providing power to a screw propeller. It was the third largest but most modern ship purchased by the Army for the Mexican War. They sailed around Cape Horn and through the Hawaiian Islands, arriving at the mouth of the Columbia River on May 9, 1849.

The *Massachusetts* discharged eight officers (seven line and one medical) and 152 enlisted men, plus wives and children, at the Hudson's Bay's Fort Vancouver on May 13. Five of the line officers were West Pointers. A 14-year-old drummer boy climbed a large fir tree, which was cleared of limbs up to 100 feet, to raise the United States flag over Camp Vancouver, the Army's first installation in the Oregon Country and on the soil that would become the Territory of Washington. Camp Vancouver would be redesignated Columbia Barracks in 1850.

On May 1, 1849, Snoqualmie Indians attacked Hudson's Bay's Fort Nisqually in a robbery attempt. This alarmed American settlers, causing the Territorial Governor to request that troops be stationed in the area. Because the 150 troops of the two artillery companies were tied up with arriving supplies and equipment, it was August 23 before Company M, First Artillery, arrived at Fort Nisqually. A vacant Puget Sound Agricultural Company farm was rented about five miles away and named Fort Steilacoom for the stream (today's Chambers Creek) that flowed nearby. The perpetrators of the attack on Fort Nisqually were tried, and the two found guilty were hanged at Fort Steilacoom that October. In January, 1851, the settlement of the Port of Steilacoom began about two miles from the Fort.

Departing Fort Leavenworth in May, 1849, the Regiment of Mounted Rifles left six companies to garrison posts along the Oregon Trail, arriving at Camp Vancouver in October with the Regimental Headquarters and four companies. There was insufficient barracks space at Camp Vancouver, so the soldiers were garrisoned for the winter at Oregon City in houses vacated by gold seekers who had gone to California. The Mounted Rifles also established Camp Drum on a stretch of the Columbia River named "The Dalles" by French "voyageurs" for the flagstone formations located there.

The people in Oregon City did not like the unruly soldiers and considered them a greater menace than the Indians. Oregon's Territorial Legislature petitioned Congress to remove the soldiers, a request that was obliged by breaking up the regiment in March, 1851, and reconstituting it in Texas. Men and horses were sent to the First U.S. Dragoons in California. On the way, they defeated Indians at two battles in southern Oregon Territory, leading the Territorial Delegate in Congress to request that mounted soldiers be returned. Soldiers returned in 1852, but not the Mounted Rifles.

The Fourth U.S. Infantry

The day was September 22, 1852, when Lieutenant Colonel Benjamin L. E. Bonneville arrived at the river landing below the Army's Columbia Barracks and Hudson's Bay's Fort Vancouver. It had been over 18 years since the Hudson's Bay Company had thwarted his attempts to follow the Columbia River to this area. Now he was the commander of all United States Army forces in the Oregon Territory, where the great Hudson's Bay Company still controlled the Indians through its monopoly on trade. Now, however, it was territory ceded to United States sovereignty, which weighed against Hudson's Bay power and control, although the Company was still protected by the Treaty of Washington.

Lieutenant Colonel Bonneville was in command of the Fourth U.S. Infantry Regiment since the regiment's elderly colonel went on sick leave rather than go with his regiment to the West Coast. Arriving with Bonneville were five of the ten companies and the Regimental Headquarters and Band. There were 11 line officers, one medical officer, and 268 soldiers plus dependents. Ten of the 11 line officers were West Pointers.

Higher headquarters, the Pacific Division, had detached three companies and the senior Regimental Major, George Wright (USMA Class of 1822) for duty in Northern California. Two companies did not leave New York Harbor until October 20 with regimental equipment and baggage. Their route was around Cape Horn, with a planned arrival of the following June.

In addition to the regiment, Lieutenant Colonel Bonneville took command of the 11th District, an area covering all of the Territory of Oregon except the Rogue River watershed in the southwest corner of the Territory. This added to his responsibilities the two First Artillery companies (Company L, at Fort Vancouver, and Company M at Fort Steilacoom), Columbia Barracks, Fort Steilacoom, and Camp Drum. One Fourth Infantry company was sent to take over Camp Drum from the small artillery detachment guarding the military property left there when the Mounted Rifles were disbanded.

With the troop buildup on the West Coast, the Pacific Division was upgraded to the Department of the Pacific. The 11th District became the District of Oregon. Columbia Barracks was redesignated Fort Vancouver, and Camp Drum was upgraded to Fort Dalles.

Chief Garry of the Spokanes came to visit and favorably impressed Lieutenant Colonel Bonneville. Subsequently, on being told by Indian agents that Chief Garry was a troublemaker, Colonel Bonneville vowed to apprehend the chief, but was persuaded against sending his soldiers on such a dangerous mission.

Second Lieutenant William A. Slaughter (USMA Class of 1848) arrived at Fort Steilacoom on February 20, 1853 to prepare the post for arrival of his company. The rest of Company C, Fourth Infantry, consisting of the company commander and 62 noncommissioned officers and rank and file, left Columbia Barracks on March 19 and arrived at Fort Steilacoom after a nine-day foot march. Company M, First Artillery, was relieved for reassignment (along with Company L) to the East Coast. The officers went east to fulfill new First Artillery requirements, while the enlisted men were transferred to the Fourth Infantry.

Washington Becomes A Territory

While Company C, Fourth Infantry was in the process of replacing the Artillery at Fort Steilacoom, the bill to create Washington Territory was moving through Congress. House approval came on February 8, and Senate passage occurred on March 2, the day before the 32nd Congress adjourned. President Millard Fillmore signed the act into law two days before leaving office, passing responsibility for establishing the Territorial Government to incoming President, Franklin Pierce. The new President's choice for Governor of the Territory was Isaac I. Stevens, the brilliant first graduate of the West Point Class of 1839.

The first governor of any state or territory is often remembered in history just for being first. But in the case of Isaac Stevens, his selection as "first governor" falls far down the list of significant achievements in this West Pointer's political and military career. The second monograph tells the story of this ambitious man of boundless energy and incessant drive, who left a successful military career to enter politics — his path to a role in the economic miracle of that day, railroad development. Railroads were the major economic thrust of the mid-1800s, inspiring visions of great transcontinental routes tying the nation to its newly-acquired lands on the Pacific Coast. In the 32nd Congress, the Senate session was almost entirely taken up with discussion of railroad projects and related problems. An amendment to the Army appropriation bill for 1853-54 added $150,000 to be expended by the Secretary of War for explorations and surveys of four potential routes for a transcontinental railway to the Pacific Coast.

Brevet Major Isaac Stevens, assigned in the highest of his two brevet ranks earned in the Mexican War, was serving in Washington, D.C. as the Executive Assistant to the Superintendent of the United States Coast Survey. This placed him in a position to participate in the mainstream of economic and political events of the day, to include involvement in the development of the government plans for surveying potential railroad routes. The Washington, D.C. assignment also provided an opportunity to get involved in the campaign of his political party's candidate for president. He had met Democrat Franklin Pierce, a lawyer and politician from New Hampshire, in the Mexican War when Pierce was a brigadier general of volunteers. Brevet Major Stevens was the adjutant for the Engineers supporting all of the commands in the victorious Army. After helping the former general to win by a large majority, he was rewarded by President Pierce with a dual appointment as Governor of Washington Territory and Superintendent of Indian Affairs for the Territory. Brevet Major Stevens resigned his Army commission effective March 16, 1853, to begin a new career as a politician.

At the same time he lobbied strenuously to head the survey for the northern railroad route. His appointment was effective on April 8, 1853; leadership of the other three routes was given to military officers. The northern route was allocated the largest amount of funds, allowing Governor Stevens to organize a well-equipped and manned survey contingent. In addition, a $20,000 Congressional appropriation was provided to Governor Stevens, with orders to build a military road from the Walla Walla Valley through Naches Pass to Fort Steilacoom.

The Northern Railway Survey

With the intense political interest in the transcontinental railways, Governor Stevens gave first priority to his Northern Railway Survey assignment, and did not reach the Territorial Capital of Olympia until nine months after being appointed Governor. The spring, summer and fall were taken up with the survey.

To make the best use of time, he divided the survey effort into two parts. The main party, led by the Governor, started in late May from Saint Paul, Minnesota, on the Mississippi River, and surveyed between the 47th and 49th parallels across the Great Plains and Rocky Mountains. He had 243 men, including scientists and artists, supported by a sizeable wagon and pack train. The western party departed Fort Vancouver on July 18 with 66 men and 173 horses, crossed over to the eastern slopes of the Cascades, and surveyed north to the 49th parallel above Fort Okanogan, then east to Fort Colville. The western party also outfitted a pack train to transport supplies from Fort Dalles to the Governor's main body as it approached the eastern slopes of the Rocky Mountains. This unit of 52 men met the Governor's party at Fort Benton. (A circa 1857 map, "Routes of Governor Stevens in 1853 and 1854," page 105, shows the routes of the main party led by the Governor, and the western party, which started at Fort Vancouver.)

After a long summer of tedious survey work, the main party slowly approached the Rocky Mountains in September. Although they were told by the Blackfoot Indians about Marias Pass, which became a major railroad route through the Rocky Mountains, Governor Stevens favored the approaches to Cadotte's Pass, named for the party's French-Canadian guide, and chose this route to cross over the Continental Divide and enter the Territory of Washington for the first time. The date was September 24, 1853, over six months after he was appointed Governor, and four months after starting from Saint Paul. A proclamation was issued by the Governor declaring the Territorial Government to be inaugurated.

The Governor pushed on west through Coeur d'Alene Pass of the Bitterroot Mountains, past the lake of the same name, and into the valley of the Spokane River, while the pack train went down the Clark Fork River, around the northern end of the Bitterroot Mountains, and past Lake Pend Oreille to the Spokane River. Several bands of Indians passed the Governor going east to hunt buffalo. In the Spokane River valley, herds of horses belonging to the Spokane Indians were seen grazing.

On October 17, Chief Garry came to meet the Governor and told him that the western survey party from Fort Vancouver was at Fort Colville. Chief Garry sent messengers to guide the pack train while the Governor and an Indian guide went to Fort Colville to meet the western party and to receive his first greeting from the Hudson's Bay Company. Chief Trader Angus McDonald welcomed the Governor with a two-day party.

The western party was down 36 men and 94 horses. They had been reduced in two increments because of the difficulties in resupplying from Fort Steilacoom, across the Cascades, and Fort Dalles, 300 miles to the south. Also the friendliness of the Indians and their chiefs had decreased the number of soldiers needed for security. They reported taking time to explore all gaps considered possibilities, but had found only two passes of likely suitability. Snoqualmie Pass was missed.[1] The

------

[1] A group from the western party went up the Yakima River and made observation at the lakes that are its source and went to the summit of Yakima pass, but failed to explore five miles further to Snoqualmie Pass, although a foot path went into that pass. From the observations around the lakes and in Yakima Pass by the leader of this party, the mountains ahead and to the north appeared

Governor learned about this pass from Hudson's Bay employees two weeks later at Fort Walla Walla.

Difficulties were encountered in getting started, since the quartermasters at Forts Vancouver and Dalles did not have enough horses and mules to meet the demands of both the supply pack train and survey party. Consequently, a large number of inferior Indian horses had to be purchased. Services and goods were contracted from Hudson's Bay at Fort Vancouver to outfit both parties. Manpower was relatively scarce, having been drawn away by the high wages paid in the California gold fields. Settlers from the Puget Sound area had started to cut a road through Naches Pass. A supply party sent through Naches Pass to Fort Steilacoom in mid-August observed that the road builders on the west side of the pass were doing a better job than those on the east side.

While surveying the extent of Naches Pass, the party sighted a lofty, snow covered mountain. The 9,415-foot peak was named Mount Stuart for Brevet Captain James Stuart (USMA Class of 1846) of the Mounted Rifles. This South Carolinian had died on June 18, 1851, from an arrow wound received while leading an attack in southern Oregon Territory.

The surveyors encountered parties of Indians and villages. Many Indians were inflicted with smallpox, arousing fear of contracting the disease among both soldier and civilian members of the party. Approaching the Saint Joseph Mission on Ahtanum Creek, they observed many vegetable gardens. The Yakimas brought in potatoes and corn to trade for food and tobacco. Four steers were purchased for beef. At the mission the party met Chief Kamiakin — a large, gloomy-looking Indian, slovenly dressed with a strongly-marked face, but reported to be honest and generous. Presents were offered, but he demurred for a time in accepting. He pointed out that a long time ago "King George Men" told him that the "Bostons" would come by someday to offer presents and then say they have bought your land. He was assured that this was not the case now. It was believed that Chief Kamiakin was under the influence of the priests and was friendly towards the survey party.

Chief Owhi and a large number of his people came to the survey party camp. The Chief was described as the best-natured Indian yet found in this country. Some flakes of suspected gold were found in sands, causing a flurry of gold fever. Chief Owhi and other Indians took members of the survey party panning for gold in various streams, but no actual gold was found. A visiting Spokane chief was decorated with scalps. On September 19, Chief Owhi and other Yakimas rode with the party as they moved north towards the Wenatchee River. Near the juncture of the Wenatchee and Columbia Rivers, the party bought more potatoes from the Indians, and watched Indian horse races.

On September 26, they came in sight of Hudson's Bay's Fort Okanogan, but still continuing their survey work and explorations for possible routes through the mountains. An element went north up the Okanogan River to the 49th parallel before the survey party continued east to Fort Colville. In the Colville River

---

rugged and impassible, and winter snows could be expected to reach depths of over 20 feet. This was determined by the markings on the trees.

Valley, settlements of former Hudson's Bay employees extended for some 28 miles. These farmers were eager to become American citizens, a prerequisite to obtaining title to their lands. Further south, an American settler from Detroit was living in an abandoned mission surrounded by a camp of about 200 Spokane Indians.

Governor Stevens established Camp Washington, his first headquarters in the Territory of Washington, near the spot where he had left the main party on October 17. On October 26, the western party arrived at Camp Washington; the pack train came in two days later. Eager to get to Olympia, Governor Stevens planned to go south to the Columbia River and down the river to Fort Vancouver. The Governor wanted the western party and others to go through the Cascade passes to Puget Sound, hoping to get information that would help minimize the wintertime dangers of routes through the Cascades in his report.

The Governor left Camp Washington on the afternoon of October 28 headed for Fort Walla Walla, leaving to his subordinate leaders the decision whether to continue west across the Cascades. No one was anxious to cross these mountains in December through rugged terrain that had not yet been explored, let alone mapped. The horses were in poor condition. Already, 16 horses of the supply pack train going from the western survey party through Naches Pass to Fort Steilacoom had broken down in September. Now a considerable amount of snow would make the trailing much more difficult. All barometers were beyond repair from rugged use, which would prevent taking needed measurements. Instead of going west to the Cascades, they divided into subgroups and started leaving Camp Washington on November 29, headed for Fort Walla Walla, and then to Fort Dalles and Fort Vancouver. Chief Garry and some of his brothers went along as guides to Fort Walla Walla.

The Tranquil Year 1854

As the monograph on Governor Stevens relates, there was euphoria in the Territorial Capital of Olympia[1] after he arrived. Citizens were eager to get their government going, and a political "honeymoon" atmosphere prevailed. The Territorial Government was organized, and the Legislature held its first session, creating counties and passing laws that were primarily adoptions from the Territory of Oregon. Governor Stevens conducted a reconnaissance of Puget Sound and visited the British in Victoria on Vancouver Island.

But the Governor felt pressured, probably by his own ambitions, to get a report on the Northern Railway Survey to the Secretary of War. He had overdrawn his budget by $16,000, which the Secretary of War refused to honor. Also, there was a growing sense of competition over which route might be selected. In March, 1854, after working as Governor for only three months of the first year, he went to Washington, D.C. for the stated purposes of turning in an initial Northern Railway Survey Report and compelling Congress to approve, as required, the acts passed by the Territorial Legislature.

---

[1]Olympia was a "city" of about 20 buildings. Many people lived in tents.

In 1854, there were no unusual conflicts between the Indians and whites. Some prominent Indians in the south Puget Sound region complained to trusted whites that the "Bostons" did not pay them enough for work. It was apparent that the Indian, in general, preferred the "King George Men" to the "Bostons." Many stories have been passed on over the years about Hudson's Bay Company employees telling the Indians about the bad ways of the American settlers and Government. Chief Kamiakin relayed one when he met the western survey party. Another, passed on in the Puget Sound area, was that the "Bostons" were very bad people, and if allowed to come they would take the lands from the Indian and take the Indians away in a large black ship to an island from which they could never escape.

The Fourth Infantry began road building activities and continued routine patrolling, but did not penetrate into the interior of the Columbia Plateau, since the Army did not have the soldiers or transportation for such operations. In the Puget Sound region, canoes paddled by hired Indians were used for patrols, ranging all the way to Bellingham Bay where coal deposits were beginning to be mined.

The Army did not have any combat casualties, but Brevet Major Charles H. Larnard (USMA Class of 1831), the Fourth Infantry Post Commander at Fort Steilacoom, drowned in Puget Sound on March 27, 1854, when his canoe overturned in a storm. His body was never recovered. He left a widow at the fort. Brevet Major Larnard had believed that the Steilacoom area where the town was being incorporated was too populated for the Army. He had intended to request permission of Division of the Pacific Headquarters in Benicia, California, to move the garrison beyond the line of settlement to Whidby Island.

Lieutenant Colonel Bonneville continued building Fort Vancouver, which in a few years became the most comfortable Army installation in the Pacific Northwest. Some effort was expended at the other two Fourth Infantry posts, Forts Steilacoom and Dalles, but Fort Dalles continued to be a frontier post without many amenities. Military family and soldier life were better at Fort Steilacoom.

In the late summer and early fall, the Inspector General from Army Headquarters in New York City, Colonel Joseph K. F. Mansfield (USMA Class of 1822), came through on a routine inspection. He complimented Lieutenant Colonel Bonneville and the other commanders on the condition of their commands, except for very low strength. All companies had fewer than 30 privates assigned, as against 74 authorized. More regimental recruiters were sent to the populated areas in the east. The Inspector General recommended that a one-company fort be placed at Bellingham Bay to protect the coal mining interests and the growing population from Indians — primarily the piratical northern tribes from the Queen Charlotte Islands and southern Russian Alaska who made annual trips to fish and plunder in the Puget Sound region.

In the late fall of 1854, Governor Stevens returned to Olympia, bringing his family to set up residence in the Territorial capital "city." The political "honeymoon" of the past winter was over; political parties had organized, and Whigs were pitted against Democrats. Governor Stevens, a Democrat, was still popular, but the second legislature, which opened a few days after his return, gave the

Governor his first taste of opposition as an executive in a political position.

The population of the Washington Territory increased at a slow rate. Oregon Trail immigration is estimated as follows:

1850	6,000
1851	3,600
1852	10,000
1853	7,500
1854	6,000
1855	500

After 1855, immigration did not exceed 2,000 in any year before the Civil War. Most of the immigrants went into the Oregon Territory. At the end of 1854, the non-Indian population of the Territory of Washington was still less than 5,500.

Treaties and Councils

At the opening of the second territorial legislative session in early December, 1854, Governor Stevens informed the assembled body that treaties with the Indians would be his primary activity for the near future. This was very popular with the legislators and their constituents. In the democratic tradition of the United States, Indian title to the land had to be extinguished before title by the white settlers could be gained, even for land claimed under the Land Donation Act of 1850 in the Territory of Washington.

While in Washington, D.C. the Governor received an authorization to spend $45,000 for treaty councils west of the Bitterroot Mountains. Also, he persuaded the Indian Bureau of the need to council with the feared Blackfoot tribes, and received another $100,000 for the tribes on the western slopes of the Rocky Mountains and the Blackfeet on the other side of the Continental Divide.

Indian Bureau instructions included keeping the number of treaties and reservations to a minimum. It was realized that the Indian tribes would resist moving from their traditional lands, and animosity between tribes would add problems to co-locating on reservations. Also, the reservations had to be remote in order to separate the Indian as far as possible from areas where white settlement was in progress or would take place in the future. The reservations would allow the Indians to progress from their Stone Age culture into civilization. In return for giving up the land, the Government promised annuities in cash and material, schools, teachers, and other means to assist the Indians in preparing and building for their future.

The treaty process had begun before the Territory of Washington was separated from Oregon. In 1851, the Superintendent of Indian Affairs for the Territory of Oregon initiated treaty councils with the Chinook-speaking people of the lower Columbia River, Willapa Bay, and Cowlitz River region. Estimates are that there were about 5,000 Lower Chinookans residing there at the beginning of the 19th Century. In the following 50 years, the population decreased by at least 90 percent. Most of the decline appeared to be in the late 1820s to mid-1830s during an epidemic of "cole sick-waum sick" — the Chinook jargon description of the intermittent fever. But the decline had started before the epidemic and continued afterwards. Treaties were signed, but the surviving Indian elders just wanted to be left alone, retaining the land where they lived, fished, and gathered food. Also, they asked to keep their burial grounds and to receive payments for only ten years — which further attested to the demoralized condition of these aborigines.

But the United States Senate refused to ratify these treaties because they did not provide for removing the Indians from an area where the whites wanted to settle. Governor Stevens was determined that *his* treaties would be ratified, and that reservations would meet the Senate's criteria. He was concerned with protecting the Indian from alcohol and other white depredations, and stopping wars and slavery. Articles were written into the treaties to stop these activities. Also, he located reservations away from Hudson's Bay access, and inhibited the Company from trading with the Indians by restrictive treaty articles.

Messengers were sent out to invite the chiefs and their followers to assemble at designated points for councils where gifts were to be distributed. Especially in the Puget Sound region, many of the Indians had very little material wealth, and the promise of gifts was enough to draw them to gatherings. Many attending the councils did not know what was going on, and their only interest was in the gifts. Some of the treaty councils were great affairs, but the first ones in Puget Sound were generally simple, characterized by speeches made by both white and Indian leaders, initialing of the treaty, and distribution of gifts. Two of the eight councils held by Governor Stevens in the Territory of Washington ended without any treaty.

The Treaty Year of 1855

As described in the monograph on Governor Stevens, the treaty year of 1855 actually began on Christmas Eve of 1854, near the mouth of She-nah-nan or Medicine Creek, about halfway between Olympia and Steilacoom, two of the largest towns in the Territory. By February 24, 1855, five councils had been held, resulting in four treaties. A fifth treaty was extracted in July by Indian sub-agents. (The council locations and dates, and areas ceded by the five treaties are depicted in the map "Puget Sound and Coastal Treaties," page 31.)

It was a rainy, blowing day on the banks of Medicine Creek not far from where the Nisqually River flows into Puget Sound, when the Medicine Creek Treaty Council began on December 24, 1854. Lieutenant Slaughter attended and is recorded in the Treaty as a "witness." Arriving to get activities started by addressing the assembled Indians, Governor Stevens came well armed with a draft treaty complete with maps ready for finalization. Local settlers had assured the Indians in the days before that the Government would pay them very well for their lands. Governor Stevens paid no heed to the absence of the Lower Puyallups, a band of around 250, who were held up by high winds and did not arrive until after the Council was over.

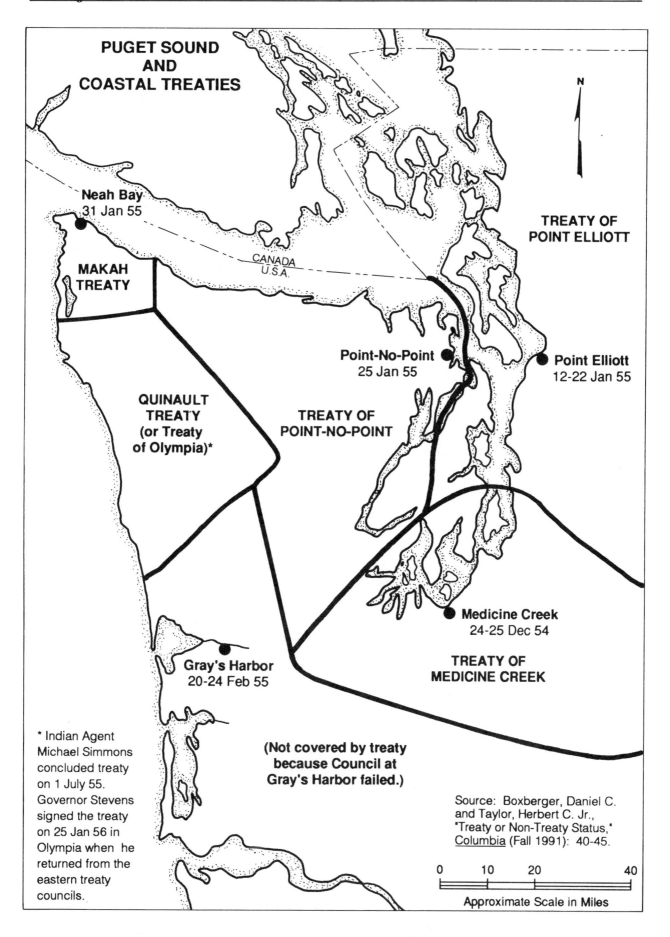

Governor Stevens wanted this treaty as the model for those to follow, since it would be sent immediately to Washington, D.C. as a test for ratification by the United States Senate. This ratification occurred the following March, providing the confidence that the Governor and his staff needed before facing the major tribes in the Columbia Plateau. (Other treaties completed in 1855 by the Governor and his staff languished until 1859 before Senate ratification.) The Governor may have been satisfied — and, undoubtedly, his constituents in Thurston and Pierce Counties were pleased — to have Indian "title" to Nisqually and Puyallup lands extinguished to allow the settlers to obtain title to their claims.

It was different among the docile Nisqually. On Christmas Day, the headmen were called forward to initial the treaty. Until the day that he died, Leschi, a prominent Nisqually who dressed in white man's clothes, claimed that he did not initial. The treaty allocated the Nisqually, a tribe of about 300, only 1,280 acres of land without water and not suitable for agriculture. In exchange, the Nisqually relinquished the Nisqually River Valley[1] where they pastured horses and fished the salmon runs. From the start Leschi, elevated to chief status in the eyes of the settlers, began to sulk and complain about this treatment as unfair.

By July, the loss of their lands had festered into open contempt and dislike for the whites. However, most Nisqually still claimed to be "tillicums," or friends, and remained firm about not joining the Klickitats in talk of war against the whites. Nisqually Chief Quiemuth complained in Chinook jargon to James Longmire, a well known settler, stating that the "Bostons" were bad people, not paying enough for work, but the "King George Men" were good. But in July, and again later in the summer, he told Mr. Longmire that he was still a "Boston Tillicum."

News of what happened at Medicine Creek preceded the Governor and his party up Puget Sound to the participants in the next two councils. With about 2,300 attending from at least six tribes, it took ten days to complete the Point Elliot Council and to finish the treaty. The Nooksack, although included in the treaty, never arrived because of the icy conditions in their foothills area. To escape the provisions of the treaty, the Semiahmoo, a tribe of about 250, went north of the 49th parallel "medicine line" to live. Otherwise, the council went well except for the foul weather.

It was different at the Point-No-Point Council where about 1,200 were assembled. There was hesitancy. Whites were logging on the lands of the Twana Tribe located at the southern end of Hood Canal. This caused the Twanas to understand that their land had some value and to want proper compensation. With coercion, they finally acquiesced and allowed the treaty to be completed.

At Neah Bay, a few miles east of Cape Flattery, about 600 Makah assembled to listen to the "White Chief," receive their gifts, and agree to the treaty. Makahs and their sub-tribe or band, the Ozettes, were the only Wakashan language family people in the Territory of Washington. Others lived to the north on the western coast of Vancouver Island. These people hunted whales, walrus and other sea mammals in addition to fishing. The white man had come many times before, but eventually left, allowing the Makahs and Ozettes to continue with their ways. The

---

[1]The river is the boundary between Thurston and Pierce Counties.

isolation of the tribes suggested that it would be the same this time. The one-day council went without incident.

After a busy January with three councils, it was nearly the last of February before the sub-agents assembled about 370 Indians a few miles up the Chehalis River from Gray's Harbor. The Governor's party consisted of 14. Indians came from the Columbia estuary, Willapa Bay, and Gray's Harbor areas, and north up the coast to about 20 miles below Cape Flattery.

The Governor's objective was to move all of the Indians remaining in the southwest quadrant of the Territory to north of Gray's Harbor. It was fine for them to work in the Willapa Bay oyster beds — already a growing business — but they could not continue to live there. Quinault and Queets Indians favored the treaty, since they would remain in their villages and receive gifts and annuities. Others adamantly opposed any relocation. Indian tempers flared, leading to at least one murder. This council lasted from February 20 to 24, but failed to produce a treaty.

While the Governor turned his attention to the tribes east of the Cascades, a sub-agent took the responsibility to establish a reservation north of Gray's Harbor and to get as many tribes and bands as possible to agree to reside there. By mid-summer, a treaty had been concluded with the Indians who normally resided in the remote area north of Gray's harbor. Sometimes, the Quinault Treaty is referred to as the "Treaty of Olympia," since Governor Stevens did not sign it until January 25, 1856, when he returned to Olympia at the completion of his treaty journeys.

Other Indians in the southwest quadrant of the Territory were not included in any treaty. The 1851 attempt by the Oregon Territorial Superintendent had failed; now efforts of the Superintendent of Indians Affairs for Washington Territory had collapsed.

Settlers and the Army in 1855

With fewer than 2,000 voters in the Territory, it was not difficult for citizens to get the attention of a member of the Legislature (which consisted of a House of Representatives and a Council) and to let the chief executive and his staff know their interests. The Democrats were the strongest party, with a majority in both houses of the Legislature. Whigs were the primary opposition; the "Free Soil" or Republican party with its strong anti-slavery platform had a small number of adherents.

Probably the most important legislation for the future, although not realized at the time, was the Militia law authorizing each council district to elect a colonel, a lieutenant colonel, and a major. The major was empowered to appoint a captain and two lieutenants; the captain's appointment authority was four sergeants and four corporals.

A failed attempt at prohibition was a measure of the power of the people. Patterned after the "Maine Law," the Legislature passed an act to prohibit the manufacture, sale and gift of spirited liquors in the Territory of Washington, with the provision that this act had to be approved by the voters before becoming law in November. The Governor signed the act. In the July general election, the voters turned down the first attempt at prohibition by a vote of 610 to 540.

In the same general election, Democrat J.P. Anderson was elected to the position of delegate to Congress with 808 votes. His Whig rival received 682 votes, the Republican candidate 41.

At Fort Vancouver, command of the Army forces in the Territory changed with the departure in the spring of the newly-promoted Colonel Bonneville. After over 39 years as a commissioned officer, he had sufficient seniority to be promoted to the colonelcy of one of the Army's 15 regiments,[1] the Third U.S. Infantry, in the Department of New Mexico. The United States Military Academy Association of Graduates' records contain a biographical sketch describing the life and exploits of this 1815 graduate in 20 paragraphs, most of them quite long. One sentence covers the period from 1849 to 1857, which includes his assignment in the Territory of Washington: "After the Mexican War his life was not particularly eventful, except a short revival of his wilderness experience when he commanded the Gila Expedition of 1857."[2] The "Gila Expedition" occurred in New Mexico.

Replacing Colonel Bonneville as Commander, District of Oregon, Major Gabriel J. Rains (USMA Class of 1827) was elevated to the senior major's slot; the former senior major was promoted to the lieutenant colonel position.[3] Major Rains previously commanded Fort Dalles, which was still a frontier outpost with hovels for barracks and quarters. Mrs. Rains was very pleased to go to Fort Vancouver where there were some acceptable living quarters for officer families.

This left Captain Granville O. Haller, also a company commander, in command at Fort Dalles, a position in which he could serve in his brevet major rank and receive additional pay as the post commander.[4] Brevet Major Haller's family was at Fort Dalles, where his Irish-born wife was a favorite. Oregon Territorial Volunteers named one of their camps Fort Henrietta for her.

Army strength in the District of Oregon was increased by the assignment of two artillery companies, a company of dragoons, and some recruits. From the Third U.S. Artillery Regiment, headquartered at Benicia Barracks, California, Company B was assigned to Fort Vancouver, and Company L, which arrived in 1854, went on to Fort Dalles. After fighting a major battle the previous fall at Hungry Hill in southern Oregon Territory, Company E, First Dragoons was sent on to Fort Vancouver. Following the Inspector General's report of his 1854 visit,

---

[1]There were eight infantry, four artillery, and three dragoon regiments, including the Mounted Rifles.

[2]G. W. Cullum, *Biographical Register of the Officers and Graduates of the United States Military Academy at West Point, N. Y. From Its Establishment in 1802 to 1890* (Boston and New York: Houghton, Mifflin and Company; Cambridge: The Riverside Press, 1891), Vol. I, p. 186.

[3]Authorizations for infantry regiments consisted of a colonel, lieutenant colonel, and two majors, with a captain, first lieutenant, second lieutenant, four sergeants, four corporals and 74 privates for each of the ten companies. There was a regimental headquarters and band. Artillery, dragoon and the Mounted Rifle regiments had similar authorizations.

[4]As a 20-year-old in 1839, Captain Haller had lost the competition for the West Point appointment allocated to his home congressional district in Pennsylvania to the son of a War Department clerk who resided in Washington, D.C. However, young Haller impressed the Army and was given a direct commission as a second lieutenant in the Fourth Infantry. This gave him a head start of four years on those entering the Military Academy that year. In the Fourth Infantry Regiment, he outranked the single graduate of the Class of 1840 and the three West Pointers from the Class of 1843, which would have been his class.

recruits were on their way to the Fourth Infantry companies at Forts Steilacoom, Vancouver and Dalles, but the number expected still left the level well below the authorization of 74 privates per company. With two infantry companies at each of the three posts, Major Rains now had nine companies.

Brevet Major Haller left Fort Dalles in June, 1855 with almost the entire garrison, going to the Boise River Valley to provide protection for the immigrants coming west on the Oregon Trail. Stock to mount this force of infantrymen and artillerymen and to have a pack train for field operations was provided by horses and mules turned in at Fort Dalles by the Northern Railway Survey party when their field work was completed.

The previous August, a band of Shoshonis had massacred a five-wagon immigrant group led by William Ward from Johnson County, Missouri. This incident began as an attempt to steal horses and ended with the Shoshonis killing all of the men and brutally murdering captured women and children. Two days after the news reached Fort Dalles, Brevet Major Haller was underway with 26 mounted soldiers and a pack train carrying rations and supplies.

Tempers raged in The Dalles, the frontier town that had grown up around this western terminus of the Oregon Trail. Nathan Olney, an Oregon Territorial Indian sub-agent and a Militia captain, easily enlisted a Militia company that soon caught up with the Regulars.

The advanced elements of the soldiers and Militia covered the 400 miles in four days, in hopes of saving any survivors; but only two boys, both wounded, managed to escape and were rescued by others. Four suspects were caught, tried, and found guilty by a military court. Three were hanged at the massacre site, and one was shot in an escape attempt. Out of rations and not prepared for a winter operation, the soldiers and Militiamen were back at Fort Dalles about the middle of October; most of the band who committed the massacre had not been apprehended.

Now, in addition to providing protection to the immigrant trains, the Fort Dalles garrison was tasked to find the rest of the fugitive band. Brevet Major Haller learned that this band had a shod horse and mule stolen from the Wards. Second Lieutenant Edward H. Day (USMA Class of 1851),[1] an artilleryman, led a contingent following this track all the way to the Continental Divide, only to lose the track in the mountains. On the way back to the Boise River Valley, the track was picked up again, and the fugitives were captured. Those identified as participants in the massacre were tried by a military court and hanged.

Brevet Major Haller developed cordial relations with the chief trader at Hudson's Bay's Fort Boise, which resulted in stopping the sale of ammunition to the Indians. But after the soldiers left Fort Boise on September 3, the chief trader

---

[1]Breveted a second lieutenant in the Second Artillery at West Point graduation in 1851, Lieutenant Day fought Indians in the swamps of Florida before being sent in June 1852 to an authorized second lieutenant position in the Third Artillery on the West Coast. The trek to capture the Ward Party murderers was probably his finest accomplishment as an Army officer. Unfortunately, Lieutenant Day became ill, necessitating going on sick leave in 1856. He died at the age of 30 in Richmond, Virginia on January 2, 1860.

and his three employees, with all of their goods, moved for safety to Fort Walla Walla, fearing that Indian resentment of the cordial relations between the chief trader and Brevet Major Haller might endanger the trader and his staff. The soldiers closed into Fort Dalles on September 18.

The First Walla Walla Council

During the winter of 1854-55, Indian sub-agent Jim Doty went among the Indian tribes of the Columbia Plateau, inviting them to a council in May and explaining the purpose of the council. These Indians knew about the efforts of Joel Palmer, Superintendent of Indian Affairs for Oregon Territory, to move tribes from the Willamette River Valley and Columbia River estuary to a reservation (Warm Springs) east of the Cascade Range. They had also heard about the hangings in the Boise River Valley of three Shoshonis by Brevet Major Haller's command and Militiamen. Their mood had changed since the Northern Railway Survey parties had passed through in 1853.

Jim Doty missed some of the tribes, such as the 350 to 400 Sinkiuse residing on the east side of the Columbia River across from the Yakimas. Hostile acts committed later by the Sinkiuse were blamed on the Yakimas and their leaders, Chiefs Kamiakin and Owhi. The Yakimas were of the Shahaptian language family where words were formed in an entirely different manner than by the Salishan-speaking Sinkiuse.

The Yakimas were not enthusiastic about attending the council, but agreed. Chief Kamiakin suggested that the council take place in the Walla Walla Valley at a traditional meeting place for the Plateau tribes. But he refused to accept any of the gifts Jim Doty offered, saying that he would not accept from the "Bostons" even the value of a grain of rice without paying for it, and he did not care to purchase any of the items offered by Jim Doty. Reluctance was expressed by both the Walla Wallas and Cayuse. Their proximity to the Oregon Trail caused anxiety over the increasing number of settlers arriving.

Only the Nez Perce were in favor, and there was some division of opinion among the chiefs. William Craig, a former Hudson's Bay employee, had married a Nez Perce woman and settled among them, learning their language. Highly respected by the Nez Perce and the whites, Bill Craig in consonance with their head chief, Lawyer, influenced the Nez Perce to continue the friendliness they had shown Captains Lewis, Clark, and Bonneville, and not to take up war against the powerful whites. Intrusion by settlers, prospectors and miners had not yet penetrated the Nez Perce homelands.

Governor and Superintendent Stevens, Superintendent Palmer, and a party of about 35 arrived at the council site on May 21, in the Walla Walla Valley (see "Map of Places and Events," endpages). Their bivouac was named Camp Stevens. Two arbors were set up, one serving as the meeting site, the other for banquets to entertain the chiefs. Tents were erected for office space and housing, and a log cabin was erected to store supplies and gifts. Major Rains sent some of his officers as observers and 47 dragoons for escort. The soldiers set up their own camp. Some Indians were already in the area, and more were arriving daily, setting up their camps in the vicinity.

On May 24, the Nez Perce made a dramatic appearance to express friendship to the whites and to demonstrate their military power. The pounding of the hoofs in the distance announced their arrival, and an American flag presented for assistance at the time of the Whitman Massacres was brought forward and planted in a hill. Next, an estimated 900 to 1,000 mounted warriors, riding two abreast, galloped into view and around the council site. When this contingent halted, Head Chief Lawyer and two others rode slowly to the knoll where Governor Stevens and others had gathered to view this spectacle, dismounted, and shook hands. Then 25 lesser chiefs rode forward and went through the same ceremony. In addition to demonstrating friendship and military strength, the Nez Perce were demanding respect.

Two days later, about 400 Cayuse warriors made a ceremonial appearance demonstrating their horsemanship and military power, but without any of the friendliness expressed by the Nez Perce. This attitude of the Cayuse continued throughout the council. Army officers visiting the various camps were always welcomed by the Nez Perce, accepted by the others, but turned away by the Cayuse.

More Indians arrived each day, including representatives of the Salishan-speaking tribes to the north and east where subsequent councils were planned. It is estimated that 5,000 Indians gathered for the First Walla Walla Council.

Formally convening on May 29, 1855, the First Walla Walla Council was one of the largest and most heterogeneous Indians gatherings ever recorded in North America. In attendance were Nez Perce, Yakimas, Walla Wallas, Cayuse, Umatilla, and numerous observers from other tribes, the Army, and missionaries. A few Palouse were there as observers, but their tribe had refused to participate. The Council began with the two Superintendents, their secretary, interpreters, criers, and sub-agents sitting under the arbor facing out. Nez Perce Chief Timothy sat near Governor Stevens, making his record of the proceedings for tribal use. Seated in semicircular rows, 40 people deep, the Indians faced back towards the two Superintendents, with the primary chiefs in the front.

Translation was a problem. Walla Walla Chief Pewpewmaxmax and others expressed major concern with the Indians' understanding of the matters being presented by the two Superintendents and their sub-agents. The limited number of words in Chinook jargon made it insufficient for this level of complex conversation. Only the Nez Perce felt comfortable, since they had faith in the interpretations provided by Bill Craig.

A few days after the Council started, the Cayuse initiated a plot to massacre the Army escort and the Governor's party, followed by a surprise attack on Fort Dalles. Informed of the plot by one of his spies, Chief Lawyer quickly moved his personal lodge after midnight on June 3 into Governor Stevens's camp. This act firmly placed the powerful Nez Perce on the side of the Governor for any conflict.

With opposition from all except the Nez Perce, both Governor Stevens and Superintendent Palmer went slowly in presenting their plans to the chiefs. They understood that these Indian leaders were shrewd and remained in their positions of leadership through political and negotiating skills. The chiefs were in no hurry to give up anything, although some wanted the wealth that could come from acquiescing to the demands of the "White Chief." It was their nature to take time to consider situations and to arrive at decisions. They did not want to hurry and preferred not to make difficult decisions.

After a week of talks, Governor Stevens presented his plan for two treaties, each setting aside a large reservation. One reservation was in Nez Perce country for the Nez Perce, Walla Wallas, Cayuse and Spokanes. A second extended from the vicinity of the Saint Joseph Mission on Ahtanum Creek west into the Cascades for the Yakimas, Palouse, Klickitat, and Columbia River tribes. Only the Nez Perce were satisfied since most of their domain was included in the reservation. No other tribe wanted to be located with and dominated by the Nez Perce. For most, the planned reservations meant giving up their lands. Even a large part of the Yakima lands were ceded. The chiefs wanted the annuities, material and gifts, but not at the price of relocating from their usual domicile areas and exclusion from their traditional food gathering locations.

Tensions mounted while the chiefs made eloquent speeches explaining their thoughts and opinions, but Chief Kamiakin remained quiet. When asked to speak, he replied that he had nothing to say, nothing to talk about. Others spoke of the Indian relationship to the land, the "Mother Earth" who nurtured the Indian. Historians claim that both Governor Stevens and Superintendent Palmer chose to remain oblivious to the Indian philosophy of the earth as a gift from the Great Spirit. Chief Pewpewmaxmax wanted to adjourn without any decisions being made. This was the opinion of many others, since decisions concerning land did not have to be made in haste; "Mother Earth" would always be here.

Governor Stevens was beginning to understand the extent of the Indian resistance to his plan, when Chief Looking Glass, a 70-year-old, very influential Nez Perce, arrived. For the past three years, Chief Looking Glass had been away hunting buffalo on the Great Plains. When informed of the council, he traveled 300 miles in seven days to participate, encountering six-foot snow drifts in the Bitterroot Mountains. Chief Looking Glass questioned his tribesman on what they were doing and why they were giving away tribal lands. Further, he demanded that the lands ceded by Chief Lawyer be returned. This provided a rallying point for holdouts in other tribes. The Superintendents now had to devise compromises or their council might conclude without treaties. This failure could unravel the entire reservation plan for the Pacific Northwest.

The Council adjourned for three days while the Nez Perce listened to tales by Chief Looking Glass and ironed out internal differences. In the end, Chief Lawyer prevailed, retaining his head chief position over rival Looking Glass. However, Chief Joseph, leader of the Lower Nez Perce, remained unpersuaded of the benefits of a treaty and the resultant reservation. He cautioned his tribesmen to think far ahead of the impacts of the treaty,[1] evidently a matter not considered by the Nez

---

[1]In 1863, Chief Lawyer bowed to additional demands and gave up most of the reservation set aside at the First Walla Walla Council, including the Wallowa region. This caused the Nez Perce to formally split into two tribes with the followers of Chief Joseph, or Lower Nez Perce, refusing to enter into the new treaty and being referred to as the "nontreaty" Nez Perce. In 1877, Chief Joseph's son and namesake led the Lower Nez Perce in war against the United States caused by being forced to give up their Wallowa homelands and move across the Snake River onto the "treaty" Nez Perce reservation.

Perce chiefs.

With the interruption of the formal council sessions, the chiefs became restless. Many wanted to follow the advice of Chief Pewpewmaxmax to adjourn and meet later for more talks before any treaties were concluded. For both Superintendents, postponement was tantamount to failure. On June 8, Superintendent Palmer proposed a compromise, offering a third treaty with a reservation about 30 miles south of the Council site in the Territory of Oregon for the Umatilla, Walla Walla and Cayuse. Governor Stevens further compromised by increasing the amount of financial disbursements for all of the treaties.

A reservation separate from the Nez Perce appeased the Cayuse, but the crafty Walla Walla Chief Pewpewmaxmax negotiated separate terms as the price for his signing. This gave him permission to establish a trading post at the mouth of the Yakima River. Also, the government agreed to provide him a house, land improvements, and a 20-year $100 annuity for his son.

Historians advance different theories on the reason that these chiefs, who were so adamant against the treaties, capitulated and agreed to sign. It was clear that the Nez Perce were going to sign, and holding out further without the powerful Nez Perce was futile. Time taken out from formal council proceedings disrupted the mutual support gained from being together in a single forum. Chiefs Kamiakin and Pewpewmaxmax came to Governor Stevens on the morning of June 9; Chief Kamiakin agreed to sign regardless of what the other did. He stated that his young people were marrying and remaining on the coast and maybe this would bring them back.

After a stormy session that day, Chiefs Kamiakin and Pewpewmaxmax signed in private, the former signing for the absent Palouse as he claimed to be the high chief for the tribe by lineal descent. Others followed, including Chiefs Owhi and Skloom, a younger brother of Kamiakin, who with Chief Kamiakin were the only Yakimas with any strong following. Under their names, Governor Stevens placed absent Columbia River tribes that Chief Kamiakin and the other Yakimas did not control. Evidently, the Governor had an impression that Chief Kamiakin was the "high chief" of the Yakimas when there was none. Each chief spoke for his band. Group or tribal decisions were made by consensus in councils.

The next day, June 10, was Sunday, and few Indians were evident. Early on June 11, Governor Stevens appealed to Chief Lawyer, and he and the other Nez Perce chiefs signed. This isolated the Cayuse, inducing their chiefs to come forward and sign the treaty establishing the third reservation.

Although stormy and difficult, the Council was successful from the government point-of-view: The strong Columbia Plateau Indians ceded most of their land and agreed to go to the three reservations (see map, "Routes of Governor Stevens in 1853 and 1855," page 105). However, the treaties were not effective until one year after ratification by the United States Senate. Ratification occurred on March 8, 1859, over three and a half years later, making the treaties enforceable on March 8, 1860 — still four and a half years in the future. The treaties were to have some very different and unanticipated results before they became the law of the United States.

The Aftermath of the First Walla Walla Council

With the First Walla Walla Council ended, Superintendent Palmer and the Army left for Fort Dalles, and the Indians melted away. Governor Stevens and his party of 21 and two Indian guides left the Council site on June 16, journeying to the next three council sites (see "Map of Places and Events," endpages).

Governor Stevens wanted to complete his treaty work by fall, but was already behind schedule. In July, after another difficult session, he concluded the Flathead Council and treaty with the Flathead, Pend d'Oreille, Kalispel and Kutenai tribes. (The Kutenai subsequently escaped the provision of the treaty by moving north into Canada.) Governor Stevens's main concern lay with the Blackfoot tribes; there the objective was not establishment of a reservation but ensuring peace between the notorious Blackfoot tribes and other tribes of the region. Although the Governor and his party arrived at Fort Benton on July 26, events not under the Governor's control delayed the Blackfoot Council until the middle of October. This delay held him east of the Continental Divide until November.

Meanwhile, the Yakima chiefs had convened at Kamiakin's place near the Saint Joseph Mission on Ahtanum Creek. Some wanted to start a war, but Chief Kamiakin prevailed with the alternate proposal of closing Yakima land to all whites rather than making war outside of their domain. Messengers were sent to warn the "Bostons" to keep out and to enlist the support of other tribes in the Columbia River plateau. From the Puget Sound area, gold seekers passed through the Cascade Range and Yakima country, going to the Colville gold mining region. Even after being warned, the lure of gold caused many to risk the danger and continue to transit Yakima lands.

At The Dalles, Governor Stevens's sub-agent for the Yakimas, Andrew Jackson Bolon, known as "A.J.," a powerful man with renowned athletic ability, learned of the Yakima announcements from Nathan Olney, the Oregon Territorial Indian sub-agent at The Dalles. Since the Yakimas were his charge, Agent Bolon decided to go to Chief Kamiakin's lodge to determine the difficulty, but stopped along the way to visit with one of the band leaders and a good friend, Chief Ice, a younger brother of Chief Kamiakin.

Chief Ice persuaded Agent Bolon to return to The Dalles rather than continuing on to find Chief Kamiakin. Along the way, Agent Bolon fell in with a party of young Yakimas going to the Celilo Falls area to trade for fish. When the party stopped to build a fire and dry out, A.J. Bolon was pinned and his throat cut. Part of their reasoning for this murder was Brevet Major Haller's forces' having hanged three of their "cousin" Shoshonis in the Boise Valley the previous fall for the Ward Massacre.

When A.J. Bolon did not return as planned, Nathan Olney sent a local Indian to find out where Agent Bolon was. In addition to learning of the murder of A.J. Bolon, the Indian spy found out that at least six prospectors had been killed while on their way to Colville. Also, Chief Ice sent an old Yakima woman to Fort Dalles to tell the story of Agent Bolon's fate.

The Army Is Defeated

After a 15-day march from Fort Boise, Brevet Major Haller and the Fort Dalles garrison closed back into their post on September 18. Anticipating a mission from Major Rains to investigate the murders in Yakima country, he moved two companies, a detachment with a howitzer, animals, ammunition, and supplies to the north side of the river, preparing to move out when the orders came. Many of the troops were newly-arrived recruits, but the officers and sergeants were experienced in Indian operations. Major Rains ordered only one company to go, but Brevet Major Haller considered a stronger force advisable, and they were already prepared to go. On October 3, the force moved north with 84 soldiers, about 20 Indian auxiliaries and guides, the howitzer broken down into mule loads, and a pack train, headed for the Saint Joseph Mission at Ahtanum Creek where Chief Kamiakin and his followers resided. Major Rains ordered a company from Fort Steilacoom to reinforce through Naches Pass.

The column was detected as it moved through the mountains to the north of Fort Dalles. Yakima War Chief Qualchan sent messengers to the Yakima bands and other tribes to send warriors to meet this intrusion. Late in the afternoon of October 6, Chief Qualchan's initial elements of 200 to 300 warriors lay in wait as the soldiers descended from the heights south of Toppenish Creek. Soon a fire fight began, and continued until dark. Brevet Major Haller sent an Indian express rider back to Fort Dalles, alerting the garrison to the battle and requesting reinforcements and ammunition.

By the next morning, the Indians had increased their numbers to about 700; but the soldiers held them until afternoon, when Indian strength increased to an estimated 1,400. Then the tide of battle turned, but the Indians, as was their custom, withdrew at dark for rest. Taking advantage of the respite, the soldiers buried their two dead and began a night withdrawal, carrying ten wounded with them. Both the main body, which withdrew first, and the rear guard got away without being detected, but lost each other in the dark. The main body waited at the summit for the others to arrive, a pause that enabled the Indians to catch up after daylight. A day-long fight ensued, with the main body holding their own except for the mule carrying the brass howitzer barrel. Traversing the difficult terrain with such a heavy load caused the animal to break down. The gun barrel was unloaded and hidden, allowing the soldier column to move more rapidly although they were carrying wounded. Indian ambush positions encountered were readily dispersed.

After dark, the main body outdistanced their foes and caught up with the rear guard. Reinforcements greeted them the next day in Klickitat Valley, but they continued to withdraw, arriving back at their starting point on the morning of October 10. Casualties were five killed and 17 wounded. Historians estimate that about 40 Indians were killed or wounded; many died later from their wounds.

First Lieutenant Slaughter was in command of the 50 soldiers of Company C, Fourth Infantry,[1] coming through Naches Pass to reinforce Brevet Major Haller at

---

[1] Actually Lieutenant Slaughter was assigned to the first lieutenant position in Company A, but none

the Saint Joseph Mission. After defeating Brevet Major Haller's command, War Chief Qualchan sent forces into Naches Pass to ambush the soldiers. The Yakima scouts detected, coming towards the summit, a lone white man, whom they soon recognized as John Edgar, a former Hudson's Bay employee married to a Yakima woman. Edgar told the Indians that he was coming to warn them of the approaching soldiers; in turn they told him about defeating the soldiers from Fort Dalles. Actually, John Edgar was Lieutenant Slaughter's scout, and returned to warn the soldiers, preventing their probable annihilation in ambush. Lieutenant Slaughter turned his force around and headed back towards Fort Steilacoom.

This was the beginning of Lieutenant Slaughter's leadership of troop units from Fort Steilacoom in the Indian Wars fought in the Territory of Washington. This West Pointer's story is told in the monograph titled, "William A. Slaughter: An Early Casualty of the Indian War, 1855-56."

The Army Fails To Defeat Kamiakin

The defeat of Brevet Major Haller caused an uproar in both Oregon and Washington Territorial Capitals. Major concerns were that the Indians would revolt and form coalitions that could hurl superior numbers against small settler communities. Newspapers told the public of the Yakima uprising and of reports from other tribes about rising opposition to the treaties. Major Rains began planning for an expedition to punish the Yakimas.

Major Rains could muster only 334 soldiers from Forts Vancouver and Dalles, and about 75 from Fort Steilacoom. He turned to the Territorial Governors for volunteers. The Acting Governor of the Territory of Washington, Charles Mason, raised two Militia companies to guard the settlements while the Regulars were gone, but released one of the companies from the Puget Sound area to participate with the Regulars. From the Territory of Oregon came four mounted companies under Militia Colonel James W. Nessmith. (Six other companies of Oregon Territorial Volunteers were sent by their governor to the Walla Walla area to counter the Walla Wallas under Chief Pewpewmaxmax and to protect a small white community there.) To provide rank over the Militia officers, Acting Governor Mason commissioned Major Rains a brigadier general in the Washington Militia.

From a staging point across the Columbia from Fort Dalles, Major Rains planned to move north to the Saint Joseph Mission on Ahtanum Creek. Coming across Naches Pass, the post commander at Fort Steilacoom, Captain Maurice Maloney,[1] was to join Major Rains with all available Fort Steilacoom troops and the Washington Volunteer Company from the Puget Sound area. With this combined force, Major Rains planned to battle the Yakimas and their allies.

---

of the Company A officers was assigned for duty at Fort Steilacoom, so Lieutenant Slaughter was placed in command.

[1]Captain Maloney enlisted in the Fourth Infantry as a private in 1836 and rose through all of the enlisted ranks to Regimental Sergeant Major. In the Mexican War, he received a "battlefield" commission to second lieutenant and earned brevet promotions to first lieutenant and captain. Now he was a regimental captain, company commander, and post commander.

Captain Maloney left Fort Steilacoom on October 19, joining Lieutenant Slaughter along the White River two days later. There he waited for three more days until the Washington Territorial Militia Company of about 90 Volunteers arrived. This contingent reached the crest of Naches Pass on October 28, and Captain Maloney decided to rest his animals for a day before continuing. After pondering the situation, Captain Maloney turned around and headed for Fort Steilacoom on the 30th, sending by express a letter dated October 29 telling Major Rains that he did not have the strength and rations to continue into an unknown situation.

Major Rains, leading a force of about 700, consisting of Regular infantry, artillery and dragoons and mounted Oregon Volunteers, began movement on October 31, and arrived at the mission ten days later. (Routes taken by Major Rains and Brevet Major Haller are shown on the map "Operations in the Fall of 1855," page 44.) They had made contact on November 8, but Chief Kamiakin, his followers and the priests were gone when the initial elements arrived at the mission. The soldiers found a half keg of powder that the priests had buried in their garden to keep it from the Indians. They burned the mission before their officers could stop them.

Some days were spent waiting for Captain Maloney to arrive, while the troops made fruitless searches for the Yakimas. Indian scouts were observed continually, and some hasty fortifications were destroyed by cannonfire. Two companies of Regulars charged an Indian position with bayonets fixed, but the Indians vanished. The warriors were covering the movement of Yakima families, livestock, and household baggage across the Columbia River and on to the northeast. Chief Kamiakin had decided not to give battle, and the soldiers, primarily dismounted infantry, did not catch them and force a fight.

The return to Fort Dalles started on November 15. Snow had fallen, concealing the trails and making travel difficult. The dragoons and mounted Volunteers broke trails through the snow for the infantry and artillery. It was a miserable march. Tempers flared among the officers, leading to charges and counter-charges. None of these ever came to trial by court-martial, but letters were published in newspapers, among them the *New York Herald*. The operation had been a dismal failure, and Major Rains's subordinates blamed him for his undue caution and lack of decisiveness.

In mid-November, the six Volunteer companies sent by the Governor of Oregon Territory established their base at Fort Henrietta. They moved north in early December to the Walla Walla Valley, where they found Fort Walla Walla abandoned. Hudson's Bay's employees had left because of unrest among the Indians. Continuing their advance towards suspected Indian locations, they saw Indians, but encountered no hostilities.

Chief Pewpewmaxmax came in to discuss stopping the Volunteer advance upon his people and was taken hostage. He sent word to his people that the Volunteers would stop if they gave up their guns and ammunition. Refusing to comply, the Indians took their stand at Frenchtown, a group of settler buildings belonging to former Hudson's Bay employees, and a battle ensued. There were a number of Oregon Volunteer casualties. According to the Oregon Volunteers,

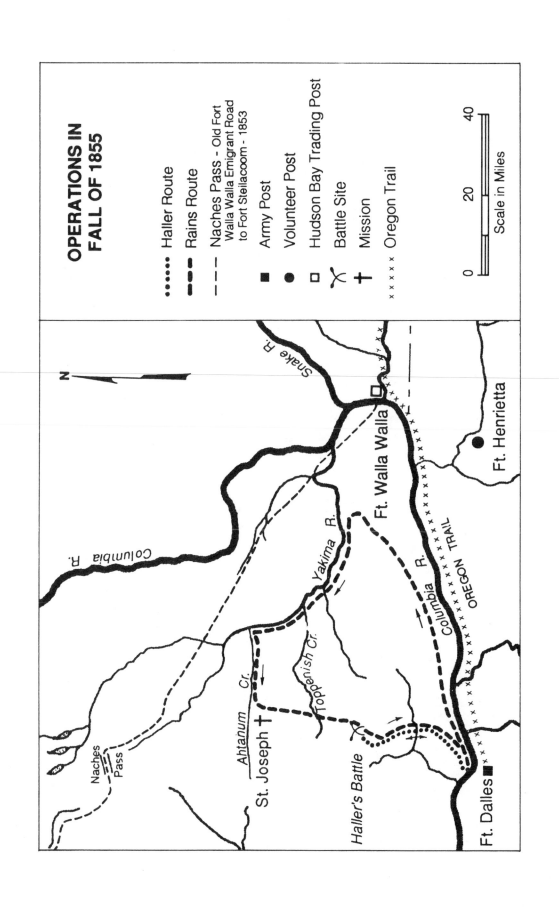

OPERATIONS IN
FALL OF 1855

••••• Haller Route
▬▬ Rains Route
─ ─ Naches Pass - Old Fort
     Walla Walla Emigrant Road
     to Fort Steilacoom - 1853
■ Army Post
● Volunteer Post
□ Hudson Bay Trading Post
⅄ Battle Site
✝ Mission
×××× Oregon Trail

0   20   40
Scale in Miles

N

Columbia R.

Snake R.

Ft. Walla Walla

Ft. Henrietta

Yakima R.

Ahtanum Cr.

St. Joseph

Toppenish Cr.

Naches
Pass

Haller's Battle

OREGON TRAIL

Columbia R.

Ft. Dalles

Chief Pewpewmaxmax and four of the five hostages resisted being tied up and were killed to prevent their escape. The Volunteers then scalped Chief Pewpewmaxmax and cut off his ears as souvenirs. After three days of seesaw fighting, the Indians left the battlefield.

War Comes to the Puget Sound Region

James Longmire was gone on October 10 when some Indians on horseback arrived with a Nisqually called Stub, who hunted for the Longmires. Rudely, they pushed the Longmire family aside, then sat in front of the fireplace talking to Stub, who listened, but said nothing. They left after Mrs. Longmire refused to feed them. After eating, Stub put his hand on Mrs. Longmire's head and said some mournful sounding words, repeated the same with the children and left. Later, they realized he was saying good-bye to go to war.[1]

The stand of Chief Kamiakin against the whites reached the Puget Sound Region in late September or early October, but the Indians were slow to begin the war. There was talk of war and peace around the fires at night, and as late as October 20, Chief Quiemuth assured Acting Governor Mason of the friendly intent of the Nisqually. Then eight days later, Muckleshoots led by their Chief Nelson massacred three settler families along the White River. The next day a Militia company attempting to reach Chief Leschi for a parley was pinned down near Connell's Prairie, between Sumner and Buckley, and was held for over four days; a lieutenant and a civilian were killed. Next, the express rider carrying Captain Maloney's October 29 letter to Major Rains and six volunteers riding with him were ambushed on the edge of Connell's Prairie. Two were killed. Chief Leschi was sighted by the riders in the vicinity before they were ambushed and was blamed for the murders. From around the countryside, settlers began to pour into Fort Steilacoom, where there were only a handful of troops for defense.

Captain Maloney's force arrived at Connell's Prairie on November 2. They found buildings burned and the body of the Volunteer lieutenant. A composite Regular and Volunteer force of 100 was sent in pursuit of about 80 Indians. At two river-crossing sites on the route of pursuit, the Indians made their stand, but on the fourth day they vanished into the thick forest. The search continued for another week, but no further contact was made. Captain Maloney closed his command into Fort Steilacoom on November 16. Regulars and Volunteers lost four killed and four wounded, including John Edgar. Indian losses were four killed outright and several more who died later from wounds. Some warriors, unnerved with the fighting, fled, taking their families away from the combat area.

The Puget Sound War had started. All military elements in the Puget Sound region worked together to confront and defeat their common foe. U.S. Government ships[2] provided arms and ammunition, sent parties ashore for

[1]R. A. Bennett, *A Small World of Our Own* (Walla Walla, Washington: Pioneer Press Books, 1985), p.186.
[2]U.S. Government ships operating on the Sound were Navy sloop-of-war *Decatur*, revenue cutter *Jefferson Davis*, survey steamer *Active*, and armed transports *Massachusetts* and *John Handcock*.

combat operations, and patrolled the Sound. The command at Fort Steilacoom stayed in constant contact with the Governor's office and the Territorial Adjutant General, both in Olympia, as the Regulars and Volunteers coordinated their operations in pursuit of the elusive Indians.

Lieutenant Slaughter took his company out again on November 24. Two days later they were reinforced by Third Artillery soldiers from California, sent into the field as riflemen. Some contacts were made, and the Indians made a raid and conducted an ambush. But after a period of about three weeks, it appeared that the warriors had disappeared into the forest. Winter rains had started, causing the streams to become swollen torrents. Constant exposure to the rain and cold brought most of the soldiers down with respiratory ailments. The troops were withdrawn to Fort Steilacoom on December 21, but Lieutenant Slaughter was not with them. He was killed in an ambush on December 4, 1855. The story is told in his monograph.

Replacing Lieutenant Slaughter was Lieutenant August V. Kautz (USMA Class of 1852). More than three years earlier, Lieutenant Kautz had been assigned at Fort Steilacoom for about six months, and had become friends with Lieutenant Slaughter. Fresh out of West Point, he was a brevet second lieutenant and was fortunate to get appointed to the second lieutenant position in the Fourth Regiment's Company H at Fort Vancouver rather than to another regiment in a different part of the frontier. Now he returned to the Fort Steilacoom garrison, promoted into the Company A first lieutenant vacancy left by his friend's death. The monograph on Lieutenant Kautz provides a sketch of this outstanding officer's professional career and achievements.

Commanding General, Department of the Pacific

It took a few days for the reports of Brevet Major Haller's defeat and Major Rains's retaliation plan to reach the Department of the Pacific Headquarters at Benicia Barracks on San Francisco Bay in California. Neither was well received by the Commanding General, Brevet Major General John E. Wool.[1]

Unlike some generals, General Wool was not political; but he was egotistical, exhibiting a contentious temperament that relegated anyone who disagreed with him to the position of a scoundrel with ulterior motives. On the other hand, in addition to having an outstanding combat record, General Wool was an honest and able administrator. In soldiers he admired discipline — a quality he found lacking in Volunteers. Congress passed a resolution on January 15, 1854, requesting the President "to cause a sword with suitable devices to be presented to General

---

These ships all were armed with naval cannons and carried stores of arms and ammunition. Also, the Hudson's Bay Company steamers *Beaver* and *Otter* were armed with small cannons.

[1] General Wool, a Regular Army brigadier general, was one of the Army's five "real" generals. Breveted and widely hailed as a hero in the War of 1812, as well as the Mexican War, this 70 year old had served with distinction both in combat and successive administrative and command positions in his 44 year career. Promoted to Regular Army major general in 1862, he continued to serve successfully to include as a Department Commander in the Civil War, some six to eight years in the future, until retiring at the age of 79 years on August 1, 1863.

Wool as a testimony of the high sense entertained by Congress" for his gallant and meritorious conduct in the Battle of Buena Vista, Mexico, and for his service in the war with Mexico.[1] Brevet Major General Wool was a national hero.

About mid-November, General Wool boarded the same ship that was carrying the Third Artillery company, which he had ordered to Fort Steilacoom from Benicia Barracks. The company commander, E. D. Keyes (USMA Class of 1832) a senior and experienced captain, was to form a new separate command, the Puget Sound District, at Fort Steilacoom, to prosecute the war that reports indicated was starting there. General Wool arrived just before Major Rains returned from his attempt to fight the Yakimas. Although he publicly stated his displeasure with Major Rains, he refused to start any court-martial proceedings, stating that he did not have the officers with sufficient rank for such a court. But he chastised Major Rains for asking the Territorial Governors for Volunteers and for accepting the Militia brigadier general appointment.

At Fort Vancouver, a company of Volunteers raised by Acting Governor Mason was waiting to be sworn into federal service. This company was to join Governor Stevens somewhere east of the Columbia Plateau for escort through the hostile areas. General Wool directed that the company be dismissed, pointing out that he did not have the budget to pay for these Volunteer troops.

Governor Stevens learned of the dismissal of the Volunteers through a message sent by express rider, with suggestions that he should go to the East Coast and return by ship and the Isthmus of Panama to Olympia. Not surprisingly, Governor Stevens took offense at General Wool's actions, starting a feud that continued into the Civil War. The primary issue was their different views of the causes and solutions of Indian problems.

In General Wool's opinions, which he aired in public, the interior was inhospitable for whites, and there was plenty of space west of the Cascades for white settlement. Indian problems were caused by the white intrusion on the Indians; leave them alone, and the problem would go away. These unpopular sentiments appeared in the press, exciting both politicians and their constituents. Wool also opined that the Army could better handle the Indian situation than the Indian Bureau and its string of superintendents and sub-agents. He repeatedly recommended that the Army become the Indians' "agent."

Governor Stevens's Return Journey

The first days of December, 1855 found Governor Stevens in Spokane Indian country. As the party traveled west from Fort Benton, an express-delivered message informed the Governor of two matters: General Wool's dismissal of the Volunteer escort company and suggestion that the Governor return to Olympia by ship; and the Yakima uprising and the presence of a Yakima war party searching for the Governor.

---

[1] W. H. Powell, *List of Officers of the Army of the United States from 1779 to 1900* (New York: L. R. Homersley & Company), p. 689.

A three-day council was held with the Spokane, Coeur d'Alene, and Colville chiefs (see "Map of Places and Events," endpages). The chiefs knew that at the First Walla Walla Council the Governor had proposed that the Spokanes relocate to the Nez Perce reservation. These were stormy sessions, since Chief Garry with his full command of the English language communicated the Indian position, placing the Governor on the defensive. Chief Garry refused to talk about land concessions or relocation. Pressing the advantages gained by Chief Garry, the chiefs told Governor Stevens that if they were to remain out of the Yakima-led uprising, they would tolerate no American military presence north of the Snake River. The Spokane Council ended without a treaty, and the Governor was severely rebuked.

After the Governor's party organized into a Militia company, it went to William Craig's place at Lapwai to gain the protection of Chief Lawyer. A one-day council was held, reaffirming Nez Perce support of the Governor. Before the council session ended, two Nez Perce chiefs arrived with news of the fighting at Frenchtown between the Walla Wallas and the Oregon Territorial Volunteers. A Militia company of 69 Nez Perce warriors was organized with Chief Spotted Eagle as captain; an additional 30 Nez Perce were included to handle the approximately 250 horses being taken along as spare mounts.

The Militia column led by Governor Stevens found many Indians and about 25 settlers, mostly French and half-breeds, in the Walla Walla Valley. These Indians had not participated in the fighting, and some chiefs came in to surrender, claiming that they were not participants. Governor Stevens addressed about 400 assembled Oregon Volunteers, thanking them for opening the way for his return, and condemning General Wool for not supporting him. The weather grew extremely cold, with temperatures recorded as low as 27 degrees below zero. Some horses belonging to the Oregon Volunteers froze to death. The Nez Perce Militia company was sent with William Craig — now the Indian sub-agent for the Nez Perce and a Militia lieutenant colonel — back to Lapwai to be mustered out. On January 1, 1856, Governor Stevens, his son Hazard, three of his men, two Nez Perce, and a Cayuse chief as a prisoner, left the Walla Walla Valley for The Dalles.

The Year 1856: In Like a Lion

Before returning to California in mid-January of 1856, General Wool laid out plans for the future. Colonel George Wright (USMA Class of 1822) was bringing the newly organized and trained Ninth U.S. Infantry Regiment to Fort Vancouver in a few weeks. The Regimental Lieutenant Colonel, Silas Casey (USMA Class of 1829), was to proceed with two companies to Fort Steilacoom and take over prosecution of the war there as Commander of the Puget Sound District. Colonel Wright was to take command of the Columbia River District from Major Rains and wait until the general returned in March to give further instructions before beginning a campaign into the interior.

Governor Stevens arrived in Olympia on January 19 to find the Puget Sound area enshrouded in gloom, but the headlines of a territorial newspaper hailed him as follows:

GLORIOUS NEWS FOR WASHINGTON TERRITORY.
GOVERNOR STEVENS RETURNED FROM BLACKFOOT COUNCIL.
LITTLE BANDYLEGGED "ROUGH AND READY" IN THE FIELD.[1]

Hostilities had subsided in the Puget Sound region. This was the rainy season, with its cold, wet, unhealthful conditions. Hostile Indians apparently had gone to hidden shelters in the forests, while the Army troops were withdrawn to Fort Steilacoom to recover from sickness caused by prolonged exposure to adverse weather. Volunteers primarily manned blockhouses, prepared to defend specific localities from the hostiles. Many men and some families had left Fort Steilacoom for their homes to protect their property and precious livestock. But this was just a lull.

Governor Stevens wanted action. He issued a special communication to the Legislature advocating a vigorous prosecution of the war. Citizens were urged not to leave their homes in the outlying areas, but to build blockhouses for protection where there were three or more families. Governor Stevens added to the scare by issuing an alert, credited to "reliable sources," stating that the piratical Northern Indians from the Queen Charlotte Islands and southern Alaska intended to come down in 16 war canoes carrying 50 to 60 warriors each, to attack settlements on the Sound.[2] Such a force never appeared.

Efforts were begun to raise a second regiment of Volunteers for service "anywhere," to replace the first Volunteer companies, which had been recruited for defense of particular localities. Indian auxiliaries were raised. Chief Patkanim of the Snohomish, assisted by Indian sub-agent John Taylor, organized a force of about 80 warriors,[3] while smaller auxiliary units were raised south of Puget Sound. Volunteers required the purchase of arms, ammunition and supplies, creating a large war debt that the Territorial Government did not have the funds to pay. Nevertheless, the Governor and the Territorial Government were determined to prepare for vigorous prosecution of the war, instead of leaving the task to the Regulars.

Governor Stevens came by the village of Seattle on January 25, aboard the U.S. Government's survey steamer *Active*, during his tour of the Sound communities. In Elliott Bay, the U.S. Navy's *Decatur* was anchored, and a lumber bark, *Brontes*, was close by. Defensive works were prepared in the village for the expected attack by "1,000" Indians led by Chief Leschi. Rumors abounded that Chief Owhi had brought many warriors with him from the other side of the Cascades to participate in the anticipated attack. Marines from the *Decatur* were part of the

---

[1]R. F. Watt, *Four Wagons West, The Story of Seattle* (Portland, Oregon: Binfords & Mort, 1931), p.232.
[2]W. P. Bonney, *History of Pierce County, Washington* (Chicago: Pioneer Historical Publishing Company, 1927), pp. 198-199.
[3]Chief Patkanim's forces did attack successfully Chief Leschi's forces on one occasion and participated with the volunteer forces on operations a few times. Chief Patkanim was paid by the officers of the Navy's *Decatur*, anchored at Seattle, for each head delivered. When he had no heads of his enemies, Chief Patkanim killed his slaves and sent their heads.

defensive force and manned a howitzer, which was positioned to fire over and beyond the range of the Marine and Volunteer rifles.

At mid-morning of the following day, the Indians began an attack, firing rifles at the manned defenses from distances, and moving about in groups. The howitzer and naval cannons[1] were fired at known and suspected locations of hostiles. For two hours the battle continued; then the hostile Indians pulled back, but stayed in the area, causing the defenders to remain cautious. During the day, the Indians took time to feast on beef roasted by their women from freshly-slaughtered stolen cattle. Two whites were killed while standing out in the open, but the Indians suffered no casualties. Food and other items were taken from vacated cabins, and cattle were driven off. During the night the Indians disappeared.[2]

Seattle was the site of the first and only deliberate assault by the Puget Sound Indians. Other contacts were raids, ambushes, meeting engagements, and hasty defenses against advancing Regulars and Volunteers. From a tactical perspective, the attack on Seattle was poorly executed, attesting to the Indians' lack of organized war skills.

The Ninth U.S. Infantry Arrives

On January 21, a few days before Seattle was attacked, the steamship *Oregon* had arrived at Fort Vancouver to discharge the Regimental Headquarters and Band, and six companies of the Ninth U.S. Infantry, under its commander, Colonel Wright. There were many accompanying dependents. Companies set up their camp on the parade field. On the following day, Lieutenant Colonel Casey's contingent of the four remaining companies and more dependents arrived aboard the steamship *Golden Age*. Two companies were sent to camp on the parade ground while the other two with baggage and equipment, were loaded onto the smaller *Republic* for transshipment to the Port of Steilacoom. The Ninth Infantry was close to authorized full strength, with more than 700 officers and men.

Puget Sound's Indian War

Departing Fort Vancouver on January 27, the *Republic* made a fast journey up the Washington coast and through Puget Sound, closing into the Port of Steilacoom on the 29th. The next day, Lieutenant Colonel Casey took command of the Puget Sound District and began planning and preparing for the Army to vigorously prosecute the war. The fifth monograph tells the story of this outstanding officer's command of the Puget Sound District during the Puget Sound Indian War.

---

[1]Sounds of the cannons, followed by explosion of the fuse of the arriving projectile and then the exploding cannon ball confused Chief Leschi's followers. They described this phenomenon as "mox-poohed."

[2]According to Captain Guert Gansvoort of the *Decatur*, Chief Leschi sent a message stating that they would be back, which caused continuing fear in the settlement, but this threat never materialized.

This was far from the most difficult Indian war situation Lieutenant Colonel Casey faced in his service. As a lieutenant and captain in the Second U.S. Infantry, he had fought Indians in the Indian Territory and in Florida, where the adversaries posed greater challenges than in the Puget Sound region — especially the Seminoles in Florida, where five years of his career were spent. After the Mexican War, where he was breveted to major and lieutenant colonel, he served in California and commanded, as a brevet lieutenant colonel, a major operation to subdue the tough Coquille Indians in southern Oregon Territory. Plucked out of the Second Infantry as a senior captain, he was promoted to the Ninth Regiment's lieutenant colonel slot without ever serving in the actual grade of major. He seemed the right leader to wrap up the Puget Sound Indian War in a few months.

Lieutenant Colonel Casey immediately sent troops to establish operational support bases and prepared the remainder of the command to put pressure on the hostile Indians to capitulate. On February 17, the Governor sent Lieutenant Colonel Casey a letter explaining plans to send 120 of the 160 Territorial Volunteers further into hostile country to build a blockhouse for an operational base. Lieutenant Kautz was already at such an operating base for the Regulars. Lieutenant Colonel Casey replied to the Governor on the same day that another company was going to join Lieutenant Kautz, and that he, Lieutenant Colonel Casey, and his entire command would be in the field by the 25th.

By March 1, the entire Fort Steilacoom garrison of five infantry companies and one artillery company were searching for the elusive hostile Indians in the vast, thick forest. Volunteer forces were also conducting operations. In the middle of March, a battalion of two infantry companies from Fort Vancouver, under the regiment's junior major, Richard S. Garnett (USMA Class of 1841), arrived to join the search.

On the Indian side, there were never more than 300 warriors, even counting those coming from east of the Cascade Range for short periods of time. The estimate of Puget Sound hostile warriors was a maximum of 175.[1] Most families went with the warriors, and many women were observed encouraging and supporting their men during fighting. As the fighting progressed, more and more of the warriors dropped out of the fight. Fighting the Regulars and Volunteers was much different than fighting another tribe, since the soldiers did not take time for war ceremonies or to ponder. Instead they pushed forward aggressively, causing casualties, and greatly disturbing the Indian and his family. This was not the way Indians wanted to fight; consequently, many took their families and went deep into the forest or relocated beyond the fighting areas.

As time progressed, the Indians were pressed more and more, and the Regulars reported an increasing number of villages abandoned. There were some sharp meeting engagements and aggressive attacks, but contacts became fewer and fewer. On April 25, a Ninth Infantry company surprised the hidden camp of Chief Nelson, the Muckleshoot leader who had led the first massacre the previous fall along the White River.

---

[1]J. A. Eckron, *Remembered Drums, A History of the Puget Sound Indian War* (Walla Walla, Washington: Pioneer Press Books, 1989), pp. 44-45.

When and how does a guerilla type war end? There is no peace conference, treaty, or ceremony in which the belligerents meet and a victor is declared. Lieutenant Colonel Casey and Colonel Wright jointly declared the Puget Sound war over on May 11, 1856.[1] There were some incidents after this date readily attributed to the war. It had been devastating to many in the Territory of Washington, both Indian and white, but the Indians had lost the most.

Stub, the Longmires' former Nisqually friend, was captured about two months into the war and hanged himself while in captivity in Olympia. It was also in Olympia that the Nisqually Chief Quiemuth was murdered. At the Indian's request, James Longmire and a group of others escorted Chief Quiemuth on a rainy night in November, 1856 to surrender to the Governor. It was about three o'clock in the morning, but Governor Stevens came down to meet them in his office, had food brought in, and gave the chief a pipe filled with tobacco. Mr. Longmire and the chief went to sleep on the floor, while the Governor went back to bed. Shortly, everyone was awakened by a shot, which left a wound in Chief Quiemuth's body, though he was actually killed by a stab wound to the heart. A suspect was tried for the murder, but was acquitted.[2] This is the only unsolved murder in the nation's history that occurred in a governor's office.

The 1856 Campaign Into the Interior

The Oregon Volunteers remained in the Walla Walla Valley after Governor Stevens left as the year of 1856 began, suffering that winter's unusual cold along with the Indians. In February, a force was sent across the Snake on a difficult and fruitless operation, in which many of their horses were lost to the shortage of grass and water or slaughtered to feed the hungry Volunteers. In April, they left the Walla Walla Valley with part of the command, taking the remaining settlers to Fort Henrietta. The remainder, a larger element, attempted to advance up the Yakima River, but they were thwarted by an estimated 300 Yakima warriors led by Chief Kamiakin. Yakimas retaliated by stampeding nearly all of the Volunteers' horses at their camp near The Dalles, which virtually immobilized the Volunteers. Indians also rustled 45 horses from the Volunteers at Fort Henrietta, and were last seen swimming their prizes across the Columbia.

Volunteers were expensive, and the Territorial Governments went heavily into debt to keep them on duty. The Territory of Washington issued over 1.6 million dollars in scrip, almost destroying the Territory's credit.[3] With the arrival of the Ninth Infantry, there were 19 Regular companies between the Puget Sound and Columbia River Districts. All but two of the Oregon companies were disbanded, turning the Yakima and other interior problems over to Colonel Wright. Even after the Puget Sound War ended in May, Governor Stevens kept the Second Washington Territorial Volunteer Regiment and some other units on duty, continuing to run up the Territory's war debt. There were plenty of Regulars,

---

[1]Eckron, *op. cit.*, p. 150.
[2]Bennett, *A Small World of Our Own,* pp. 186, 191-192.
[3]Eckron, *Remembered Drums*, pp. 109-110.

paid for by Congress, to handle the situation; but Governor Stevens could not tell the Regulars what to do, and he perceived a need to have military forces responsive to his requirements.

When General Wool arrived, Colonel Wright was already moving supplies up the Columbia River through the Cascades, where the drop in the river level created about 12 miles of rough water impassible to river steamers. Goods and passengers were portaged through this stretch, where the Army had established three block houses and other buildings — collectively called Fort Cascades — to protect the three transshipment sites. Flat-bottomed boats — bateaux — manned by local Indians — were used between the lower and middle landings. A horse-drawn tram ran from the middle landing to the upper site. Although there were sufficient river steamers on the lower river, there were only two, *Wasco* and *Mary*, on the upper part of the river.

Settler communities and businesses such as stores and boarding houses sprang up at these three landings, because the Army provided protection and wage-paying jobs, including employment for the Cascade Indians. These local Indians were noted for their hard work and for reporting to work early in the morning. There was no reason to suspect any hostility. In moving companies around to meet operational requirements, General Wool left no security force at Forts Vancouver and Cascades except for the nine soldiers manning the Fort Cascades blockhouse at the middle landing. These were considered safe rear areas.

Colonel Wright's command passed through Fort Cascades and was staging at Fort Dalles by the middle of March. His plan, influenced by Governor Stevens, was to go to the Walla Walla Valley, establish a post, and then move into the heart of Yakima country where the Naches River joins the Yakima. But these intentions were changed. Yakima warriors observed the departure of the soldiers from Fort Cascades and received Chief Kamiakin's approval for about 30 to raid the military and civilian stores accumulated there awaiting transshipment. The Cascade Indians were enticed to participate for a share of the booty, and some 20 Klickitats joined for the same reason.

On the morning of March 26, the attack began at the upper landing. Settlers fled to the local store, a two-story log building, to defend themselves. Tied up at the landing, the *Mary* barely escaped and joined the *Wasco* which was already on the river; both headed upstream towards Fort Dalles about 60 miles away. Shots near the middle landing alerted the settlers and the soldiers, and they gathered for safety in the Middle Blockhouse. There were settler casualties at the upper landing and both settler and Army casualties at the middle landing. But at the lower landing, warning came from an observer of the attack on the middle landing. This allowed time to evacuate women and children by bateaux and to form a defense force, which stayed until dark before leaving by a schooner and bateaux.

It was after midnight when, at Fort Vancouver, the river steamer *Belle* took aboard 40 dragoons commanded by Second Lieutenant Philip E. Sheridan (USMA Class of 1851) and headed upstream. At the lower landing, they fought a sharp engagement, driving the Indians back up the road which ran on the north bank to the middle and upper landing. Instead of continuing up the road, the dragoons crossed to the south bank, then crossed back over when they were opposite of the

Middle Blockhouse.

As related in his monograph, Colonel Wright's command came downriver on the *Mary* and *Wasco* from Fort Dalles and stormed ashore at the upper landing, dispersing the Indians in a short engagement. The counterattack to the middle and lower landings was commanded by Colonel Wright's second-in-command, Brevet Lieutenant Colonel Edward J. Steptoe (USMA Class of 1837), whose monograph follows Colonel Wright's. At the Middle Blockhouse, Brevet Lieutenant Colonel Steptoe met up with the dragoons and pushed on down the road to the lower landing, clearing the area of hostiles. The battle was over, though Regular and Volunteer reinforcements continued to arrive afterwards. Oregon Volunteers were unhappy and complained bitterly that there were no Yakimas there to kill. This was published in Oregon newspapers.

The Cascades Massacre was a surprise even after the boldness of the Indians in opposing the Oregon Volunteers during the preceding few months. A company was sent back to Fort Vancouver for security of the many Army dependents residing there, and a second company was left to garrison Fort Cascades. Minus these two companies, Colonel Wright's command went back to Fort Dalles to stage for future operations.

The Cascades Massacre changed Colonel Wright's priority from the Walla Walla Valley to the Yakimas, and the column of troops and their supporting pack train went north on the same trace taken by Brevet Major Haller the previous October. Near Ahtanum creek some scouts were encountered, and a band of Yakimas including women and children were overtaken. But Chief Kamiakin and his followers had left the Saint Joseph Mission area after being driven out by Major Rains and were now located to the north of the Naches River. After sending a messenger to the Yakima chiefs to parley, the command waited a day for their arrival and continued on to the Naches when they failed to show.

Spring runoff made the Naches a roaring torrent, causing the Army column to stop at this barrier with a large number of Indians visible on the other side. A messenger was sent across the river asking the chiefs for the second time to parley, and again the chiefs did not come in, although messages were sent back and forth. Colonel Wright sent for Brevet Lieutenant Colonel Steptoe to bring all of the forces at Fort Dalles forward, and for Lieutenant Colonel Casey to release Major Garnett and his battalion to join the forces gathering on the Naches. These reinforcements increased the strength from just under 500 to over 750 soldiers. Colonel Wright built Fort Naches as the supply base.

On the other side of the Naches, a large number of warriors gathered to watch the soldiers on the south side. A council of chiefs was discussing war and peace. The visiting Chief Pewpewmaxmax, the namesake of his murdered father, wanted to fight until fall; others were not sure. Chief Owhi, his son Qualchan, the war chief, and some others swam across the river for discussions with Colonel Wright and some of his officers. Brevet Major Haller talked to Chief Qualchan about helping to retrieve the howitzers hidden during his retreat from the Chief's warriors. Chief Owhi professed not to want war and promised to bring his people in to Colonel Wright's camp. They left and did not return. Chief Owhi did not keep his promise to Colonel Wright.

Bridging the Naches, the Army units were able to get to the other side, but found only a few strays and possible spies remaining in the area. Evidently, the Yakimas and their allies had decided not to fight. Later it was learned that Chief Kamiakin and his followers had gone to the Palouse River, about 120 miles north of the Walla Walla Valley, to live; and Chief Owhi and his band had just left the area to get away from the soldiers. Leaving a garrison at Fort Naches under Brevet Lieutenant Colonel Steptoe, Colonel Wright continued the campaign north as far as the Wenatchee River region, encountering many bands of Indians where parleys, not war, took place.

Hostilities in Yakima country ended forever with Colonel Wright's show of force and understanding of the Indians' needs. Many chiefs and their followers were enticed by the Colonel to follow the soldiers to Fort Dalles for resettlement in accordance with government policy. They came voluntarily. As it was the time of year for one of the salmon runs, many were left to catch and preserve this dietary staple. Colonel Wright reported that Indians in this region needed a large area to find sufficient food to sustain their existence.

On the way back to Fort Dalles, Major Garnett was detailed to build Fort Simcoe, a post for four companies, near the battlefield where the forces of Brevet Major Haller and War Chief Qualchan fought the previous fall. The purpose of Fort Simcoe was to keep the peace gained by this summer's campaign in Yakima country. Other companies were left in the field until fall to monitor the Indians fishing for salmon and to protect the good from the bad. Colonel Wright closed into Fort Dalles in August. The successful "bloodless" summer campaign was over.

The Second Walla Walla Council

The next step for the Army was to establish a post in the Walla Walla region. At the request of Governor Stevens, the first units arrived during the first week of September to replace the Washington Territorial Volunteers sent there for the Governor's next meeting with the Indians. The Volunteer enlistments were over, and they were about to be mustered out. Brevet Lieutenant Colonel Steptoe was assigned to build the fort and to remain in command, as related in his monograph.

The story of the Second Walla Walla conference began months before the meeting opened in September. Governor Stevens had failed to make a treaty with the Spokane, Coeur d'Alene, and Colville tribes when Chief Garry refused even to talk about land concessions at the testy Spokane Council in December, 1855. Since then, the Yakima-initiated defiance to the treaties was spreading now that the chiefs, other headmen, and warriors had time to ponder and discuss the issue. Reports from Sub-Agent William Craig carried disturbing information of the growing Spokane defiance infiltrating the Nez Perce. Athough Chief Lawyer remained firm, younger men and some of the lesser chiefs were openly challenging Chief Lawyer for giving up lands. It was obvious that the Governor and Superintendent of Indian Affairs had failed to dominate the Columbia Plateau tribes.

In his numerous letters to the Secretary of War, Jefferson Davis,[1] the Governor admitted problems with the Nez Perce, but felt that he could keep both the Nez Perce and the Spokanes friendly. He chastised both General Wool and Colonel Wright, stating that the Army operations were characterized by indecision and procrastination, and did not contribute to placing the hostiles under domination. In his opinion as stated in the letters, the hostiles needed to be forced into submission in order to preserve the peace in the Columbia Plateau. Messages were sent out to the Columbia Plateau chiefs to meet the Governor in the Walla Walla Valley on August 25, and demanding that all hostiles surrender unconditionally.

In June, the Governor sent the Second Regiment of Washington Territorial Volunteers to Walla Walla with one column moving from The Dalles and a second, under Lieutenant Colonel Benjamin F. Shaw, from Puget Sound through Naches Pass. Lieutenant Colonel Shaw offered to join Colonel Wright, but was refused; the Volunteers continued on, joining the others on July 7 at their camp site on Mill Creek in the Walla Walla Valley.

From the Nez Perce, Lieutenant Colonel Shaw learned of a village across the Oregon border in the valley of the Grande Rhonde River where the Walla Wallas, Cayuse, and Umatillas had gone to get out of harm's way. A Nez Perce chief guided them to the village. There were no chiefs present to make decisions, and the women became nervous when the approach of the Volunteers was detected. They packed all of their family belongings and foodstuffs, loaded their pack animals, and began to leave the area in a long pack train.

The approaching Volunteers sighted the dust from the pack train and prepared their attack. A brief attempt was made by the Nez Perce chief to parley, but Lieutenant Colonel Shaw was afraid that the pack train would get away; he swung the Volunteers into a cavalry attack running the pack train and its escorts for 16 miles, causing the Indians to lose most of their belongings and livestock.[2] The few warriors present fought back, killing two Volunteers, but the Indians lost about 60; those killed were almost entirely women, children, and old men.[3]

In his August 14, 1856, letter to the Secretary of War, Governor Stevens boasted of the great victory at Grande Rhonde, and stated:

> I push in person to Walla Walla tomorrow to meet the Indians, and establish relations of friendship with the tribes generally, and especially those struck by Lieut. Col. Shaw.[4]

---

[1]Washington National Guard Pamphlet ARNG 870-1-2/ANG 210-1-2, *The Official History of the Washington National Guard*, Vol. 2: *Washington Territorial Milita in the Indian War of 1855-56* (Camp Murray, Washington: Headquarters, State of Washington, Military Department, 1961), pp. 74-78, 86-88, 95, 97-98.

[2]Washington National Guard Pamphlet ARNG 870-1-2/ANG 210-1-2, *The Official History of the Washington National Guard*, Vol. 2: *Washington Territorial Milita in the Indian War of 1855-56*, pp. 98-100.

[3]D. L. Nicandri, *Northwest Chiefs, Gustav Sohon's Views of the 1855 Stevens Treaty Councils* (Tacoma, Washington: Washington State Historical Society, 1986) p. 28.

[4]Washington National Guard Pamphlet ARNG 870-1-2/ANG 210-1-2, *The Official History of the*

But on arrival at the council site he found the Indians seething. Only Chief Lawyer and his adherents among the Nez Perce were friendly.

The enlistment period of the Volunteers was up, and they left to be mustered out, with Governor Stevens expecting Brevet Lieutenant Colonel Steptoe to provide security of the council site with his four companies. However, the Army camp was located about eight miles away, so one of the Volunteer companies recruited in Oregon was called back for council site security. Chief Lawyer provided about 60 Nez Perce auxiliaries under Chief Spotted Eagle.

The Second Walla Walla Council opened on September 11. Representatives of the Nez Perce, Yakima, Cayuse, Umatilla, and Walla Walla tribes attended, but some of the ranking chiefs were missing, such as Looking Glass, Joseph, Kamiakin, and Owhi. The Spokane, Coeur d'Alene, and Colville chiefs refused to come. It was a stormy session, with the Governor often on the defensive. Chief Lawyer told the Governor that his people had entered the treaty in good faith, but *all*, not just the Indian, must adhere to its provisions. Many just wanted to cancel the treaties and keep settlers off their lands. The Governor insisted that the treaties be honored and wanted all warriors committing hostile acts turned over to him, but did not answer questions on what happened to whites committing depredations.

Security was a major concern as the Indians held councils among themselves. As suggested by Brevet Lieutenant Colonel Steptoe, the council site was moved on the fourth day, closer to the Army camp. On the way to the new location, the party encountered a Yakima war party led by Chiefs Kamiakin, Owhi and Qualchan, but the Yakimas withdrew on seeing the dragoons escorting the wagons. On the night of the 16th, there was fear of an attack from the Yakimas camped a mile away. The Nez Perce auxiliary beat drums all night and formed security around the Governor's camp.

The Second Walla Walla Council ended on September 17, and the next day the Governor's wagon train started for The Dalles, but had gone only about three miles before it was attacked by Yakima, Palouse, Walla Walla, and Cayuse warriors, and some disillusioned young Nez Perce. A defensive position was taken near a source of water. Threatened with reprisals to their families nearby, the Nez Perce auxiliary withdrew, leaving the Volunteer company to fight the battle. The next day, Brevet Lieutenant Colonel Steptoe sent his company of dragoons supported by infantry and artillery to escort the Governor's party into the Army camp. The Indians followed and attacked the soldier's camp, but were easily driven off by the Regulars. A few days later, Brevet Lieutenant Colonel Steptoe left one company to secure the supplies, and with the other three companies escorted the Governor, wagon train, and Volunteers to The Dalles.

The Year 1856: Out Like A Lamb

Brevet Lieutenant Colonel Steptoe and his command arrived back at their camp in the Walla Walla Valley on October 17, accompanied by Colonel Wright and his escort. During the Second Walla Walla Council, Brevet Lieutenant Colonel Steptoe had held talks with the Indian leaders, explaining the Army's plan to live among them in peace. In an order dated August 2, General Wool closed the Columbia Plateau to all whites except missionaries, Hudson's Bay employees, and Colville miners. This was disseminated in a proclamation by the Brevet Lieutenant Colonel.

Colonel Wright's purpose was to assure the chiefs and warriors of the Army's desires to maintain peace. Not many answered his call to parley, but he learned the Indian version of the Grande Rhonde incident and listened to the anxiety of young warriors. In return, the Colonel asked them to bury the past and live in peace in the future. He reported to General Wool by letter, relating the Indian version of the Grande Rhonde and reiterating his stand against ratification of the treaties which, in his opinion, were the cause of the hostilities. General Wool took this opportunity to send a long, scathing report to Army Headquarters on the mishandling and mismanagement of the Indians by Governor Stevens. In turn, the Governor complained to the Indian Bureau that Colonel Wright was usurping the prerogatives of the Superintendent of Indian Affairs for the Territory of Washington.

Colonel Wright returned to Fort Dalles in November and relocated his District and Regimental Headquarters to that post. Brevet Lieutenant Colonel Steptoe began the construction of Fort Walla Walla, working to get all four companies under shelter before the extreme cold set in after Christmas. For the Army, the campaigns of 1856 were over. Soldier and beast were in garrison for the winter. The primary activity was building barracks, quarters and other buildings.

Governor Stevens still had to face the Legislature, which opened on December 5. In addition to the failure of the Second Walla Walla Council, there were other lingering targets for his political enemies, the Whigs — such as the martial law imposed by the Governor on two counties.

During the previous spring, settlers near the Nisqually River accused retired Hudson's Bay employees, now settlers themselves, of aiding the hostiles.[1] Five were arrested and placed in the Fort Steilacoom stockade, but the Army released three, and the Militia placed the remaining two in confinement. Governor Stevens proclaimed martial law in Pierce County to prevent a trial in Steilacoom from granting their release by *habeas corpus*, and later in Thurston County to forestall a trial in Olympia for the same purpose.

The Legislature censured the Governor for proclaiming martial law and restored to duty a Volunteer company that he had dismissed for disciplinary reasons. More wounds were inflicted for the Second Walla Walla Council. The Legislature sent a recommendation to Congress asking for the Offices of Governor and Superintendent of Indian affairs to be separated. For Governor Stevens, that ended the stormy year of 1856.

---

[1]The settlers were losing livestock to night-time thievery by Indians who had taken refuge in the foothills to get away from the fighting. This situation disrupted their normal way of gathering food. To get meat, the Indians stole livestock from the "Bostons" and not the "King George men."

1857 — An Easy Year

In January 1857, Governor Stevens had returned from his great treaty expedition and was hailed in newspaper headlines as the conquering hero. This past year had successes and failures, also heralded in newspaper headlines, but he was still very popular with the voters. After the admonishments, the Legislators fell in line with the Executive's legislative program. On January 28, 1857, the Legislature passed a law incorporating the Northern Pacific Railroad Company with the name of Isaac I. Stevens as the first of 58 incorporators.

Before leaving for the futile Second Walla Walla Council, Governor Stevens had visited some displaced Puget Sound Indians on Fox Island across the sound from Steilacoom. At this July, 1856 meeting, he had listened as these confused people answered his questions on why the Indians went to war. Their answers concerned the need for land with water and grazing, and for access to fish and other native foodstuffs.

The Governor's staff was put to work on solutions, which were approved by Governor Stevens in December, 1856 and sent on to Washington, D.C. An Executive Order, dated January 20, 1857, corrected some of the inequities of the Medicine Creek Treaty. For the Nisqually, their 1,280 acre reservation was set aside for 4,717 acres in the Nisqually River Valley, consisting of ground on both sides of the river. Puyallup Reservation acreage was increased from 1,280 to 18,069 acres, to include land for the lower branch of the tribe which was left out of the Medicine Creek Treaty. The Muckleshoots were recognized with an allocation of 3,532 acres between the Green and White Rivers. So there was, after all, some gain for the Indians from the Puget Sound Indian War.

The Nisqually leader Leschi was tried for murder in March. He was accused of the October 31, 1855, ambush slaying of one of the express party carrying Captain Maloney's message to Major Rains. In the late spring of 1856, Chief Leschi and other Indian leaders of the Puget Sound War fled east across the Cascades into Yakima country. He returned in the early fall to be a fugitive in his own homeland, until November when a nephew tied him up and then turned in his uncle for a reward of 50 blankets. The first trial, held immediately after capture, resulted in a hung jury. The verdict in the second trial was guilty as charged in the indictment; Leschi was sentenced to be hanged on June 10 at Steilacoom. This was appealed to the Territorial Supreme Court while Chief Leschi was confined at Fort Steilacoom.

As told in the monograph on Lieutenant Colonel Casey, the Colonel and almost all of his officers, including Lieutenant Kautz, joined many others in opposing the execution, which caused the hanging to be delayed until February 19, 1858. In the end vengeance won out; but even the highly respected Chief Seattle of the Duwamish Tribe pointed out that Chief Leschi had to fight because his people were cheated at Medicine Creek.

After the hanging, the executioner, who had spent considerable time with Chief Leschi before his death, made a public statement that he felt convinced an innocent man was put to death. Previously, Lieutenant Kautz had proven that Chief Leschi could not have been at the point of the ambush, following trial testimony of another who claimed that he saw Chief Leschi in the area of the ambush.

Now changes in personnel — and personalities — took place. Late the previous year, General Wool requested reassignment and went to command the Department of the Missouri. His replacement, Brevet Brigadier General Newman S. Clarke, the Colonel of the Second Infantry Regiment, arrived at the Department of the Pacific Headquarters in March. About this time the Democrats of the Washington Territory nominated the Governor as their candidate for Delegate to Congress, which he won by a comfortable margin in the July 13 election. Arriving in Washington, D.C. later in the year, Delegate Stevens was looked upon as the authority on the Pacific Northwest. He used this prestige to attack General Wool and the General's exclusion policy for the Columbia Plateau. But in areas such as the Territory's war debt and treaty ratification, the realities of the Congressional process caused delays and frustration. Delegate Stevens devoted much of his boundless energy to completing his final report on the Northern Railway Survey.

General Clarke continued his predecessor's exclusion policy, but without creating the furor of the past, although the Washington Territorial Legislature and newspapers still expressed considerable opposition. From his headquarters at Fort Dalles, Colonel Wright refused to send his soldiers to arrest Indian leaders as demanded in newspapers and by the Territorial Governors. The previous year, about the time that he had selected the site for Fort Simcoe, Chiefs Quiemuth, Leschi, Nelson and others came to see the Colonel, requesting his intercession on their behalf. He suggested that they go home to their people and live in peace. Instead of offering amnesty to these Puget Sound War leaders, Governor Stevens and other politicians chastised the Colonel for not arresting them.

For the Army, the major activity of 1857 and into late spring of the following year was the building of their military installations. This construction activity created jobs and brought badly-needed money into the Territorial economy. In the Puget Sound District, a major rebuilding program was in progress at Fort Steilacoom, and two new posts were in the process of being built.

One of these, Fort Bellingham, was established by Captain George E. Pickett (USMA Class of 1846). Captain Pickett had arrived at Fort Steilacoom in June, 1856, after the Puget Sound War was over. Instead of deploying with the Ninth Infantry during the previous winter, he had been on detached service at a court martial. The monograph on Captain Pickett tells of his establishment of Fort Bellingham in Whatcom County, to protect the coal-mining community from Indians, primarily the piratical Northern Indians.

The second new post was just outside of Port Townsend to provide a buffer against the Northern Indians at the major entrance to Puget Sound. Colonel Wright's takeover of Fort Dalles for his headquarters and inland depot displaced Brevet Major Haller and his Fourth Infantry company to establish and build Fort Townsend. Patrolling the Sound for Northern Indians in the Government steamships was an activity for the Brevet Major and his company.

In the Columbia River District, money continued to be spent in developing Fort Vancouver and its supply and ordnance facilities into the best military installation in the Pacific Northwest. At Fort Dalles, the Army quartermaster building program included construction of a large house with an ornate facade as quarters (and office) for Colonel Wright. He and his quartermaster were reprimanded for building elaborate officers' quarters at a frontier post. The building program continued at Fort Simcoe, similar in architecture to Fort Dalles; however, the Commanding General of the Department and higher headquarters quartermasters never reached this isolated post, allowing Major Garnett to escape such criticism.

In the Walla Walla Valley, the situation was quiet. A small community was growing to meet the needs — labor and entrepreneurial — of the post, causing Brevet Lieutenant Colonel Steptoe to relocate the fort away from the settlers' cabins. The town was known as Steptoeville until the community organized politically and established local government. Vices abounded, a situation found at The Dalles and to a lesser extent in Steilacoom. But there was peace.

Beyond the frontier forts on the Columbia Plateau, Indians continued living as before in a society dominated by the warrior. Bands migrated to their food-gathering areas; hunting parties crossed the Continental Divide to hunt buffalo; and salmon runs provided the staple for most Indians. There was still livestock rustling, an age-old avocation of young warriors. But there were some changes: a Yakima chief returned some rustled livestock to Fort Simcoe to preclude retaliation by the Army. North of the Spokane River, the isolated mining community of Colville continued to flourish, connected by the Colville Road which ran almost due north for about 250 miles from Fort Walla Walla or Steptoeville to Colville.

News of the Frazer and Thompson River gold strikes in southwestern Canada reached Steilacoom, the largest "city" in the Territory of Washington, on March 25, 1858, while images of the California gold fields were still fresh in people's minds. Settlers left their homes in the Territory of Washington and went north across the international boundary. A flood of gold seekers came by sea and landed at Bellingham Bay and other coastal areas, creating a "bonanza" for entrepreneurs who could get their produce and goods to this market. Some enterprising prospectors came through The Dalles and passed by Fort Simcoe on their way to the lands of this new "El Dorado." Many gold seekers disappeared at the hands of marauding Indians (and probably others). For the Army commanders on Puget Sound, desertion became a problem, as young soldiers left to join the gold seekers bound for the Frazer and Thompson Rivers.

Miscalculations By the Chiefs in 1858

At Fort Walla Walla, Brevet Lieutenant Colonel Steptoe commanded the largest and most potent force of any post commander in the Pacific Northwest. It consisted of three dragoon companies, with another due to arrive soon, and two infantry companies. General Clarke, by correspondence through his adjutant, alerted the Fort Walla Walla Commander to plan an operation to the southeast along the Oregon Trail into the Snake River Plains. The operation was to begin after the dragoon horses returned from winter pasture at Fort Vancouver, escorted by the newly-arriving fourth company of Dragoons. They arrived on April 24.

Brevet Lieutenant Colonel Steptoe decided to change the operation. Palouse Indians raided in early April and ran off 13 head of Army beef cattle and some horses and cattle belonging to citizens of Steptoeville. These Indians had to be punished lest they became bolder. Also, some 40 citizens at Colville were concerned for their security and petitioned for Army forces to be stationed there. Oregon Trail immigrant trains did not reach the Snake River Plains until August, so the Army could handle their security after returning from Colville.

Setting out from Fort Walla Walla on May 6, Brevet Lieutenant Colonel Steptoe's force consisted of seven officers (all West Pointers), a medical officer, 152 soldiers, some Nez Perce scouts, and a pack train of civilian packers and herders with 85 mules and some beef cattle. The primary capability was the three dragoon companies. There were 25 mounted infantrymen with two six-pound howitzers. They did not anticipate any unusual reaction to this reconnaissance, beyond some police-type activity with the Palouse cattle rustlers.

They were not well armed even in comparison with the Columbia Plateau Indians, who carried Hudson's Bay Company trade rifles. Two companies of dragoons carried musketoons, which were useless beyond 50 yards. The third had Mississippi Jaeger rifles, which had adequate range but could not be loaded from horseback. Some of the dragoons had revolvers; most had antiquated muzzle-loading pistols. The mounted infantry had ten good carbines, while the others carried Mississippi Jaeger rifles. Sabers were limited to officers and noncommissioned officers. Due to an error in loading the pack mules, only 40 rounds of ammunition per man were taken — a serious error if trouble were encountered.

At the Snake River, Chief Timothy's band ferried the party in canoes and swam the horses and cattle across the river. Instead of following the Colville Road, the column went farther east to find the Palouse raiders of their livestock. This was the region where Chief Kamiakin and his followers now lived. Some 20 miles north of the Palouse River, a large war party (estimates range from 600 to 1,200) appeared to their front at about 11:00 Sunday morning, May 16. The Indians were all mounted, and most were armed with rifles. The two forces halted about 200 yards apart, and some chiefs came forward to parley. From his conversations with the Indians, Brevet Lieutenant Colonel Steptoe knew it was suicide to continue, and made camp for the night. The Indians taunted the soldiers, saying it was Sunday, but they would fight tomorrow.

It was not Brevet Lieutenant Colonel Steptoe's intention to fight this superior force, and he began a march south at sunrise, generally following the path of the previous day. At about 8:00 a.m., warriors appeared and followed closely behind the rear guard. Father Joseph Joset from the Sacred Heart Mission, located with the Coeur d'Alene Tribe, came in, suggesting another parley. Brevet Lieutenant Colonel Steptoe agreed, but pointed out that his command would keep moving. Only one Coeur d'Alene chief came in, and he left just before the Indians began shooting, first from long distances at the rear guard.

The Battle at Tohotonimme (the Nez Perce name for a stream now called Pine Creek) was fought on Monday, May 17. The monograph on Brevet Lieutenant Colonel Steptoe contains his report of the battle, a first-hand observation of how this day was saved by the discipline and determination of the greatly outnumbered Army officers and men. It was a day-long running battle, with the Army units keeping their moving defense oriented on the pack train. Howitzers were used when the situation favored their employment. Indian warriors swarmed like bees while the dragoons held their formations. Only once did a dragoon company fall back in disorder from the onslaught of superior numbers. In reference to this incident, Brevet Lieutenant Colonel Steptoe stated in his report that the company fell back "in confusion and could not be rallied." Modestly, he failed to record that he personally rallied them back into the fight.

The companies of the First Dragoons and Ninth Infantry acquitted themselves well. With ammunition running out in mid-afternoon, the command took up defensive positions on a large hill overlooking the Tohotonimme. Twice the Indians made dismounted attacks, only to be beaten back both times. After dark, the command executed a night withdrawal that went undetected by the Indians. They rode about 75 miles to reach the Snake River at dawn. Chief Timothy set up security, and his band ferried them across the river early the next morning.

The Army command lost five killed, six badly wounded, and seven lightly wounded. In his report, Brevet Lieutenant Colonel Steptoe gave Indian casualties as nine killed and 40 to 50 wounded. This claim is modest; probably the soldiers did not have the time to count Indian casualties. At least 12 Indians were killed at one time by charging dragoons, and the Coeur d'Alenes lost three important chiefs.

A Ninth Infantry company, coming by forced march from Fort Walla Walla, reached them just after the ferrying was completed. The next day, as the Army column was continuing its march towards Fort Walla Walla, a sizable band of Indians with a large American flag for a standard galloped into view. Chief Lawyer came forward and offered to join the Army in defeating the hostiles. The offer was acknowledged with appreciation, but Brevet Lieutenant Colonel Steptoe's command was not in condition to return. The Army column closed into Fort Walla Walla on May 22.

The Battle at Tohotonimme was the Columbia Plateau Indians' great miscalculation. It caused the political mood in Washington, D.C. to change radically against these Indians, resulting in the loss of Army support. Delegate Stevens used the defeat as proof of the failure of Army Indian policies in the Territory of Washington and justification to push for Senate ratification of the treaties. Political pressure resulting from the defeat caused the Army to open up the interior to settlers even before the Senate ratified the treaties about ten months later on March 2, 1859. The Battle at Tohotonimme was the beginning of the end for the "warrior way of life" in the Territory of Washington.

The Army Has Its Days

General Clarke arrived at Fort Vancouver on June 23 to set up a separate headquarters under his personal control to plan and direct the retaliatory operation. In an earlier report, Colonel Wright had informed the general that all

Indians in the Columbia Plateau could be expected to join the uprising, stating that a force of 1,000 men would be necessary to subdue the large number of warriors available. Based upon this advice, companies from the Fourth Infantry and Third Artillery stationed in California were on their way as reinforcements. Colonel Wright, Brevet Lieutenant Colonel Steptoe, and Major Garnett were summoned by General Clarke for consultations.

The Catholic priests at the Sacred Heart Mission were enlisted as intermediaries to transmit letters to the Indians and to send back their replies. The missionaries readily accepted this role and wrote back of their futile attempts to open the eyes of these misguided savages to the need for peace and the horror of war. According to the missionaries, Chief Kamiakin was exciting the warriors into eagerness to fight the soldiers again. Through the missionaries, the chiefs were told that the Indians must admit and atone for their crimes; allow Army troops in their lands; turn in all government property in their possession; and surrender all warriors who fired on Army troops against the wishes of their chiefs. This last condition meant hanging to the Indians. They preferred death in battle to the dishonor of being hanged. Chief Garry and other chiefs sent word back through the missionaries that they would not turn in their warriors. Obviously, the Indians, fresh from another victory over the Army, were defiant, with no desire to listen to reason.

General Clarke sent out orders on July 4 directing Colonel Wright to take command at Fort Walla Walla and to commence operations with at least 600 men in early August, leaving Brevet Lieutenant Colonel Steptoe with an adequate strength to defend the post. In addition to the Fort Walla Walla garrison of four companies of the First Dragoons and two of the Ninth Infantry, six companies of the California-based Third Artillery were added to his force. Authorization was given to employ friendly Nez Perce for the mission and to supply them with arms, ammunition, and old Army uniforms. A vigorous war was to be conducted against all hostile Indians, driving the dissidents into complete submission.

Orders to Major Garnett, sent out two weeks later, contained the same instructions tailored to his operational area. His reinforcements were two Fourth Infantry companies, also from California. One company was to remain at Fort Simcoe for security of the post. Major Garnett asked for 30 to 50 dragoons, but since these were not provided, he planned to mount about 40 infantrymen on the horses belonging to Fort Simcoe to perform the calvary function.

Preparations for operations occupied the commanders, their officers and men even before General Clarke arrived at Fort Vancouver. It was a large undertaking to take 900 to 1,000 troops on a campaign for 60 or more days of operations — one that had not been done before in the Columbia River District. Equipment was inspected at the forward posts, and supplies and ammunition inventory taken to determine amounts to be ordered. At Fort Dalles, Army quartermasters received material from Fort Vancouver by river steamer and contracted for transportation of supplies, ammunition and pack animals to the forward posts. Extra money was pouring into the Territory's economy from the Army's preparations for war.

By the last week in July, reinforcing companies were at Forts Simcoe and Walla Walla after long, hot, dusty marches from the river port at Fort Dalles. The

Fort Vancouver

[Special Collections Division, University of Washington Libraries]

first order of business was training in marksmanship and tactical skills to counter the warriors' method of fighting. Four of the artillery companies were designated foot soldiers and were trained for this role. (Delegate Stevens stated in Washington, D.C. that the Indian could be defeated only by mounted troops. Ten of the 16 companies were foot troops, two were artillery, and four were dragoons.)

In contrast to Brevet Lieutenant Colonel Steptoe's force, the troops were equipped with arms and ammunition adequate to the task. The dragoons were issued breach-loading Sharps carbines, Colt revolvers or older cavalry pistols, and they carried sabers. For their foot-soldier role, the artillerymen carried the new Springfield .58-caliber 1855 model rifle musket. The infantrymen's improved Mississippi Jaeger rifle fired the same efficient minié ball as newer guns. Some men were relatively new recruits, but the training brought them equal to the veterans for this mission.

The Secondary Attack

Major Garnett planned to go north to the juncture of the Wenatchee and Columbia Rivers, and then follow the west bank of the Columbia to Hudson's Bay Company's Fort Okanogan. From there his route went east along the north bank of the Columbia before crossing that river near the mouth of the Spokane. The final leg was a thrust north up the east side of the Columbia to Kettle Falls before returning to Fort Simcoe (see map, "Operations in 1858," page 153). Assigned tasks included apprehending members of the Sinkiuse tribe involved in the June attack on a party of California miners going to the Frazer River gold strikes. Instructions stated that anyone determined guilty of participating in the attack would be executed. It was expected that all hostile Indians who escaped from the troops from Fort Simcoe would be driven into Spokane country where Colonel Wright would deal with them.

The light infantry force moved out from Fort Simcoe on August 10, in four companies. There were nine line officers,[1] one medical officer, and 306 enlisted men. Provision for 50 days was packed on 225 pack animals, both mules and horses, tended by 50 packers and herders. A few head of beef cattle were taken along. Officers left behind their swords and carried pistols and rifles. Bayonets were considered not practical for the type of warfare anticipated and were left behind. "Hudson's Bay shirts" were substituted for the regular tunic as a more practical uniform. In the lead were 15 of the mounted infantrymen commanded by Second Lieutenant Jesse K. Allen (USMA Class of 1855), staying 300 yards to a mile ahead and placing out flank guards as dictated by the terrain. The companies followed in single file with a 50-man rear guard protecting the pack train.

On the fourth day out, Indian scouts reported that several warriors who had attacked the miners were at a camp some 20 miles ahead. Lieutenant Allen set out after dark with 15 of his mounted infantrymen to surround and capture the Indian camp before daylight. One warrior was killed as he tried to bolt through the circle

---

[1]Five were West Pointers, and four of the nine officers became general officers in the Civil War, one for the Union and three for the Confederacy.

of soldiers, but the rest of the band, consisting of 21 men, about 50 women and children, 70 head of horses, and 15 head of cattle, was captured. Lieutenant Allen was mortally wounded in this action, probably in the cross-fire of his own soldiers. He died early in the afternoon — the only Army battle casualty of the operation.

Three Indian men were identified as participants in the attack on the miners and shot while tied to trees. Another participant was shot while eluding capture. Four days later, at another village, five more participants were tied to trees and shot after four admitted their guilt and implicated the fifth in a military trial.

By August 25, the light infantry was near the mouth of the Wenatchee.

The Main Attack

Colonel Wright's plan was to make a deliberate crossing of the Snake River at the mouth of the Tucannon River, a short distance downstream from where the Palouse River joins the Snake. After his force was across the Snake, it would go generally north through Palouse country to the Spokane River, and into the heartlands of the Spokanes and Coeur d'Alenes. The command started leaving Fort Walla Walla, 75 miles to the south, on August 7 for a planned deliberate crossing on August 23.

At the crossing site, the Snake River was about 275 yards wide with a swift current, but this was low-water season, and crossing conditions were as good as could be expected. On the south side of the river, overlooking the crossing site, Fort Taylor[1] was constructed to garrison an artillery company with two six-pound howitzers as security for the crossing site. The expedition quartermaster had constructed a large flat-bottomed boat and made a ferry by lashing together some boats brought from Fort Walla Walla. Nez Perce Indians were hired to drive animals across by swimming after them. Fort Taylor, boat and ferry were to stay in place until the command returned.

A violent storm delayed the crossing for two days until the Third Artillery began crossing at 5:00 a.m. on August 25. Next came the two Ninth Infantry companies and part of the pack train. On the following day, the dragoons and the rest of the pack train crossed. Both days went without incident.

The expedition began its movement the next day, August 27. The order of march began with three dragoon companies, also providing flank security and point, followed by the artillery howitzer company with two 12 pound-howitzers. Next came the four-company battalion of artillery foot soldiers, followed by the infantry battalion of two companies, pack train, command headquarters, quartermaster pack train and a company of dragoons as rear guard. There were 190 dragoons, 380 infantrymen and artillerymen, 23 officers,[2] and two medical officers.

---

[1]Fort Taylor was named for Brevet Captain Oliver H. P. Taylor (USMA Class of 1846), the commander of Company C, First Dragoons, who was killed during the Battle of Tohotonimme on May 17, 1858. Also, in memorial, the high basalt cliffs that guide the Tucannon into the Snake were named on one side for Brevet Captain Taylor and on the other side for Second Lieutenant William Gaston (USMA Class of 1857), the commander of company E, First Dragoons, killed about 30 minutes before Brevet Captain Taylor.

[2]Twenty-one of the officers were West Pointers, including former cadets. Seventeen became general

There were 30 Nez Perce scouts proudly dressed in Army uniforms. This command was embarking on the largest and most significant military operation ever conducted on the soil of the Territory of Washington.

The monograph on George Wright covers the next 40 days as this West Pointer led his command in two battles in which the Columbia Plateau Indians were decisively defeated and suffered a large number of casualties[1] while the Colonel's force had only one soldier slightly wounded. (The route Colonel Wright's command followed is shown in the map on page 153.) The monograph follows Colonel Wright as the terms of peace were dictated, the guilty were punished, and compassion was shown for the good. After this campaign in the late summer and early fall of 1858, no more battles were fought on the soil of the Territory or State of Washington. Colonel Wright brought peace.

When the soldiers arrived at Fort Walla Walla on October 5, Colonel Wright's West Point classmate, Colonel Joseph K. F. Mansfield, the Army Inspector General, was waiting. The Inspector General was highly complimentary on the condition of the men's arms and equipment, especially after over 40 days on a major combat operation. This was further testimony to Colonel Wright's successful methods of command and leadership.

The Secondary Attack Is Completed

Major Garnett reached the mouth of the Okanogan River on September 7. His command had no significant contacts after August 25. When informed by express that Colonel Wright had already defeated the Indian coalition, he realized there was nothing to gain by continuing. Supplies were running low, and the men's footwear was wearing out. Major Garnett started back on September 15 and arrived at Fort Simcoe a week later, releasing the two companies from California on September 25.

The Inspector General, Colonel Mansfield, arrived to inspect Fort Simcoe on October 15; but Major Garnett was not there. During the campaign, his wife and their infant son had died of fever at Fort Simcoe. He had left to take their bodies to New York City for burial — where he, too, would be buried some years later: Brigadier General Robert S. Garnett, Confederate States of America, was the first general officer to be killed in action during the Civil War.

Department of Oregon

Over a week after Congress adjourned on June 9, the news of the defeat of Brevet Lieutenant Colonel Steptoe's command on May 17 at the Tohotonimme reached the East Coast. The news sent reverberations through the Government, the War Department in Washington, D.C., and Army Headquarters in New York City. Next came General Clarke's June 2 letter informing the Army's Commander-in-Chief, Major General Winfield Scott, of the advanced headquarters at Fort Vancouver,

---

officers in the Civil War; 12 were in the Union Army, and five served the Confederacy.

[1] Chief Kamiakin was badly wounded and went to Canada to recover.

from which General Clarke would personally direct the situation.

The separate command headquarters for the troubled Pacific Northwest provided a way for the Secretary of War and Army Commander-in-Chief to show response to the situation. Using General Clarke's concept, the Department of Oregon, headquartered at Fort Vancouver, was established on September 13, covering the Territories of Washington and Oregon (excluding the Rogue River watershed in southwestern Oregon, which remained in the Northern District of California). The remainder of the Department of the Pacific was redesignated the Department of California.

The Army's newest "real" general, Brigadier General William S. Harney, was appointed to command the Department of Oregon. Just promoted on June 14 to brigadier general, the controversial General Harney was politically adept and effectively used the Congressional delegation from his home state of Tennessee.[1] Promoted to the Regimental Colonelcy of the Second Dragoons in 1846 at the beginning of the Mexican War, he was acclaimed at the April 18, 1847, Battle of Cerro Gordo, receiving a brevet to brigadier general for "gallant and meritorious conduct." But General Harney was arrogant and had a propensity for following his own bidding rather than the direction of his superiors. This led to incidents in which units under his command were placed in difficult situations that a more prudent commander would have avoided. Adeptly, General Harney used his political connections to escape from problems with his superiors.

In reputation, General Harney was considered by some as a foremost Indian fighter, while others tagged him "squaw killer." In the Seminole War, he allegedly hanged Indians arbitrarily after a disastrous action in which his command suffered numerous casualties. His treatment of Indians caused a rift with the Army's Commander-in-Chief, Major General Winfield Scott, which he escaped only through his political connections. More recently, in 1855, General Harney had led a brutal attack on a band of Brulé Sioux in which many of the 85 Indians killed were women and children. A Congressional inquiry condemned the attack, but General Harney's promotion was confirmed by the Senate less than four years later.

General Harney arrived at Fort Vancouver on October 24, 1858, after passing through the Army Headquarters in New York City and the War Department in Washington, D.C. The Secretary of War's[2] orders, prepared without knowledge of the results of Colonel Wright's campaign, ordered harsh action against the hostile Indians of the Columbia Plateau, emphasizing their vulnerability in the winter because of a regular shortage of food and forage. In addition to striking the hostile Indian, these instruction directed capturing their families and destroying their herds of horses and cattle; no overtures of friendship were to be made before chastisement to instill in the Indians the evils of war. This coincided with General

---

[1] As a young officer, General Harney was a protegee of President Andrew Jackson of Tennessee, which led to the appointment of Infantryman Harney, after only three years in grade as a major, to the lieutenant colonel position in the Second Dragoons when the Regiment was first organized in 1836. This promotion propelled General Harney ahead, providing a significant advantage over his contemporaries.

[2] John B. Flood came in with the Buchanan Administration, replacing Jefferson Davis as Secretary of War.

Harney's approach to Indian problems. In San Francisco, he learned of the success of Colonel Wright's campaigns.

It was General Harney's first inclination to begin the campaigns again; however, an October 28 report from Colonel Wright assured the General that the Nez Perce, Spokane, Coeur d'Alene, Palouse, Walla Walla and other tribes along the Columbia and its tributaries were now all friendly. General Harney sent the letter and copies of Colonel Wright's treaties to Army Headquarters, endorsing Colonel Wright's views. One of General Harney's first acts was to allow expanded settlement in the Fort Walla Walla vicinity.

Accompanying General Harney on arrival at Fort Vancouver was a Belgian Jesuit priest named Pierre Jean de Smet, who was sent to visit the formerly belligerent tribes where he had been a missionary some 12 years earlier. At Fort Walla Walla in November, he obtained the release of the hostages and prisoners held there, to accompany him to their tribes. For six months in the winter of 1858-59 and the spring of 1859, he went to various tribes to talk peace.

Father de Smet found the Indians confused and restless, but wanting peace as a result of Colonel Wright's campaign. In May he brought eight chiefs from the Flathead, Coeur d'Alene, Kalispel, Colville, and Spokane tribes to Fort Vancouver, but Chief Kamiakin of the Yakimas and Palouse became suspicious at Fort Walla Walla when warned by an Indian agent of the possible consequences, and slipped away. The others visited the Fort Vancouver area for three weeks, seeing at first hand the power of the whites.

1859: A Year Without Fighting

In the interior of the Department of Oregon, the focus turned farther east in 1859 as General Harney reasoned that any Indian problems that might arise would occur there. Fort Simcoe was closed, with the last two companies leaving on May 28 for a 383-mile road march through Fort Walla Walla to a site 14 miles east of the Hudson's Bay Fort Colville. A third company joined at Fort Walla Walla, and the force arrived on June 20 to establish Harney's Depot, later designated Camp and then Fort Colville. Next a composite force of infantry, artillery, dragoons and engineers left Fort Dalles on May 28, going up the John Day River and across the Blue Mountains trying to find a shorter route for the Oregon Trail. They went all the way to the Great Salt Lake, but returned on the regular immigrant trail, having decided that it was the best route. Finally, in June, the District and Ninth Regimental Headquarters was relocated from Fort Dalles to Fort Walla Walla to place Colonel Wright closer to the Oregon Trail and potential Indian problems.

In the Puget Sound region, road work was continuing. As an alternative to the difficult Naches Pass, the Legislature sent a memorial to the Congress justifying a wagon road through Snoqualmie Pass. A bill authorizing $75,000 was introduced in Congress, but it was not passed because of the Civil War.[1] Consequently, the road through Snoqualmie Pass continued to be little more than

---

[1]R. F. Watt, *Four Wagons West: The Story of Seattle* (Portland: Binfords & Mort, Publishers, 1931), pp. 266-277.

a trail. Road projects from the Columbia River north past Puget Sound to Bellingham were funded, however, and work was in progress.

Water was the most economical mode of transportation in the Puget Sound region, and numerous vessels operated on the sound. The *Julia* was the newest steamship and considered the flagship of the commercial fleet. A significant capability was gained by the transfer of the *Massachusetts* back to the Army with Steilacoom as its port; the ship was now a part of the District of Oregon's forces available for patrolling, troop transport, afloat headquarters, and other uses. Its armament was four 32-pounder naval cannons.

In May, the U.S. Deputy Director of Customs, residing on San Juan Island, the major island of the San Juan Archipelago, sent a letter to General Harney requesting the stationing of 25 soldiers on San Juan Island for protection from marauding Indians. He also visited Captain Pickett at Fort Bellingham to make the same request. The previous year, Brevet Major Haller had sent a detachment over to San Juan Island on the *Jefferson Davis* because Indians had garroted two unknown white men, probably Frazer River gold seekers. A short time later, British Marines from Esquimalt, the naval base on Vancouver Island, went to one of the islands in the San Juan Archipelago to rescue from marauding Indians a large party passing through to the gold fields. Obviously, both the British and the Americans thought the San Juans were their sovereign property.

In 1846, the Treaty of Washington established the 49th parallel as the boundary from the Rocky Mountains to the Pacific, with the exception of Vancouver Island, which went to the British. But the treaty failed to identify which of the two principal channels, running generally north and south between Vancouver Island and the mainland, was the boundary. The British claimed that Rosario Strait, the eastern channel closest to the mainland, was the boundary; while the Territory of Washington chose Haro Strait, the western channel. Both claimed the San Juan Islands lying between the two channels. Consequently, the Hudson's Bay Company set up ranching operations on what the British called Bellevue, while the Legislature of the Territory of Washington included the same islands, called San Juans, in Whatcom County. Tax collectors came from both sides; a standoff was inevitable.

Another point of difference was the population. Although charged by the British Government with the responsibility of colonizing, the Hudson's Bay Company was not successful at it; while from the American side settlers came on their own looking for a place to live and, most often, a plot of land. The few British subjects in the San Juans worked for Hudson's Bay, while there were probably close to 50 Americans permanently residing on the main island.

There were far more Americans than British even on Vancouver Island. About 23,000 Americans had arrived by sea over the past year to seek gold along the Frazer and Thompson Rivers. Another 8,000 came by land. After the realization that very little gold was to be found, many Americans ended up on Vancouver Island. In correspondence to Army Headquarters, General Harney indicated that Vancouver Island could be taken over, because there were far more Americans and foreigners there than British.

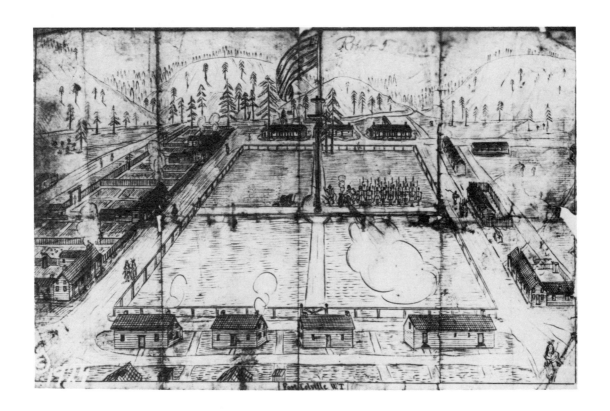

Fort Colville, circa the 1860s.

[Special Collections Division, University of Washington Libraries]

Arriving aboard the *Massachusetts* in Bellingham Bay on July 6, General Harney and his adjutant, Captain Alfred Pleasonton (USMA Class of 1844) and his quartermaster, Captain Rufus Ingalls (USMA Class of 1843),[1] spent the evening with the Fort Bellingham Commander, Captain George E. Pickett. From Bellingham Bay, they went to Victoria, where the General was received with full military honors. The next stop was San Juan Island where General Harney asked the Custom Collector to draw up a petition for protection from the Indians and forward it with as many signatures as possible to his Headquarters; this petition arrived at the Department of Oregon Headquarters sometime after July 27.[2] The return trip included a stop in Olympia, where General Harney visited Territorial Governor R. D. Gholson and Delegate Stevens, who was back in the Territory to seek reelection for a second term to Congress. Both favored asserting U.S. sovereignty over the San Juan Islands.

By a July 18, 1859 letter sent by the Department Adjutant General (Captain Pleasanton), General Harney directed Captain Pickett to deploy his company to Bellevue or San Juan Island and perform two missions: to protect inhabitants from marauding Indians, and to protect the rights of American citizens. In separate instructions, Lieutenant Colonel Casey was directed to dispatch the *Massachusetts* for the deployment of Captain Pickett's company. Upon release of the vessel by Captain Pickett, Brevet Major Haller and his company from Fort Townsend were to board the *Massachusetts* and patrol the San Juan Islands area to protect United States interests.

General Harney precipitated an international crisis, with Captain Pickett as his "point man," in a period of Washington Territorial history referred to as "a war that was never fought" or the "Pig War." The monograph titled "George Edward Pickett: Defender of the San Juans" cites the July 18, 1859 letter and then relates the role of Captain Pickett in this confrontation.

Local newspapers in the Territory of Washington applauded General Harney and Captain Pickett, pointing out that the Hudson's Bay Company was again using American soil, which was not their right. But when the news reached the other Washington (arriving first through British diplomatic channels), President James Buchanan was "flabbergasted." The President, as the Secretary of State, had been the American author of the Treaty of Washington, which reached a diplomatic solution to a difficult border problem. The San Juan Islands were a mere technical correction to the Treaty, which should be solved through diplomacy, not war. Further, the President did not know that General Harney had increased his force on the San Juans to five infantry and four artillery companies,[3] about 450 men, and artillery and naval cannons under Lieutenant Colonel Casey.

President Buchanan's emissary, Army Commander-in-Chief Major General Winfield Scott, arrived unannounced at Fort Vancouver by ship late on October

---

[1] Both Captains Pleasanton and Ingalls became Union generals in the Civil War.
[2] D. B. Richardson, *Pig War Islands* (Eastwood, Washington: Orcas Publishing Company, 1971), p. 56.
[3] After Colonel Wright's successful campaign ended in October 1858, General Harney retained the Third Artillery companies at Fort Vancouver instead of allowing their return to California except for one company, which went to the Artillery School of Practise at Fort Monroe, Virginia.

20, 1859. About 2 a.m., General Harney and his staff were notified to meet with General Scott at 8 a.m. aboard the Commander-in-Chief's ship. The situation was cordial, but soon deteriorated when General Harney opposed General Scott's plan for joint occupancy of the Islands pending a diplomatic solution. He was proud of the successful confrontation with the British. It appeared to General Scott that the vain General Harney was out to make a name for himself and would risk a war rather than pursue the less dramatic route of diplomacy.

Using the *Massachusetts* as his headquarters, General Scott went to Dungeness Harbor (Port Angeles) and negotiated with Sir James Douglas, the Governor of British Columbia, by messenger across Fuca's Strait. They agreed to joint occupancy of not more than 100 riflemen without heavy arms from each side until a diplomatic solution was made. Lieutenant Colonel Casey was ordered on November 9 to return all companies to their original posts except one of the Fort Steilacoom companies staying on as the American occupying force. Governor Douglas responded by ordering the British warship laying off of San Juan Island to return to its base at Esquimalt, but the British occupying force did not arrive until March 27, 1860, after approval was received from London for the joint occupancy.

General Scott left on the long journey to the Army Headquarters in New York City. In the Territory of Washington, politicians and newspapers lambasted the diplomatic approach. Governor Gholson went before the Legislature to express his displeasure, stating that it was like having martial law over part of the Territory.

1860: Return to Peace and Stability

General Scott was very concerned about the commander and staff of the Department of Oregon Headquarters. In his February 14 letter to Secretary of War John B. Flood, he reported that it was difficult to monitor a headquarters far away across the continent. This single visit uncovered numerous irregularities in addition to the deliberate precipitation of a dangerous diplomatic situation that was not in the best interests of the United States. It was obvious to General Scott that the ranking British naval officers and Governor Douglas had prevented bloodshed. Their warships easily could have bombarded the American troops, with immunity from reprisal. The venerable "old war horse" was concerned for the "gallant officers and men" subjected to the "ignorance, passion and caprice" of the Department of Oregon Headquarters.

With the gold rush in British Columbia over, the San Juans became a refuge for wanderers and brigands of all types. A West Pointer, Captain Lewis C. Hunt (USMA Class of 1837)[1] and his occupation company became the only semblance of law and order in the Islands. A major source of trouble was the illegal spirits being sold to whites and Indians, as drunkenness, vice and crime appeared to be the major activities on San Juan Island. Captain Hunt took the offensive against the spirit merchants, to the point of initiating court actions to force them out of

---

[1]Less than two and a half years later, Captain Hunt was a brigadier general of volunteers in the Union Army. When he died at age 63, he was the Colonel of the Fourteenth Infantry Regiment.

business. Ten of the spirit merchants sent a petition to General Harney, alleging that Captain Hunt was interfering with their pursuit of business. General Harney welcomed this opportunity to get rid of Captain Hunt, and sent Captain Pickett and his company back to San Juan Island. In response, Captain Hunt sent a letter to General Scott. Upon receiving the letter, the astounded and angry General Scott sent his recommendation to the Secretary of War that General Harney be relieved. On June 6, the British registered a protest with the Secretary of State about the return of Captain Pickett. It was unusual for an officer with General Harney's rank and political following to be relieved, but President Buchanan directed such action. General Harney left the Territory of Washington in the middle of July, following orders to report in person to both the Secretaries of State and War. His instructions also directed turning over command of the Department of Oregon to the next ranking officer.

From Fort Walla Walla, Colonel Wright arrived at Fort Vancouver on July 5, to take command of the Department of Oregon, followed by the Ninth Regimental Headquarters and Band on July 20. Since Captain Pickett now had developed good relations with the British occupation force on San Juan Islands, Colonel Wright decided to make no changes, which satisfied Governor Douglas. At the request of the Territorial Legislature, Company A, Fourth Infantry was sent to Gray's Harbor in February to protect the Indian agency being established there. Just back from a year's sabbatical to Europe, Lieutenant August Kautz was at this post, Camp Chehalis, unhappy to be stuck in such a dull, isolated place.

After a half of century of doing business in the Pacific Northwest, the Hudson's Bay Company closed its operations in the Territory of Washington. Resentment of the trading company and its subsidiary, the Puget Sound Agricultural Company, had grown with the increase in settlers. Hudson's Bay wanted to sell, but there were no buyers. Settlers in Pierce and Thurston Counties submitted memorials to the Legislature and Congress to gain political support for removing the foreign Agricultural Company from American soil. In the interior, the Army clamped down on the sale of arms and ammunition to the Indians, and chastised the Company for its traders' purchasing stolen livestock. Business had deteriorated, causing abandonment of trading posts. At Fort Vancouver, the expanding Army installation was taking Company lands without compensation, with the Secretary of War's official approval. The President of the Council of Hudson's Bay Company in North America announced in May the Company's intent to close Fort Vancouver. On June 14, the Chief Trader handed the keys of the trading post buildings to Department Quartermaster Captain Ingalls,[1] and sailed away in the *Otter* to Victoria, British Columbia. A claim of $5,449,936.67 was submitted. The United States and Great Britain established a joint commission, which in 1869 awarded Hudson's Bay $450,000 under the provisions of the 1846 Treaty of Washington, and $200,000 to the Puget Sound Agricultural Company.[2]

---

[1]Captain Ingalls was the Army's Quartermaster General during 1882-83 in the grade of Regular Army brigadier general.

[2]J. A. Hussy, *The History of Fort Vancouver and Its Physical Structure* (Portland, Oregon: Robert Kerns & Bell Company, 1957), pp. 105-114.

As the years went by, Shoshoni and Bannock Indians of the Snake River Plain became bolder each year, approaching wagon trains to beg, barter, and steal. Small wagon trains with limited manpower for defense were especially vulnerable, a situation that the Indians exploited. Beginning in 1859, dragoons from Fort Walla Walla were deployed in the summer to protect immigrant wagon trains passing through the Snake River Plain. A small wagon train traveling across the plains in September, after security forces had left the area, was attacked by Shoshoni Indians who killed 12 of the 45 immigrants and stole all of the livestock and baggage. Remaining immigrants fled on foot from the looting Shoshonis. Two of the survivors made their way to the Umatilla Agency; another was rescued by an Indian agent. Fort Walla Walla dragoons and infantry mounted on mules, led by Captain Frederick T. Dent (USMA Class of 1843),[1] rescued 12 survivors, some of whom had resorted to cannibalism to survive. Others had met their fate at the hands of unknown Indians after escaping the initial attack. The Army force with the survivors closed back into Fort Walla Walla on November 7.

Colonel Wright recognized that forces needed to be stationed in the Snake River Plains until the Shoshonis and Bannocks turned away from robbery. Supplying forces stationed there would be a major transportation problem and expense; the Department of Oregon Quartermaster Department was in debt by about $400,000 already, just supporting the present stationing of forces. Colonel Wright recommended centralizing his forces at a few posts to improve training and cut down on expenses.

But far from the Territory of Washington, clouds of war were forming. Southern leaders threatened dissolution if Abraham Lincoln was elected President. South Carolina led the way, seceding on December 17, 1860. The others followed in early 1861.

1861 and 1862: From Regulars To Volunteers

On January 15, 1861, the Department of Oregon was downgraded to a military district and combined with the Department of California into the Department of the Pacific under the brigadier general in San Francisco. This caused little change in the headquarters at Fort Vancouver or in the Territory of Washington. But changes *were* caused in the regiments by the news of Southern States seceding from the Union. The first West Pointer to resign in the Territory of Washington was Second Lieutenant Samuel W. Ferguson (USMA Class of 1857),[2] assigned to the First Dragoons at Fort Walla Walla. The effective date was March 15, three months after his native state of South Carolina seceded from the Union; others followed quickly. There were demonstrations of loyalty to the Army, such as company commanders refusing to leave until their replacements had arrived; but the crisis plaguing the country called the Southern officers to their home states.

---

[1]Brother-in-law of his West Point classmate U. S. Grant, 18th President of the United States, Captain Dent became a brigadier general of U.S. Volunteers in the Civil War.
[2]Lieutenant Ferguson became a brigadier general in the Confederate Army and commanded a cavalry brigade in the Atlanta campaigns.

Captain Pickett left in June, replaced by Captain Thomas C. English (USMA Class of 1849). Assigned as the Regimental Adjutant, Captain English had deployed with the Ninth Infantry in 1855 to the Territory of Washington. In the summer of 1858, he was sent to the eastern part of the country on recruiting duty and returned the next year with a bride. The English family was living at Fort Steilacoom.

In May of 1861, a detachment of two noncommissioned officers and 100 rank and file from the Ninth Infantry was detailed for escort duty with the party building the "Mullan" military road from Fort Walla Walla to Fort Benton.[1] Building of the road had begun in March of 1859. Originally conceived at the time of the Northern Railway Survey, this road became the project of Lieutenant John Mullan, Jr. (USMA Class of 1852). Assigned to the Second Artillery, Lieutenant Mullan did the work of a topographical engineer for the Northern Railway Survey and with Colonel Wright's campaign from August to October of 1858.

The story of the Mullan Road is told in the last monograph, covering the career and life of Lieutenant Mullan. During the winter, Chief Garry delivered mail to the snowbound Mullan Road party and took readings at snow-depth markers that the party had placed out. The Mullan Road was completed in August, 1862, and the remaining 66 soldiers returned to their Ninth Infantry companies.[2] Left behind by contemporaries who had gone to war, Lieutenant Mullan left the Army for a civilian career.

The Exodus of the Regular Regiments

While Lieutenant Mullan was pushing his road through the Rocky Mountains, the exodus of Regular units from the Territory of Washington was underway. This began in earnest with the Fourth Infantry company at Camp Chehalis pulling out for California on June 19, 1861, on the first leg of its journey to the battlefields on the East Coast. Deployments continued from the Territory of Washington, company by company, until the end of 1861, when only two remained, one of the Ninth Infantry at Fort Vancouver and a Third Artillery company in the San Juans.[3] Colonel Wright left for California in September, 1861, and in November was a brigadier general, U.S. Volunteers, commanding the Department of Pacific. He retained the Regular Army appointment of Colonel, Ninth Infantry. This regiment and four companies of the Third Artillery remained on the West Coast in the Department of Pacific while the Fourth Infantry and First Dragoons (redesignated the First Cavalry) were part of the defense of Washington, D.C. in January, 1862.

---

[1]F. R. Brown, *History of the Ninth U.S. Infantry, 1799-1909* (Chicago: R.R. Donnelely & Sons Company, 1909), p. 89.

[2]Brown, *op. cit.*, p. 91.

[3]The Ninth Infantry company at Fort Vancouver replaced the Third Artillery company in the San Juans in February 1862 and remained for the duration of the Civil War. The Third Artillery company went to California. Two other companies of the Ninth Infantry returned to the District of Oregon and remained through the Civil War years.

Above: **Fort Steilacoom, circa 1860.**

[Historic Fort Steilacoom Association]

Below: **Third U.S. Artillery on San Juan Island, 1861.**

[Provincial Archives, Victoria, British Columbia]

The citizens of the Territory of Washington were far removed from the political and military conflicts of the Civil War. News of battles and other events took weeks to arrive, and even then it was far from their doorsteps. More pertinent were the hard work and local activity that impacted their daily lives. Most with an interest in politics were Democrats, who did not understand this new Republican President and his party's platform. Democrats were opposed to interference with slavery, and were inclined to sympathize with the slaveholders. But the people of the Territory of Washington did not want slavery in their Territory. Except for a few "diehards," there was little interest in marching across the continent to fight in a war for purposes that did not concern their daily existence or appear relevant to their future.

The conflict of cultures remained, regardless of the military victories of the past. Military forces were needed to replace the Regular Army forces withdrawn for the battles in the East and other requirements. The solution was for the Territory of Washington to raise volunteer forces for federal service.

Volunteer Service

In October, 1861 the War Department initiated action for the Territory of Washington to raise volunteer troops. A survey of the Territory's 10,000 white residents determined that only three companies could be raised in the Territory. Consequently, only 264 of the 1,021 commissioned officers and enlisted were from the Territory of Washington. About 83 percent of the remaining 757 came from California, and the remainder from Oregon. The ten companies were organized between March 21 and December 5, 1862, and formally mustered into federal service on December 31 as the First Washington Infantry Regiment of Volunteers.[1] Lieutenant Colonel, U.S. Volunteers, Thomas C. English was the Regimental Lieutenant Colonel until mustered out on April 18, 1865.[2]

When General Wright left Fort Vancouver for California in September of 1861, command of the District of Oregon passed through three commanders until orders arrived for Major Benjamin Alvord (USMA Class of 1833) to be promoted to brigadier general, U.S. Volunteers and take command of the District. The Army Headquarters orders were dated April 15, 1862, but it took until July 6 to reach Fort Vancouver, where General Alvord was an Army staff major assigned as the Paymaster for the District.

Before being promoted in 1854 to major in an Army Staff authorization, General Alvord was a career infantry officer with combat service in the Florida Indian Wars and the Mexican War. In the latter, he was breveted to captain and major for "gallant and meritorious service" in battles. The intellectual General

---

[1]Last elements of the staff and units were mustered out on October 31, 1865, six months after the surrender at Appomatox.

[2]After being mustered out, Brevet Lieutenant Colonel English served on Army Headquarters boards and in command positions in Kansas and Alabama. While on sick leave to his home in Philadelphia, Pennsylvania, Lieutenant Colonel English, Second Infantry, died on June 10, 1876, at age 48.

Alvord wrote scientific papers that were published and widely distributed. Between Florida Indian War tours, the General was an assistant professor at West Point, first in mathematics and then Principal Assistant Professor of Natural and Experimental Philosophy. Governor Stevens was one of his students, and they became close friends. In 1852, in command of a company of the Fourth Infantry, he deployed with Lieutenant Colonel Bonneville to Columbia Barracks (Fort Vancouver), but continued on to Camp Drum (Fort Dalles) to take command there in his grade of brevet major. He brought his wife, a hometown girl, and their family to this post. The promotion and assignment to the Paymaster Department transferred them to Fort Vancouver in 1854.

General Alvord and Lieutenant Colonel English were the only two West Pointers to remain in the Territory of Washington for the entire Civil War. The senior captain of the Ninth Infantry, Brevet Major Pinckney Lugenbeel of the Class of 1840, was in command at Fort Colville when the Civil War started. Although promoted to major in the newly organized Nineteenth Infantry in December, 1862, he was retained at Fort Vancouver to command the post and to train newly recruited volunteers being mustered into service. In the summer of 1863, he establish Fort Boise, projecting District of Oregon forces father east along the Oregon Trail where immigrants still came regardless of the great war in progress. Returning to Fort Vancouver in the fall, he was the Assistant Provost Marshal General for the Territories of Washington and Oregon until reassigned to the east in late 1864, arriving too late to participate in any of the battles.

General Alvord worked diligently at his assignment, gaining respect from the press and Territorial Governments, and earning praises from his immediate superior, General George Wright, the commander of the Department of Pacific. A difficult period occurred just after taking command. In 1860, whites prospecting illegally on the Nez Perce Reservation found gold. A major war did not stop gold fever. By the fall of 1862, there were over 18,000 whites on the Nez Perce Reservation. Nez Perce Indians worked for the miners, some becoming rich by tribal standards. Alcohol became a serious problem, and Indians, often deliberately made drunk, were cheated, robbed, and murdered. The chiefs were becoming belligerent because dishonest Indian agents stole part of the payment finally being made for the 1855 treaty and because goods delivered under the treaty were shoddy.

General Alvord sent troops to establish Fort Lapwai near the reservation to protect the Indians from the whites and went to speak to the Nez Perce. As he recalled, these were a proud people who honored their past association with Captains Lewis and Clark, and Colonel Bonneville, and who had assisted the Army over the years. General Alvord's admiration for the tribe went back to his first meeting with Chief Lawyer in 1853 when the young warriors knelt on the ground and said their prayers. Now it was a sad occasion to observe what was happening on the Reservation. General Alvord delivered a speech to the assembled chiefs on October 24. Among many subjects covered, he told them the following:

. . You will never have a worse enemy than the whiskey sellers and the bad whites who intrude upon you and commit outrages upon you and your families. . . .

General Alvord ended his speech with these words:

. . It takes fire to temper steel. Temptation is the test and trial of virtue. If a Nez Perce's lodge will stand rain and storm and hail and hurricanes, it is well pitched; it is then firmly secured to the earth. The sun may shine, but fair weather and sunshine are no test for it. It required all this severe and harassing treatment by the gold diggers to show how true and honest and straightforward a Nez Perce can be. Such fidelity shall always have my praise. We wish in return for it only to be fair, not only be just, but to be also as kind and as generous as possible towards you.[1]

In the Territory of Washington, the year 1862 ended with the great Nez Perce nation fighting for its very existence against evils from the civilization of the whites. Policing Indians and gold seekers and completing the mustering of the Washington Territorial Volunteer Regiment were the main activities of General Alvord's command. The cannons of the Civil War were far away, and not heard by many in the Territory of Washington.

General Alvord stayed in command of the District of Oregon until he resigned the commission of brigadier general, U.S. Volunteers on August 8, 1865, and went to a paymaster assignment in New York City. He was recognized with brevet promotions to lieutenant colonel, colonel, and brigadier general for "faithful and meritorious service," allowing him to be addressed as "General." In 1872, General Alvord was appointed Paymaster General of the Army in the grade of colonel, staff; in 1876, the position was upgraded and he served the last four years before retirement as a Regular Army brigadier general.

Epilogue

On March 2, 1863, Washington completed its first ten years as a Territory. Thirty-six more years would pass before statehood. But it was during that first decade of the territorial period that the most West Pointers came to employ their profession in the Territory of Washington, as the fledgling political entity sought its path to the future. They were never settlers, because their profession would not let them stay; but the West Pointers were frontiersmen.

Like the settlers, they brought their wives and children to share life in the wilderness of the new Territory, and had to build their domiciles from the wilderness. But there was a difference. The settlers and their Territorial Government, led by the West Pointer Governor and Superintendent of Indians Affairs, wanted to accelerate the implementation of government policy forcing the

---

[1]Washington National Guard Pamphlet ARNG 870-1-3 /ANG 210-1-3, *The Official History of the Washington National Guard*, Vol. 3: *Washington Territorial Militia in the Civil War* (Camp Murray, Washington: Headquarters Military Department State of Washington, 1961), pp. 206-207.

Indians through treaties onto reservations. This would release large tracts of land for settlement and white culture economic development. Army leaders, by contrast, opposed white intrusion on the Indian way of life. This divergence of viewpoint made the Army stationed in the new Territory of Washington, and its West Pointer leaders, a kind of buffer between the settler and the Indian. Sadly, the Indian never saw the Army's role in this light, and as a result, many battles were fought, beginning an end to the Indian way of life in the Territory of Washington.

West Pointers brought some measure of prosperity to this economically poor region where opportunities to earn money were scarce. Army posts were built; goods and services were procured; material was transported from supply depots to the outlying forts; and military field operations were supported. These created jobs, bringing cash into the territorial economy. Many of the roads they built may still be found throughout Washington, identified as "military road." Heralding the future, the Northern Railway Survey was the base study for the railroads that came during the last two decades of Washington's Territorial years, crossing the Territory and later the State with avenues of economic prosperity.

This book memorializes some of the contributions of West Pointers to the development of the Territory of Washington before and during its first ten years. Many other West Pointers and their contributions — during this period and the subsequent territorial and statehood years — remain to be covered another time, in other books. But West Pointers have never stopped coming to Washington. They continue today — some in the military, others in business or the professions — to use skills acquired at a great national university, the United States Military Academy, to sustain the prosperity of a great state: Washington.

Colonel Charles N. Howze
U.S. Air Force, Retired
USMA Class of 1931

Major General John A. Hemphill
U.S. Army, Retired
USMA Class of 1951

MONOGRAPHS

Brevet Brigadier General Benjamin Louis Eulalie Bonneville

B. L. E. BONNEVILLE:
MORE THAN A FAMILIAR NAME

Bonneville is one of the most familiar names in the West today. A mountain in Wyoming, a salt flat in Utah, a county in Idaho, a town in Washington, a dam and lake on the Columbia River, a federal power administration — all celebrate the memory of the first graduate of the United States Military Academy to explore extensively the central Rocky Mountains and the Pacific Northwest.

Publicity about Benjamin Louis Eulalie Bonneville's exploits led to emigration to the Oregon Country and the establishment of the Territory of Washington north of the Columbia River. Just before the organization of Washington Territory, Bonneville brought U.S. Army troops to reinforce the sparse garrisons, to establish new garrisons required by the expanding population, and to construct military roads to connect settlement areas.

He was born in or near Paris, France, on April 14, 1796, the son of Nicholas de Bonneville, a gentleman of culture, a politician, a member of the National Convention, and an intimate personal friend of the Marquis de Lafayette and Thomas Paine. The political upheaval of the French Revolution prompted de Bonneville to send his wife and children to New York in 1803. They lived near New Rochelle, in Paine's household and as his beneficiaries.

Young Benjamin was knowledgeable in French, Latin, Greek, and mathematics when he entered the United States Military Academy at West Point on his 17th birthday. He was graduated on December 11, 1815, and commissioned as a brevet second lieutenant of light artillery.

For the next four years he served on recruiting duty at New England posts. In 1819 he was transferred to the Eighth Infantry, and a year later to the Seventh Infantry. There he saw his first duty, on what was then the western frontier — duty that was much more appealing to his ardent temperament and adventurous spirit.

This was the beginning of a lifelong association with the trans-Mississippi frontier. By 1824, Bonneville had helped in the construction of military roads and of Fort Gibson, in present-day Oklahoma, then the westernmost military outpost, a base from which the Army sought to establish control over the Osage Indians.

When the Marquis de Lafayette returned to the United States for a triumphal visit in 1824-25, he renewed his long and close friendship with the de Bonneville family in New York. Toward the end of his visit he asked that the newly promoted Captain Bonneville be permitted to accompany him on his return to France as the "Secretary of General Lafayette." Permission was granted, and Captain Bonneville returned to France, becoming the guest of the General until the following year. In 1827, Bonneville returned to his duty station at Fort Gibson. For the next three years he was occupied with the Indian affairs of the garrison.

He had long been interested in heading a fur trading expedition into the Rocky Mountains when, in 1831, he met Joseph Reddeford Walker, a thoroughly experienced frontiersman and trapper. Together they made plans for an expedition into the Rocky Mountains and on to Oregon Country, with Walker as Bonneville's lieutenant. Accordingly, on May 21, 1831 Bonneville wrote to the General-in-Chief, Major General Alexander Macomb, requesting a leave of absence for the purpose of making such an expedition. On August 3, 1831 the leave was granted until October 1833, on the condition that Bonneville would provide for a complete expedition including maps, instruments, gear, and provisions — all at no expense to the government. He was to ascertain the agricultural and mineral resources, and the geographic and geological character of the Great West.

He was also charged with determining the nature, character, and mode of warfare of the Indians. Indeed, he was charged with obtaining information that took at least another seven decades to obtain. Another possible purpose to Bonneville's mission has never been absolutely confirmed or refuted: Was Bonneville, in addition to his stated purposes, charged with reporting secretly on the British holdings and operations in the Pacific Northwest, and similarly on the Mexicans in California? Why, otherwise, would he have asked for, and received, United States and Mexican passports prior to his departure? The financing of Bonneville's private undertaking is shrouded in obscurity. One investor is known to have been Alfred Seton, who some 20 years earlier had been a clerk at John Jacob Astor's post at Astoria. Another former clerk at Astoria, Gabriel Franchere, may also have contributed; and it is possible that Astor himself assisted financially.[1]

By the end of April 1832, Bonneville had completed the organization, manning and provisioning of his expedition. On May 1, 1832 he left Fort Osage, about 10 miles from present-day Independence, Missouri, with 110 men, and 20 ox- and mule-drawn wagons loaded with ammunition, provisions, and colorful cloth and trinkets for trade with the Indians. He made his way up the Platte River without incident, following a well-known route used by the fur traders, to South Pass. Here he crossed the Continental Divide on July 24, 1832 — the first crossing of the Rocky Mountains with wagons, on the route that would later become known as the Oregon Trail.[2]

For the next three years Bonneville attempted to establish a profitable fur trading company. His efforts toward that end inspired Washington Irving's book, *The Rocky Mountains; or, Scenes, Incidents and Adventures in the Far West; Digested from the Journal of Captain B. L. E. Bonneville of the Army of the United States, and Illustrated from Various Other Sources.*, published in Philadelphia in 1837.[3] During his first year — until the summer of 1833 — he built a rough stockade in the vicinity of the Green River, which he later had to abandon. He sent out at least two trapping brigades, while he moved to a second winter camp at a lower elevation on the North Fork of the Salmon River, in present-day

[1]It is curious that Bonneville, upon his return to civilization in 1835, went to see Astor in New York, before reporting to the Army authorities in Washington, D.C.

[2]South Pass, Wyoming, elevation 7,550 feet, is located about 50 miles southwest of present-day Riverton, on Wyoming State Highway 28.

[3]Later editions, to which the reader is referred for a lively account of adventure in the Far West of the 1830s, were published under the title *The Adventures of Captain Bonneville*.

Idaho. The results of his trapping efforts were mediocre at best, and he soon learned that his American rivals, the Rocky Mountain Fur Company, led by Jim Bridger, and the American Fur Company, under Milton Sublette, were fierce competitors who would spare no effort to cause mischief.

During his second year, until the summer of 1834, Bonneville fared no better in his efforts to establish a profitable fur trade. In fact, it is doubtful that the furs he sent back east could have covered the salaries of his employees and the supplies that his financial backers sent him each summer. However, Bonneville did two important things during this year. First, he sent his lieutenant, J. R. Walker, with a party of about 40 men — fitted out for a full year — ostensibly to explore the fringes of the Great Salt Lake and to trap in the beaver streams in the vicinity. Second, Bonneville decided to make his first "reconnoitering expedition" into the tightly controlled domain of the British Hudson's Bay Company in the Oregon Country of the Pacific Northwest.

Walker started his trip in July, 1833 but did not tarry long near the Great Salt Lake.[1] Instead he moved southwest along the north bank of the Humboldt River. His route took him through Idaho, Utah, Nevada, and California, near the present-day towns of Virginia City, Berkley, Oakland, Monterey, and Bakersfield, then east of Mt. Whitney and back to Virginia City, and finally on to his rendezvous with Bonneville on the Bear River, in eastern Idaho. During his 11-month trip Walker had blazed a trail through the Great Basin, across the Sierras and into California. This same route, but along the _south_ bank of the Humboldt River, would become the "California Emigrant Trail" of the Gold Rush Era.

Bonneville spent the summer of 1833 in the general vicinity of the Yellowstone River. On Christmas morning he set out for the Oregon Country, taking with him only three men and five horses and mules. They followed the Snake River downstream but soon found themselves in the treacherous defile of Hell's Canyon. By backtracking they exited Hell's Canyon and moved northwest into the Wallowa Mountains where, in the winter's cold, they nearly died of exhaustion. Finally, with the help of some of the local Indian tribes, they reached the Hudson's Bay post near the mouth of the Walla Walla on the Columbia River. The date was March 4, 1834, and Bonneville had made this journey through unmapped mountains, valleys, and plains in midwinter.

Some of Indians they met along the way had induced the captain to believe that there were good prospects for an American trading company along the Columbia. However, while Bonneville and his bedraggled men were hospitably treated at the Hudson's Bay outpost, the factor, Pierre Pambrun, acting on company orders, would sell no supplies or provisions to a competitor. Bonneville stayed only two days, but took the time to respond to a Nez Perce Tribe request to discuss with them religion and morals. Bonneville was indignant with Pambrun and resolved to return with a stronger and better provisioned party. By June 16, he was back on the Bear River, where Walker was waiting for him.

---

[1] Walker's clerk, Zenas Leonard, later stated that Walker, "was ordered to steer through an unknown country toward the Pacific."

In July 1834, near Bear Lake, Bonneville by prior arrangement met Michel Cerre, who had taken their furs to St. Louis the previous summer and was returning with goods and equipment from the East. However, Cerre had not brought any written orders prolonging the captain's leave, which terminated in October 1833.[1] No one will ever know whether or not Bonneville thought that his leave had actually been extended. In any event, five days after meeting Cerre, he departed with 23 men on his second attempt to explore the Hudson's Bay Company empire. This venture kept him busy through the summer and fall. He reached a point on the Columbia River about 50 miles below Walla Walla; however, the result was as disappointing as his previous attempt to reach the mouth of the Columbia and Willamette Valley. Denied provisions once again by the Hudson's Bay post at Walla Walla, and facing starvation, he found no assistance from the Indians, all of whom were under pressure from the Hudson's Bay Company to have nothing to do with Bonneville. Reduced to eating some of his own horses, he abandoned hope of reaching the Willamette River and withdrew to the valley of the Bear River, where he spent the winter of 1834-35 camped near the friendly Utes and Shoshonis. Bonneville's two journeys both generally followed the trace of the future Oregon Trail (see map, "Bonneville's Routes," page 89). Bonneville had maintained strict military discipline, but was popular with his men, Indians and trappers. He was a successful leader, not losing a single man from any party under his personal command.

In the spring of 1835, he kept a rendezvous with all of his men on the Wind River (in today's state of Wyoming). Leaving Walker with about 50 men to continue trapping, Bonneville returned to St. Louis on August 22, 1835. After visiting Astor and others in New York City, Bonneville reported to the War Department where he learned, to his amazement, that he had been dropped from the rolls.[2] Bonneville applied immediately for reinstatement. While there was opposition from some officers at Fort Gibson, his name was transmitted from the Secretary of War to President Jackson for reappointment. It is said that when Bonneville showed his maps to the President, Jackson exclaimed, "By the Eternal, Sir. I'll see that you are reinstated to your command. For this valuable service to the War Department and the country you deserve high promotion." The Senate confirmed Bonneville's reappointment, and he resumed his army career.

He participated in the second Seminole Indian War in Florida, and in 1846, now a major in the Sixth Infantry, he fought in all the principal battles of the Mexican War, from Vera Cruz to the capture of Mexico City. In August he was wounded in action and awarded a brevet to lieutenant colonel for "gallantry and meritorious service;" in October he was court-martialed for "misbehavior before the enemy." Found guilty of three of the 10 counts with which he had been charged, he was reprimanded by the Commander-in-Chief. Bonneville

---

[1]Cerre had also gone to Washington, D.C., where he delivered to General Macomb, a long report written by Bonneville. The report, Bonneville expected (or hoped), would be the basis for an extension of his leave.

[2]In fact, General Macomb had reported the captain absent without leave on May 28, 1834, and he was dropped from the rolls of the Army of the United States on May 30, 1834.

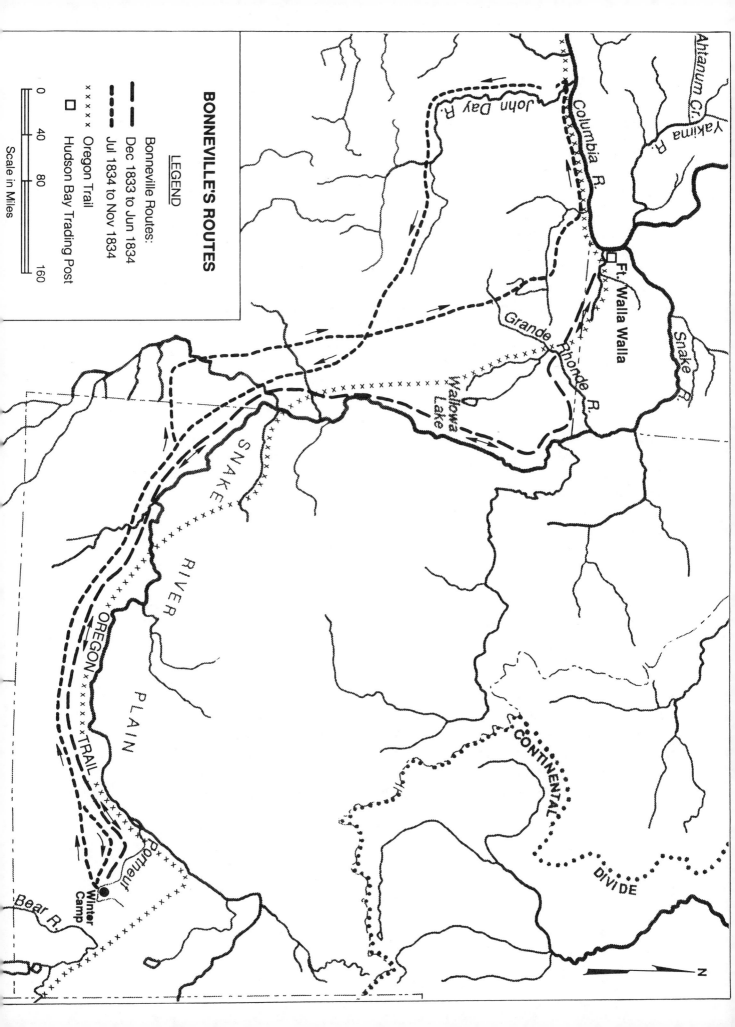

BONNEVILLE'S ROUTES

LEGEND

Bonneville Routes:
- Dec 1833 to Jun 1834
- Jul 1834 to Nov 1834
- Oregon Trail
- ☐ Hudson Bay Trading Post

Scale in Miles

0   40   80   160

Ahtanum Cr.

Yakima R.

Columbia R.

John Day R.

☐ Ft. Walla Walla

Snake R.

Grande Rhonde R.

Wallowa Lake

SNAKE RIVER PLAIN

OREGON TRAIL

Portneuf

Winter Camp

Bear R.

CONTINENTAL DIVIDE

N

subsequently served as Commander of Fort Kearney on the Oregon Trail, and several other garrisons. He was promoted to Lieutenant Colonel, Fourth Infantry Regiment, on May 7, 1849.

It is a kind of justice that about 18 years after his unsuccessful attempts to reach the mouth of the Columbia River and Willamette Valley, Lieutenant Colonel Bonneville would, as commander of all United States military installations on the Columbia River, witness the beginning of the decline of the Hudson's Bay Company, which had twice thwarted his sorties into the Oregon Country. On September 22, 1852, Lieutenant Colonel Bonneville arrived at the Hudson's Bay Company's Fort Vancouver with four companies of the Fourth U.S. Infantry Regiment and the Regimental Band. He took command of the U.S. Army's Columbia Barracks (located on a hill above the Hudson's Bay Company's post), the Military District encompassing the entire Oregon Territory (Pacific Coast to Continental Divide), and the other two Army posts and garrison forces located in the district. Also, construction of military roads was begun, to connect settlement areas.

Bonneville actively supported Oregon Territorial Governor Joseph Lane, (whose domain included Washington until 1853), lending the governor a howitzer that was credited with awing the warring Rogue River Indians into negotiations in 1853. Washington's first Territorial Governor, Isaac I. Stevens (USMA Class of 1839) was Lieutenant Colonel Bonneville's guest at Fort Vancouver in November 1853, before the Governor's initial entry into the capital town of Olympia. Lieutenant Colonel Bonneville supported many of Governor Stevens's military equipment needs.

Lieutenant Colonel Bonneville relinquished command of Fort Vancouver and the Military District to Major Gabriel J. Rains (USMA Class of 1827) in spring, 1855, accepting promotion to Colonel, Third Infantry Regiment, assigned to the Department of New Mexico. He led the Gila Expedition in 1857, and stayed in the Department of New Mexico, commanding when no general officer was present, until he retired in 1861.

After two wars, numerous Indian skirmishes, and 46 years of service, primarily on the country's frontiers, Colonel Bonneville retired from active duty on September 9, 1861, as the record reads, "For disability, resulting from long and faithful service, and from sickness and exposure in the line of duty." However, he immediately offered his services for the Civil War, and was recalled to active duty at the age of 68, serving as a colonel in recruiting and garrison duty in and around Saint Louis. He retired again in October 1866, with more than 50 years' active service, and was elevated to the rank of Brevet Brigadier General for "long and faithful service in the Army." Benjamin Louis Eulalie Bonneville died at Fort Smith, Arkansas on June 12, 1878 — at age 85, the last surviving member of West Point's Class of 1815.

Some historians have declared that Bonneville did not make history, but rather was made *by* history — and, of course, by Washington Irving's popular book. Other historians disagree, pointing out that while Irving's book promoted Bonneville's name-recognition, his exploits roused in thousands of Americans an intense interest in travel to the West. Bonneville proved that wagons could be taken over the Continental Divide; he established through what is now Idaho and Oregon the route that, starting in 1842, became the Oregon Trail. He mapped the headwaters of the Missouri, Yellowstone, Green, Sweetwater, Snake and Wind Rivers. He provided a second map, at a smaller scale, of the area of Walker's passage to the Pacific Ocean. He probed the area of operations and holdings of the Hudson Bay Company, as well as those of the Mexicans in California. He provided information regarding the nature, mode, and character of the warfare of the Indians.

On balance, while Captain Bonneville was an ineffective trapper and businessman, he was a critically important explorer of the interior of the Pacific Northwest and bordering areas in today's Wyoming and Utah. His party, led by Walker, blazed an important trail into California. He played an important role establishing the route of the Oregon Trail from South Pass to the Columbia near its juncture with the John Day River. He accomplished much of what the War Department charged him with — and at no expense to the United States. This included reporting on geographical data and economic possibilities. Bonneville's maps were made available to the public. These were instrumental in gaining public interest to emigrate to the Oregon Country.

Brevet Brigadier General Bonneville initiated strong United States Government interest in the Oregon Country, directly causing further government-directed explorations, leading to settlement of the boundary question with the British and opening the Pacific Northwest to American settlement. Immigration began in earnest in 1843, overcoming the Hudson's Bay Company policy of discouraging Americans from going north of the Columbia when part of the 1844 group continued on into the Puget Sound region in 1846. When the Territory of Washington was created in March, 1853, Brevet Brigadier General Bonneville was in command of the Army forces that provided law and order as the fledgling Territory began moving toward its destiny — statehood.

Today, besides the many western locations that bear his name, Camp Bonneville, a 3,018-acre military training area on the Columbia River, also celebrates his memory. Vancouver Central Park — which includes Fort Vancouver, now a National Historic Site — covers much of the 640 acres that Bonneville surveyed and mapped as the U.S. Army's first major post in Washington. The Bonneville Power Administration and the Bonneville Dam on the Columbia River give testimony and tribute to the influence of B. L. E. Bonneville on the history of Washington.

Colonel Fayette L. Worthington
U.S.Army, Retired
USMA Class of 1945

Isaac Ingalls Stevens
First Governor, Territory of Washington

[Special Collections Division, University of Washington Libraries]

ISAAC INGALLS STEVENS:
FIRST TERRITORIAL GOVERNOR

On the evening of November 25, 1853, a solitary tired, dirty, hungry stranger arrived in Olympia from Fort Vancouver. He was barred from entering the only open eating place with the terse explanation: "We are going to have doin's here and we can't feed strangers til after they're over." Protesting his hunger, the traveler was given some scraps at the kitchen table. After eating his fill, he returned to the street to learn that the "doin's" were planned for the overdue new Governor. Responding to complaints about the guest of honor's late arrival, the stranger opined: "Then I suppose I am the man you are looking for." A complainer's hasty beating on an old saw hung on a post brought men from all directions to the dinner in honor of the new Governor. Isaac Ingalls Stevens (USMA Class of 1839), the first Governor of the new Territory of Washington, presided at the head of the table, watching the others eat.[1]

Isaac Ingalls Stevens, the West Pointer who most influenced and shaped the development of Washington, was born March 25, 1818 at North Andover, Massachusetts, the first son of Isaac and Hannah Cummings Stevens, a farm family of modest means. The Stevens family had been yeoman farmers in England until John Stevens and his wife emigrated from Oxfordshire in 1638 to settle in the Massachusetts Bay Colony. In 1642 they helped found the town of Andover, where they and their descendants remained as prominent farmers, active in the community for 200 years.

Young Isaac, the third of seven children, grew up with a younger brother and two older and three younger sisters. His stern, abstemious father believed children should be hardened for life's trials. One story of Isaac's childhood tells of him being routed from his warm bed every morning and plunged into cold water as part of his hardening process. His mother, depressed from a serious injury and the birth of a stillborn baby, died when Isaac was nine years old. Isaac found solace in study, especially mathematics. A prodigy, he astonished teachers by solving all problems presented to him. He attended public school from the age of five until ten, when he entered Franklin Academy, a private school built on land donated by his grandfather. Shortly thereafter he went to work in his uncle's woolen mill where, within a year young Stevens could manage four looms at a time — double the number of the average adult.

At 15 Stevens entered nearby Phillips Academy, paying his own expenses with earnings from odd jobs. At Phillips he excelled in mathematics, engineering, and surveying. He also learned to apply himself to human problems in the real world. For example, attributing a bashful disposition to the discomfort he felt in the presence of certain types of people, he overcame the problem by deliberately engaging such people in conversation. His brilliant mind and driving energy more

---

[1]This legendary account contains considerable truth and appears to be a characteristic reaction of Stevens.

than compensated for his diminutive stature. He developed an extremely strong will and nearly inflexible determination from his ability to resolve problems, combined with traits learned from his father. The problem-solving skills, drive and supreme self-confidence Stevens acquired in his youth proved to be both assets and liabilities in later life. They served him well as an administrator, planner, executive, and legislator, but tended to bring out a stubborn intransigence and impatience when faced with situations calling for patience, diplomacy, tact, compromise, and understanding in dealing with others holding opposing points of view.

Isaac Stevens broke from the confinement of his world of some 40 square miles when, at the age of 17, he received an appointment as a cadet at the United States Military Academy at West Point, New York. Entering the academy in 1835, Stevens flourished there, completing the curriculum at the head of his class in every course of study — a remarkable achievement against fierce competition. He graduated number one in the Class of 1839 and received a commission as a second lieutenant of engineers in the United States Army. While a cadet he also excelled in horsemanship. His extra-curricular activities as a leader in the Cadet Dialectic Society turned him into an accomplished speaker and debater and enhanced his literary style and his knowledge of the liberal arts. Isaac Stevens's record at the Military Academy dominated the achievements of several generations of West Pointers in his time in the same manner as that of Douglas MacArthur in the early twentieth century.

As an engineer officer Stevens rapidly demonstrated high competence and an ability and willingness to assume responsibility in carrying out important, diverse assignments while engaged for seven years in repairing and building fortifications along the New England Coast. He was promoted to first lieutenant July 1, 1840, one year after his graduation from West Point. The following year, on September 8, 1841, the young officer married Margaret Hazard, daughter of Benjamin Hazard, a prominent Rhode Island lawyer. Isaac and Margaret Stevens enjoyed a happy marriage; they were blessed with five children, three of whom survived well into adulthood. The eldest, and only son, Hazard, accompanied his father during much of the Governor's activity in Washington Territory, and served the Union with distinction during the Civil War, becoming a Medal of Honor winner and the youngest officer to be awarded a brevet promotion to general officer. He also wrote a notable biography of his father.

In the small peacetime Army of the early 1840s, ambitious Lieutenant Stevens saw few opportunities for rapid advancement. With the help of his father-in-law, Isaac began to study law and considered leaving the military. The unexpected death of Benjamin Hazard disrupted his plan to resign his commission and enter a prestigious law firm. The outbreak of the Mexican War in 1846 brought new military opportunities to Stevens. For both patriotic and professional reasons he eagerly sought and secured an assignment where he would see action in the coming campaign.

During the war Lieutenant Stevens served as Adjutant of Engineers on Major General Winfield Scott's[1] staff, participating in all operations with Scott's army from the siege of Vera Cruz to the capture of Mexico City. Though a staff officer, Stevens frequently served at the front, boldly reconnoitering enemy positions, selecting routes of attack, and locating American gun positions. He impressed his superiors, peers, and subordinates with his exemplary intelligence, sound judgment, and impetuous daring on the battlefield. For gallant and meritorious conduct at the Battles of Contreras and Churubusco on August 20, 1847 he was breveted to captain. Less than a month later his distinguished service in the Battle of Chapultepec won him a brevet to major. The following day, September 14, Stevens was severely wounded while fighting to secure the fall of the enemy capital in the San Cosme suburb of Mexico City. It was the last day of combat in the war.

Besides earning him a personal commendation from General Scott, Stevens's great competence and courage in Mexico won him the admiration of several associates who would rise to national prominence in the years ahead. On Scott's staff he worked with, and sometimes under, another distinguished engineer officer, Captain Robert E. Lee (breveted to colonel by the end of the war), the number two graduate of the USMA Class of 1829, later the great commander of the Confederacy's Army of Northern Virginia. Second Lieutenant (Brevet Captain at the end of the war) George B. McClellan,[2] the second graduate of West Point's Class of 1846, served in Mexico with the United States Army's first company of engineers, conceived and largely recruited by Stevens.[3] During the Mexican War Lieutenant Stevens served with the man who would exert perhaps the most influence on his future: Brigadier General Franklin Pierce, later the 14th President of the United States.

Stevens's wound forced his evacuation from Mexico, required months of recuperation, and periodically bothered him the rest of his life. Though still on crutches, he returned to his engineer duties in New England. On September 14, 1849 the 31-year-old officer, just 10 years out of West Point, accepted an appointment to the important position of Assistant-in-Charge of the United States Coast Survey[4] Office in Washington, D.C. With the recent acquisition of so much

---

[1]The Army's Commander-in-Chief and only major general at the outbreak of the war, Scott was breveted to lieutenant general effective March 29, 1847.

[2]During the Civil War McClellan rose to the rank of Major General, Regular Army, serving variously as Commander of the Union Army of the Potomac and General-in-Chief of the Union Armies 1861-1862, for a time holding both commands simultaneously. As the Democratic Party's Presidential Candidate in the election of 1864, he opposed and lost to Abraham Lincoln. In 1877 McClellan was elected to and served a term as Governor of New Jersey, declining to run for re-election.

[3]Further exemplifying his vision, initiative, versatility, and contribution to the Army, Stevens advocated, after the war, more improvements in the Corps of Engineers and reform of the artillery, mounted troops, and infantry, suggesting a general reorganization and re-education of the Army, and criticizing the lack of care of their men shown by some company officers in various regiments.

[4]Later the U.S. Coast and Geodetic Survey, now incorporated within the National Oceanic And Atmospheric Administration (NOAA) of the U.S. Department of Commerce. At first Stevens assumed this position reluctantly, with the proviso that he retain concurrently for a year his Army

new national territory, the Survey's work drastically increased. New shore lines and rivers to chart, new lighthouses to site, and expanding navigational problems requiring expanding scientific research presented ideal challenges to the new appointee.

Applying his customary vigor, administrative ability, and problem-solving genius to his new task, Brevet Major Stevens, to his great credit and the lasting benefit of his country, soon improved the organization and efficiency of the Survey, substantially increasing its productivity. In his new capacity Stevens met and dealt with many prominent scientists, engineers, and politicians of the time and acquired a practical working knowledge of how politics and government functioned at the national level.

Isaac Stevens's restless ambition next led him to politics. A lifelong Democrat, he actively campaigned for his Mexican War comrade-in-arms Franklin Pierce in the presidential election of 1852. Stevens's efforts helped to defeat the Whig candidate, his old wartime commander, Winfield Scott. He felt that Scott lacked the vision Pierce showed in embracing the popular national doctrine of "Manifest Destiny" — the destiny of the United States to spread the blessings of American liberty and progress across the continent allotted to it by "Providence." He believed that Scott exhibited insufficient enthusiasm for developing the vast western acquisitions to our domain. Stevens's defense of Pierce's challenged war record was critical to the President-elect's victory, paving the way for a political reward for the ambitious young Army officer.

On March 2, 1853, two days before Pierce's inauguration, a new territory, Washington, was carved from that part of the Oregon Territory north of the Columbia River.[1] Stevens's work in the Coast Survey had instilled in him an appreciation of the tremendous opportunities awaiting able, innovative men in the largely untapped country west of the Mississippi. He firmly believed it was America's manifest destiny to create a vast great nation between the Atlantic and the Pacific, and he intended to take a leading role in the creation. Mystifying less-visionary influential friends who supported his candidacy, Major Stevens eagerly sought and won from the new President the joint appointment as the first Washington Territorial Governor and Superintendent of Indian Affairs. Appointed on March 17, 1853, he tendered his resignation from the Army and the Survey on March 21, effective retroactively to March 16.

It was a time of growing serious thought about a transcontinental railroad, with four routes under consideration. Isaac Stevens recognized that on Puget Sound in Washington Territory the closest American ports to Asia would be located, making the northern rail route appear to be the most important. If he could survey that route terminating in the territory he would govern, he would gain national prominence and exert tremendous influence on United States trade with the Orient and the development of the American Northwest. Besides being

---

responsibility for the construction of Fort Knox, Maine, before deciding which career he wished to pursue.

[1]The 46th parallel of North Latitude formed the boundary between Washington and Oregon Territories from the southeastern bend of the Columbia to the Continental Divide.

supremely qualified, he could ideally conduct the survey enroute to his new post in Washington Territory. Having marshalled strong political and professional support in his behalf, on March 25, 1853, his 35th birthday, Stevens was put in charge of the survey of the northern rail route from Saint Paul, Minnesota to Puget Sound by the Secretary of War, Jefferson Davis (USMA Class of 1828).

Governor Stevens plunged into the formidable task of organizing the railway survey with his usual ardor. To meet the deadline imposed by Congress, he divided the survey operations into eastern and western divisions, allowing for simultaneous explorations in each division. He secured the assignment of Brevet Captain George B. McClellan, a friend since the Mexican War, to his expedition and sent him with a small party by way of Panama to Fort Vancouver, Washington Territory, to head the western division, working eastward. McClellan's primary mission was to explore the Cascade passes for possible rail routes through that range to Puget Sound. He also was charged with exploring and evaluating Puget Sound and building a road from it to Walla Walla. J. Patton Anderson, appointed United States Marshal for Washington Territory, also preceded the main Stevens party to the territory to take a census in preparation for the coming election of a legislature. He found 3,964 white residents, of whom 1,682 were eligible to vote. Before leaving Washington, D.C. on May 9, 1853 the new Territorial Governor, Superintendent of Indian Affairs, and head of the Northern Railway Survey, to the satisfaction of all concerned, practically wrote the instructions of the State, War, and Interior Departments to himself and secured essential funds from the Congress to begin to carry them out. He also found time to select, purchase, and ship a large variety of books (some 5,000 in all) to Olympia to start a territorial library. He also solicited all state and territorial governors to donate excess volumes from their own libraries to Washington Territory.

Completing preparations in a remarkably short time, Stevens led his main group of 243 men — including 11 Army officers, 76 soldiers, and a staff of scientists and artists — westward from its base near Saint Paul in June, 1853. The Governor's party crossed the Continental Divide (then the eastern boundary of Washington Territory) at Cadotte's Pass in what is now Montana on September 24. Upon entering the new territory, Governor Stevens issued a proclamation declaring the inauguration of the Territorial Government. To examine all known passes through the Rocky and Bitterroot Mountains, he split his group into several smaller ones. He took his own group through Coeur d'Alene Pass and down the Spokane River to the Fort Colville trading post of the British Hudson's Bay Company, where he met McClellan's western division expedition. Though disappointed with the inadequate results of McClellan's half-hearted explorations, Stevens leniently withheld judgment, affording his western division chief further opportunities to do his job.[1]

From Fort Colville the two parties on October 29 proceeded south to Fort Walla Walla. The Governor and his chief artist, John Mix Stanley, moved out in

---

[1]The dilatory, hesitant, timid characteristics and tendency to magnify obstacles that subsequently caused McClellan to fail as an Army Commander in combat early in the Civil War were much in evidence during his work under Governor Stevens in Washington Territory.

advance from there and continued by canoe down the Columbia to Fort Vancouver. Stevens enjoyed a short respite at Vancouver as the guest of the Post and Fourth U.S. Infantry Commander, Lieutenant Colonel Benjamin L. E. Bonneville (USMA Class of 1815), already a legendary western explorer. The Governor made the final leg of his long journey from Saint Paul to Olympia, the territorial capital, by canoe and horseback, arriving there on November 25, 1853 to the delayed reception already described.

Isaac Stevens is vastly underrated as an explorer. His Northern Railway Survey was a magnificent achievement, far superior to the three other rail surveys of the period. Stevens's report was the first comprehensive survey of the feasibility of a route submitted to Congress. Although the final report was not completed until 1859, Stevens compiled and submitted a preliminary one in 1854, the basis for his early lobbying against great odds for constructing the first railroad to the West Coast over his course. Formidable opposition, including that of Jefferson Davis of Mississippi, interested only in a southern crossing, successfully blocked an early decision favoring Stevens's route. Finally, the political importance of California during the Civil War led to the 1862 decision to first construct the Union Pacific and Central Pacific, connecting Omaha, Nebraska and Sacramento. Not until 1883 did a United States railroad, the Northern Pacific, join the upper Mississippi with Puget Sound.

Nevertheless, Governor Stevens's brilliant reconnaissance provided a powerful stimulus to the future settlement, development, and prosperity of the Northwest. It expanded the work of Lewis and Clark a half century earlier and augmented that of Bonneville. Stevens's expedition explored a region some 2,000 miles long and 200 miles wide through a wild and mostly unknown country. His party examined nine Rocky Mountain passes and determined the navigability of the upper Missouri and Columbia Rivers. It held friendly councils with Indian tribes along the way, including the feared, powerful Blackfoot, and produced lucid descriptions of the natives encountered. The survey compiled extensive priceless data on the climate and on collected and observed flora and fauna of the vast area covered. It tested soils and probed the geography for agricultural and mineral potential. The topography of the country was mapped, the lakes and rivers charted. The Governor's versatility and authority added a scientific aspect to the survey and ensured that the utility of the phenomena examined was evaluated as well as their descriptions recorded. A perhaps unique aspect of Stevens's report was its magnificent art work, portraying the landscape, group and individual scenes, settlements, and western pioneer and Indian life like no words alone could do. These accomplishments, including this bonus, were due in no small part to Stevens's own skills and his generally wise selection of and influence over the various experts that comprised the expedition.

One of the first things Governor Stevens wanted to do after his arrival in Olympia was to compile the report on his Northern Railway Survey and present it to the national government prior to those of the other routes. First, however, he needed a valid reconnaissance of at least one of the Cascade passes to complete his initial survey — a reconnaissance that would provide essential data that Captain McClellan had failed to gather. When McClellan again procrastinated on a new mission to explore Snoqualmie Pass and recommended against that route, without having traversed or even entered the pass, Stevens was furious. To get the information he needed, Stevens assigned the task to one of his best engineers, Abiel W. Tinkham who had worked for him in New England. With dispatch, Tinkham completed a reconnaissance on February 1, 1854, reporting that Snoqualmie Pass indeed was suitable for an all-year railroad, winding up the Governor's basic transcontinental survey. McClellan, whose feelings were hurt, though he "got off easy," thereafter was cool to Stevens, never forgiving him for the imagined insult.[1]

The burst of energy Isaac Stevens displayed upon his arrival in Olympia dazzled the settlers and won the loyalty of most of them, who saw in him a leader who was on their side and could get things done. Guidance to proceed came from the United States law that created the territory. It provided a working constitution which, with amendments, served for 36 years until statehood in 1889. Under that law the Governor first established election districts and elected a bicameral territorial legislature and delegate to Congress on January 30, 1854. He then organized an Emergency Indian Service, appointing the three best qualified men available as members — men trusted by both Indians and whites. Meanwhile he organized the compilation of the initial rail survey report, giving detailed guidance on its component parts to those responsible to him for drafting them.

At the earliest opportunity in January the Governor set out on a sailing trip to explore a rough Puget Sound, experiencing weather that had deterred a dilatory Captain McClellan from performing this part of his threefold mission. Stevens was anxious to appraise the potential of the Sound for commerce, industry, and recreation. He judged the tiny fishing-hut village of Seattle to be the best local harbor on the Sound and the most logical site for the main terminal of the future northern transcontinental railroad. Indian villages along the shore were visited and future councils arranged with the natives. Stevens took a rough census of that portion of the indigenous population. The Governor predicted that Puget Sound would be a wonderland.

Isaac sailed to Victoria on Vancouver Island to meet and confer with Sir James Douglas, head of Hudson's Bay Company in the Northwest and Great Britain's Governor of the Island. The two Governors agreed to disagree. Sir James appraised Hudson's Bay holdings in Washington and Oregon Territories at $3,000,000, Stevens at $300,000.[2] Governor Douglas was amazed that the brand new

---

[1]Nor had McClellan satisfied Stevens with his efforts to initiate the proposed road from Puget Sound to Walla Walla. Captain McClellan failed to carry out his missions perhaps because of his declared frustration at Stevens's habit of giving explicit, minutely detailed instructions to subordinates, a practice considered by McClellan as interference into his own professional prerogatives. Stevens did not cashier McClellan or render a bad report on him for his dereliction of duty. Despite the fact that Stevens and McClellan were close friends for seven or eight years, and shared a professional relationship for nearly four of those years, the episode seems to have so embittered McClellan that he did not even mention Stevens in his memoirs *McClellan's Own Story: The War for the Union* (New York: Charles L. Webster & Company, 1887).

[2]These appraisals included values placed on the Puget Sound Agricultural Company, a Hudson's Bay subsidiary. The U.S. Secretary of State agreed with Stevens's figure, but Congressional

Washington Governor already had personally visited and evaluated most of his company's major sites in Washington Territory. Stevens resolved to thwart Sir James's efforts for Hudson's Bay Company to operate in Washington and Oregon Territories with the same rights and privileges it had exercised prior to possession of the area by the United States, in violation of the Treaty of 1846. The company's desire to maintain practically a wilderness in Washington to protect its fur and Indian trade clashed with Stevens's plans for settlement and development.

Governor Stevens convened the first session of the territorial legislature at Olympia on February 28, 1854. The legislature — a Council of nine and a House of 48 members — was an able body, reflecting excellent choices by the voters. Averaging 28 years of age, the lawmakers looked upon their nearly 36-year-old Governor as a patriarch. The "Old Man's" first message struck a responsive chord. His entire program, except the recommendation for a permanent territorial Militia, was passed (subject to U.S. Congressional veto). Among the major proposals approved were the adoption of a code of laws; organization of counties east of the Cascades; establishment of a school system for all children; the revision of all land laws to ensure speedy, clear, permanent property titles; and the extension to single women of the property rights already held by their married counterparts. Other important recommendations adopted included improvement of the mail service; construction of roads to Walla Walla, Vancouver, and Bellingham Bay; a grant of land for a university; and the continuation of geographical and geological surveys already underway. Congress would be requested to provide a surveyor general and land office to ensure rapid settlement of claims and to authorize and aid construction of three transcontinental railroads, including one over the northern route Stevens had reconnoitered.

Where appropriate, the enactments were in the form of memorials to Congress for action. Not least in importance, the Governor urged passage of memorials to Congress for prompt resolution of Indian land problems, settlement of Hudson's Bay Company claims, and the establishment of firm, accurate international boundaries. He also succeeded in convincing the legislature to include all of the beautiful San Juan Islands within Whatcom County, with United States taxation authority over them, a move that would help block British designs on the islands in a forthcoming boundary dispute.

Having accomplished in one month as much of his legislative program that he could do in the territory, Governor Stevens got a leave of absence from the legislature to return to Washington, D.C. to expedite congressional approval and support to put it into effect. For one thing, his presence in the national capital was needed to combat Jefferson Davis's strong, ruthless opposition to the northern rail route. The Secretary of War had ordered the cancellation of the Northern Railway Survey, falsifying estimated costs and substituting George B. McClellan's defeatist,

---

procrastination and the work of Hudson's Bay attorney, Washington Territory settler Judge Edward Lander, resulted in the U.S. awarding Hudson's Bay $650,000 in 1870. On May 24, 1872 the House of Representatives sent a resolution to the President asking why the State Department hadn't complied with the House's February 21, 1871 appropriation bill. The State Department paid the entire second installment of $325,000 appropriated to the Hudson's Bay Company, without deducting $50,000 owed in back taxes to the U.S. by the Puget Sound Agricultural Company as the House had directed.

inaccurate reports on Cascade routes and Eastern Washington geography for Stevens's factual data.

The Secretary's order came too late to prevent the Governor's rapid compilation and submission of his preliminary report. Further, enough data had been accumulated and work on the final document had progressed to a point that ensured its completion without Davis's support. Isaac Stevens's direct approach, convincing, accurate reports, and his flair for lobbying enabled him to beat Davis on every issue.

As usual, he made lasting favorable impressions on most government agencies and workers, high and low, that he contacted. Among the benefits he reaped for Washington Territory during his stay in the national capital were funds for a road from Fort Benton on the Missouri River to Walla Walla and congressional approval and funds to make treaties with the Indians, including the important Blackfoot Tribes, which dominated the region east of his territory. Congress also approved amendments to the land laws, Stevens's recommendations for a territorial surveyor general, funds for general surveys, and liberal expansion of the territorial mail service. The Governor's activities in Washington, D.C. enhanced both his personal stature and the development of the territory he governed. In reality, he did much of the work normally performed by a territorial delegate to Congress.

Flushed with success, Governor Stevens, with his wife, son, three daughters, and a nurse, sailed from New York on September 20, 1854, en route back to Washington Territory via Panama. They arrived in Olympia in December, the women of the party in various stages of recovery from serious bouts with yellow fever contracted while crossing the isthmus. After some initial misgivings at the primitive conditions encountered during a Washington December, the family, on the whole, adjusted to their pioneer life. They soon came to appreciate the scenic beauty of Western Washington and the spirit of the hardy settlers in their new home.

The second session of the Territorial Legislature opened on December 5, 1854. The Governor reported his successes in Washington, D.C. and recommended favorable action on his second legislative program, an extension of the first: requesting congressional approval and funding for more roads, enlarged and better mail service, steamer lines on Puget Sound and navigable rivers, and finding and monumenting the Canadian boundary at the 49th parallel of north latitude. Aware of an ever-present potential Indian threat, Stevens again advocated a territorial Militia. In view of congressional dawdling, he continued his opposition to Hudson's Bay Company's trade at the expense of the Territory. Governor Stevens ended his message with a promise of a great railroading future for the Pacific Northwest and then successfully invoked the aid of the legislature and the support of the public for the essential Indian treaty negotiations he was about to undertake at the direction of the Congress.

This legislature, unlike the first, was no rubber stamp for Stevens's proposals. When the lawmakers accused him of succumbing to Governor Sir James Douglas's wining and dining, resulting in Stevens's exorbitant $300,000 appraisal of Hudson's Bay territorial holdings, Stevens silenced that opposition by revealing

Sir James's demand for $3,000,000. Some members took exception to Stevens's plan to sow grass seed on strategically-located bare prairie lands for animals of the coming influx of wagon trains. They were against "planting grass where God did not grow it." The strongest opposition centered on Stevens's proposed Indian policy to be enforced through forthcoming treaties. The Governor explained the policy in idealistic terms — a humane solution to the potentially explosive problem which would realize the prosperous settlement and development of the great Northwest. Despite sometimes fierce opposition, Stevens, as Indian Affairs Superintendent for Washington Territory, negotiated 10 treaties with the formidable Indian tribes in the territory. According to one view those treaties, in effect, saved the native tribes from extinction and gave permanency to the territorial Indians. Significantly, the 10 treaties essentially remain in force today. Critics claim the haste with which their unfavorable terms were forced on the tribes brought on the violent wars which soon followed.

The volatile, active opposition comprised a minority of the territorial citizens. Many critics, including those who profited from selling liquor to the Indians and Hudson's Bay Company employees and settlers influenced by the company, obviously saw in the treaties an end to their unfettered commerce with the natives. Those who had profited most from Indian exploitation did not want to see the wilderness settled and developed and the tribes tamed and corralled on reservations, no longer totally available for their machinations. Some merely resented the Governor's high handed impatience and envied his dynamic display of energy and ability in carrying out his mandate from his superiors in the national government to expedite the task. Stevens exerted his usual considerable best effort to carry out a national Indian policy that was not peculiar to Washington Territory. In judging this part of Isaac Stevens's career, the successes and failures of his treaties should be put in context with the fruits of similar efforts elsewhere in the nation throughout our history.

Fundamentally, the deeply infused concepts of red and white men of the ownership and use of land were too far apart to allow an easy, peaceful reconciliation. The Indian wars attributed by some to Isaac Stevens were the outcome of the collision of the two different cultures. Similar collisions, with similar results, had occurred from the earlier contacts between the two races on the Atlantic Coast centuries before, had continued with the westward movement of the white invaders, and would occur again after Stevens's day, wherever and whenever the stronger, dominant whites imposed their civilization on newly desired lands occupied by the aborigines. Perhaps a partial case could be made for the charge that the impetuous, forceful character of the Governor hastened the inevitable — the violent reaction of the natives who were persuaded with implied force to radically change the way of life they and their ancestors had known for centuries. Worse, this radical change had to be accepted at once and to begin in a matter of months or weeks. But why make Stevens the only, or even the principal scapegoat? He was the able agent of federal policy, and his work pleased most Washingtonians and many other Americans of the time. To judge his handiwork by today's mores is an exercise in futility. The commonly accepted attitude of white Americans of Stevens's time — and indeed of many today — was expressed by

Lieutenant Colonel Benjamin Franklin Shaw, Indian interpreter, Indian fighter, an alleged friend of the natives, and a member of the Governor's Emergency Indian Service: "Does the earth belong to those who first find it, or does it belong to those who best use it?" The prevailing attitude was that civilized white men would develop and use the land to support many, where the Indians would leave it idle while only a few of them roamed over it.

Indian resentment against white encroachment increased in the Pacific Northwest with the passage of the United States Land Donation Act of 1850, which allowed settlers, individually and in groups, to take over Indian lands before the Government had acquired title to them. This procedure prevented the pioneers from getting proper deeds to their claims. Partly due to Stevens's urging, Congress belatedly acted for the Government to acquire alleged legal title to northwestern Indian lands through the device of treaties so the United States, in turn, could grant legal deeds to the settlers' land claims. Urgency in the vast undertaking resulted from the large influx of new land-hungry immigrants into the Northwest, spurred on by gold discoveries, abundant resources, and the faulty Land Donation Act. For these reasons Congress authorized Stevens to negotiate the desired treaties with the simmering, apprehensive Indians "with the least possible delay."

Armed with Federal instructions, the Washington Territorial Governor and Superintendent of Indian Affairs set out to resolve the dilemma to ensure the rapid development of the Pacific Northwest. The following salient features of the United States Indian policy guided Stevens in his treaty negotiations: (1) Confine the Indians to adequate reservations where they would be protected and controlled and would be encouraged to cultivate the soil and adopt settled, "civilized" habits. (2) Pay Indians for confiscated lands not in money, but in annuities of blankets, clothing, and other useful articles for a long period of time. (3) Provide Indians with schools, teachers, farmers, farm tools, blacksmiths, carpenters, and shops. (4) Prohibit dangerous wars and disputes between tribes and tribal groups. (5) Abolish slavery among the natives. (6) Prohibit, as far as possible, Indian consumption of alcoholic beverages. (7) Make the Indian transition from a nomadic to a civilized life a gradual one. The Indians were to retain their fishing, hunting, and berry-picking rights at their accustomed places and were to be permitted to pasture stock on unoccupied lands as long as it so remained. Added as a final assurance of good faith and future full United States citizenship, the reservation lands were, when the natives were fitted for it, to be allotted to the Indians in severalty (a condition quite foreign to native custom and philosophy at that time). Qualified interpreters would ensure all participants in the councils understood the discussions and terms of agreements. Indians could voice their own views, objectives, and wishes; they could ask questions and discuss the issues among themselves before deciding to sign or reject the proposed terms.

Given the premise that white settlement eventually would overwhelm the indigenous population and white culture would prevail, it was argued at the time that either of two basic alternatives should govern settlement. The United States/Stevens concept would treat the tribal groups as nations and formally coerce them from their lands by legal treaties to which they would be signatories. The tribes would be restricted to designated reservations where they would be protected and supported and given the opportunity to embrace white civilization. The other system of settlement, under the original Land Donation Act, was favored by territorial pioneer Ezra Meeker and other critics who refused to consider the tribes as nations with possessory title rights to their lands, but would permit white settlement on them. This concept afforded no way for the settler to gain a legal title to his claim and left the aboriginal peoples to adjust as well as possible to each new encroachment, with no assurance regarding their future holdings. The Stevens proponents felt their policy would save the Indians from being driven into the earth or into the sea, whereas the other led to chaos and extermination of all semblance of Indian tribal culture, eventually of the Indian as a separate entity. Another solution to the problem, unacceptable to most Americans, was that desired by Hudson's Bay Company and the Indians, that is, curtail white settlement and development and maintain the wilderness for the fur trade. Certainly, few whites really understood or gave serious consideration to the deeply troubled Indian reaction to the approaching end of their way of life, surely not enough consideration to give the Indian an equal voice in determining the path of the future.

Logically, Superintendent Stevens began his treaty-making activities in the Puget Sound region, the heart of American settlements and site of his capital. His *modus operandi* consisted of arriving at a prepared council site with a draft treaty which he presented practically as a *fait accompli*. After allowing sometimes brief Indian discussion, questions, and objections with counter proposals, he would ask for native acquiescence and signatures on the document. The Indian unfamiliarity with land titles and treaty negotiation, especially our concept of Senate ratification to make them effective, and Stevens's patronizing, forceful manner, hardly invited deep Indian understanding and discussion.

Stevens held four councils, averaging about four days each, west of the Cascades between Christmas Day, 1854 and February 26, 1855, completing three treaties with the Nisqually, Steilacoom and neighbors, and Puyallup;[1] the Duwamish, Suquamish, Snoqualmie, Skagit, Lummi and allies; and the Clallam, Skokomish, and Chimakum tribes. He failed to win over the Quinault, Chehalis, and other Southwest Washington tribes, due to mounting Indian resistance to giving up their homelands.[2] One view was that Indian resistance was hardened by whiskey salesmen and Hudson's Bay Company sycophants. In all, Stevens established nine reservations comprising over 60,000 acres and promised annuities of clothing and other goods amounting to $300,000 to 8,500 treaty Indians of Puget Sound for 20 years. The Nisqually and Puyallup Indians alone ceded 2,500,000 acres to the United States at the first council at Medicine Creek.

---

[1]This treaty, Medicine Creek, was ratified by the U.S. Senate March 3, 1855, a little more than two months after the council. The others made in Washington Territory were held up until Stevens secured their ratification in 1859.

[2]Special territorial agents brought the coastal tribes north of Grays Harbor under the Treaty of Olympia on July 1, 1855; Governor Stevens approved this treaty January 25, 1856 upon his return from his councils east of the Cascades.

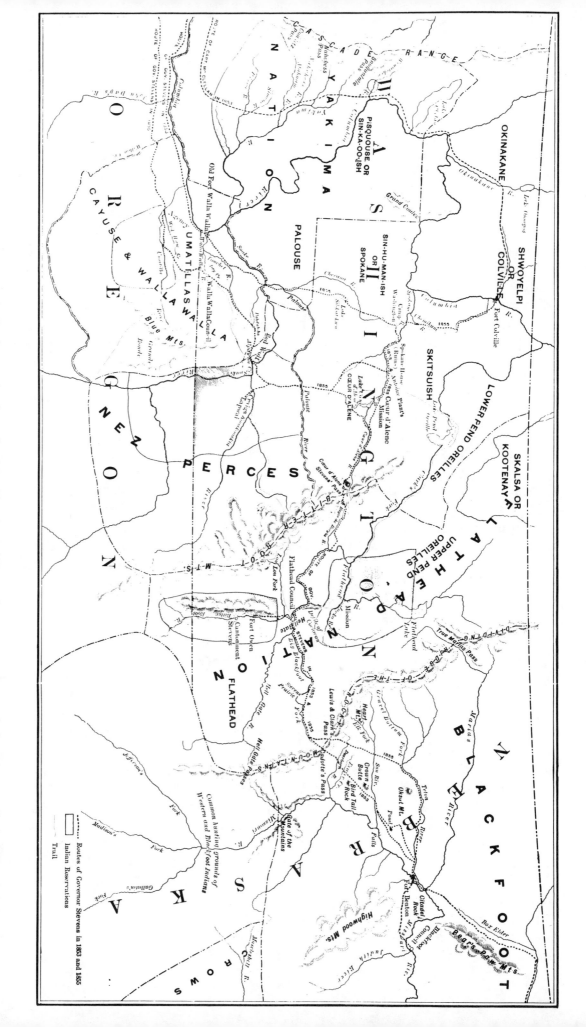

Routes of Governor Isaac Stevens during the Northern Railway Survey, 1853 and the Treaty Councils, 1855

[Special Collections Division, University of Washington Libraries]

The apparent ease with which most of the Puget Sound councils were conducted did not alert Stevens to a pattern of problems that was developing in the negotiations before he headed across the mountains to Central and Eastern Washington. Like most white men, the Governor had little or no real understanding of tribal structure, their loose social and political organization. Consequently, his practice of sometimes designating certain chiefs to legally represent a tribe or tribal group in council could result in his dealing with a chief or leader who had little or no authority to speak for his people. Not all chiefs had the power to govern; some held their titles and prestige for bravery or hunting ability. Some best known to whites were less powerful among their people than others not so well known. Stevens and his advisers would not always select the key man who had the greatest power and influence in his tribe. Further, the arbitrary assignment of several tribes who might be historical enemies to the same reservation met with resistance, as did the idea of abandoning ancestral homes and indigenous cultural practices. Failing to perceive the warning signs, Stevens saw his successes as the results of skillful negotiation of fair terms which would prove advantageous and beneficial to the aborigines. As Lieutenant Colonel Shaw put it, the day would come when, "he [the Indian] has been paid for all his rights, and has no reason to complain unless it be he is no longer considered a savage."

Turning his attention to the 14,000 natives in the vast region east of the Cascades, Superintendent Stevens approached those powerful tribes in the same way he had dealt with the Puget Sound Indians. Because the well-defined homelands of several native groups of that area sprawled over both Washington and Oregon Territories, responsibility for making the treaties with those tribes was shared with Joel Palmer, Superintendent of Indian Affairs for Oregon. Both Commissioners followed the same United States guidelines, of course, and both shared the same views. However, Stevens definitely was the dominant United States representative at that council. In the East the problems created by the proposal to move those stronger, wider-ranging tribes to reservations were multiplied by the greater impact such restriction would have on them. The eastern Indians also were aware of growing unrest and dissatisfaction among the tribes in Oregon who had as yet received no payments for their ceded lands. They also were aware of the failure of the Chehalis Council and had heard rumors that white treaty-makers had given presents to Indians and then pretended that they had purchased the land. On the plus side, a great bonus from the eastern councils is the survival of the collection of magnificent drawings of the proceedings and many of the principal Indian chiefs by the artist, Gustav Sohon, whom Stevens had borrowed from the Army to accompany his party as an interpreter and illustrator.

The first treaty council east of the Cascades convened on May 29, 1855. Known as the First Walla Walla Council, it was one of the largest and most heterogenous Indian gatherings in history. Nearly 5,000 Yakima, Nez Perce, Walla Walla, Palouse, and Cayuse chiefs and warriors attended, some reluctantly and suspiciously. Some tribes were not represented by their most influential leaders; others in the region were not represented at all. Stevens presumed that a Yakima leader not in high standing among his own people, should represent various small tribes. As in earlier and later councils, the United States position was based on the premises that the tide of white immigration would continue, indeed swell, and that Euro-American civilization had and would continue to improve the lot of the red men with horses, cattle, and trade goods. It was emphasized that treaties and reservations were essential now, while there remained plenty of land for both races, to save some measure of Indian homelands for their future.

The proceedings were long and difficult. The Indians were extremely apprehensive about selling their lands; they especially feared receiving much less than full value for what they would lose. Nor did they always like the sites selected for their reservations or the allocation of certain tribes to share them. At first, only the Nez Perce, friendly to Americans since the Lewis and Clark expedition, wanted a treaty, but even they split on the issues during the proceedings, delaying the final decision. Ultimately, Stevens and Palmer had to agree to provide a separate reservation for the Cayuse, Walla Walla, and Umatilla Tribes. This change released those three tribes from sharing the Nez Perce reservation, and made a total of three instead of the originally-proposed two reservations for the region. That concession, and a promise to increase the amount of payments for ceded lands, brought general agreement. All chiefs signed their treaties, ceding a total of 45,000 square miles of their lands to the United States. It was widely believed that the council nearly erupted in warfare, or at least an Indian attempt on the lives of the American delegation; such a disaster was averted by loyal Nez Perce, led by the staunch United States ally, Chief Lawyer.[1]

With such obvious Indian distaste for the white solution to the problem, why did the proud chiefs finally sign their treaties? Probably the wise, more mature ones realized that the white infiltration could not be stopped. They saw that white power would make resistance futile, and that probably it would be to their long-term advantage to make the best deal they could, preserving as much of their tribal existence and culture as feasible. Perhaps some foresaw an eventual Indian adoption of white civilization. The treaties would prolong that fate while preserving and preparing future generations to live as whites. Another view claims that their capitulation at the council bought time to prepare for the inevitable war which would decide the issue, at least for the short term.

Believing he had pacified the participants in the Walla Walla Council, Stevens, on June 16, 1855 set out to treat with the friendly, highly regarded Flatheads, Pend d'Oreille, and Kutenai between the Bitterroot and Rocky Mountains, six miles west of present-day Missoula, Montana. These more remote tribes had not experienced the racial tension of those previously dealt with by the Governor. They were far from the Oregon Trail and had not been infused with white settlers. Treaties with them would open up the country for the northern

[1] A prime mover in the Indian unrest at the Walla Walla Council was the Palouse leader Kamiakin, married to a Yakima woman. Although Kamiakin ultimately was a signatory to the treaties, he later denounced them and used his widespread influence among the tribes to foster the Indian revolt against white encroachment on their lands. He remained a thorn in the side of the Americans throughout the resultant Yakima War, the difficulties stemming from the Second Walla Walla Council, and the subsequent campaigns against U. S. Regular Army troops. Having eluded capture throughout the hositilities, Kamiakin fled to Canada when the tribes finally were subdued by the American military.

railroad and subsequent development. Though the usual proposals for reservations and land cessions would be tendered, Stevens's main inducement to these groups would be the prospect of peace with their feared, age-old enemies to the east, the Blackfoot Tribes. The United States would end Blackfoot raids into the Bitterroot Valley and Blackfoot harassment of the Washington Territory tribes while hunting east of the Rockies.

The Flathead Council opened on July 9; 1,200 natives attended. Though initially cordial, discussion became heated over the siting of reservations. None of the tribes wanted to move from their homes to jointly occupy a reservation in the homeland of another group. In fact, inasmuch as there had been no hostility between these tribes and the whites, the Indians saw no reason for a treaty, which to them meant an alliance. Impatient to move on to what he considered a more important session with the Blackfoot Tribes, Stevens conducted his worst council here. Finally, on July 16 the Flatheads and Pend d'Oreille agreed to the Governor's temporary "solution" to put the reservation on Pend d'Oreille land and let the President decide whether or not the Flatheads should join them there permanently. The Kutenai were offered a place on the Pend d'Oreille reservation; disillusioned, they evaded the treaty by moving to Canada.

Isaac Stevens put that disagreeable council behind him and pushed on to his rendezvous with the Blackfeet across the Continental Divide at Fort Benton. He arrived July 26 to find the Indians ready to talk but no sign of his co-participant United States representative, Alfred Cumming, Superintendent of Indian Affairs for the Territory of Nebraska, home of the Blackfoot Tribes. Cumming was more than two weeks late with the necessary supplies. Stevens went down the Missouri River and met him enroute to Fort Benton without the supplies. The two sensitive commissioners found little common ground for the coming council. Cumming believed whites should steer clear of the predatory Blackfeet, who could not be trusted, and was against dealing with them. Stevens had found them friendly in 1853, liked and admired them, and argued that their lands were so potentially valuable that the Government had to treat with them. Of course, a friendly Blackfoot tribal group was a key to pacifying and stabilizing the region, in turn a key to a successful northern railroad. Stevens persuaded Cumming to acquiesce in his leadership and at once ordered the council site moved downstream from Fort Benton to the junction of the Judith River with the Missouri to await the long-overdue food, presents, and other goods that had been ordered.

When the essential supplies finally reached the new site, the Blackfoot Council convened on October 16, 1855, more than two months late. Fifty-nine prominent chiefs from 10 tribes attended, including 27 from west of the Rockies. A total of 3,500 Blackfeet, Nez Perce, Flathead, Kutenai, and Pend d'Oreille Indians participated; the delays caused others who had intended to sit in to depart before the proceedings began, much to Stevens's dismay. The approaching winter precluded their remaining for the council. After only two days of discussion, with few disagreements, the participants signed the treaty, at last achieving welcome peace between those plains and western Indians. Ironically, Stevens's greatest treaty-making achievement occurred here, outside his gubernatorial jurisdiction.

The Blackfoot Council rates as "the most important intertribal gathering ever held on the northwestern plains." Several important factors smoothed the path of negotiations: The council's intent was to produce a "peace," rather than a "land," treaty through multi-tribal agreements. Unlike the previous treaties, the United States neither sought nor received territorial cessions at this council. Significantly, too, the always contentious reservation issue did not enter the negotiations.

As whites had not yet seriously encroached on the Blackfoot country, partly because of their fierce reputation, those Indians paid relatively little attention to the treaty's provisions for opening the region to white passage and settlement. Nevertheless, because of this treaty, the Blackfeet, who had been implacable foes of Americans since Lewis and Clark, permitted the flow of subsequent wagon trains, and, of course, the railroad through their country, avoiding an unknown number of savage conflicts in the area. The United States Senate ratified the Blackfoot Treaty April 15, 1856, six months after Stevens had produced it.

"The Great Soldier Chief," as the Blackfeet dubbed Governor Stevens, with some justification despite trying moments, considered his treaty-making tour more successful than he had thought possible. Most of the indigenous population in the northern United States, from the northwest plains to the Pacific were under treaty and the way was cleared to grant legal titles to the land claims of Washington Territory settlers. Presumably most of the tribes believed the treaties were in their own best interests. He had met the Government's criterion of a few multi-tribal reservations. Exerting single-purposed diligence against many great obstacles, he had accomplished his mission in less than two years. Senate ratification of his efforts should follow as a matter of course, putting the "icing on the cake."

Stevens's "bubble" burst when he was one day east of Fort Benton, en route to his final scheduled council with the Spokane and neighboring tribes before returning to Olympia. On October 29 a messenger staggered into camp with the terrifying news that the Yakima Indians were on the warpath, expecting to be joined by other tribes.[1] Although hostile Indian patrols were looking for him, the Governor scorned advice to return to Olympia via the East Coast and Panama and pushed on, crossing the Bitterroot Mountains in deep snow, suddenly appearing at the Coeur d'Alene Mission, surprising the local Indians whose loyalties were wavering. Determined to keep these groups from expanding the hostilities, Stevens called for a council with the Coeur d'Alene, Spokane, Kettle (or Colville), and Isle de Pierre tribes.

Stevens broke up the Spokane Council, one of the stormiest of his tour, on December 5, the day after it began. Though no treaty came from this meeting, more importantly, it kept those northern tribes neutral in the Yakima War. A concession to Indian demands provided that American military forces would stay south of the Snake River. Besides Stevens's haste to return to Olympia, this partially unproductive council was so turbulent and short-lived because of the

---

[1]The Yakima War followed the slaying by young Indians of five miners crossing their country enroute to the Colville gold fields, and the murder of the U.S. Indian agent, A.J. Bolon, who went to determine why Yakima Indians had become hostile after the First Walla Walla Council.

influence of the principal Indian negotiator, "Spokane Garry." Unlike most of the previous Indian negotiators, Garry fully understood while the proceedings were in progress what Stevens's treaty proposals meant. He had been educated by the Hudson's Bay Company and was fluent in English. He rejected outright the terms of the treaties and the patronizing manner of their presentation.

Augmented by a group of white miners gathered at the council site, the Stevens party hastened south to learn the intentions of the Nez Perce. To their relief, they found them still loyal American friends. Under the protection of a Nez Perce escort, Stevens's group moved to contact a unit of Oregon Volunteers that recently had defeated hostile Indians in the Walla Walla Valley after Regular United States troops, reinforced by Volunteers, had not brought an end to the hostilities. Discarding hopes for an immediate winter campaign due to severe cold, the Governor dismissed the Nez Perce, thanked the Volunteers for clearing the way, and continued by forced marches to Olympia. He arrived at his capital on January 19, 1856 to find the residents panic-stricken from recent hostilities on Puget Sound. They were so demoralized that only their inability to get away kept many of them from abandoning the country.

Characteristically, Stevens revitalized the settlers. In his special message to the legislature the Governor justified his Indian treaties and called for an all-out winter campaign, without mercy, against every Indian in arms against the United States. Because the whites' fall harvest had been disrupted, absolute victory before the spring planting began was essential to prevent famine. He convinced the lawmakers and the public of the necessity for the settlers themselves to fight for their homes and families due to what he described as a disgraceful abandonment of duty by the Regular Army and Brevet Major General John E. Wool, Commander of the Department of the Pacific, with headquarters in San Francisco.[1] The legislature rallied behind the Governor's leadership, and within its power, gave him unlimited authority to take whatever measures necessary to save the settlements from extinction.

Stevens immediately put into effect a nine-point military program that: (1) called for 1,000 volunteers to serve for six months under territorial command,

---

[1]Actually, west of the Cascades, under-strength Regular troops from Fort Steilacoom took the field at the beginning of hostilities in the autumn of 1855 and opposed the Indians until withdrawn in December because of sickness. In the east, an Army expedition under Major Gabriel Rains, reinforced by Volunteers, failed to subdue a Yakima group, reportedly due to Rains's alleged incompetence. As shown in the text, further attempts by the Regulars to support or cooperate with Volunteer actions were rebuked and halted by General Wool. At the time Wool was the second ranking officer in the Army, next to Commander-in-Chief Winfield Scott, and had distinguished records in the War of 1812 and the Mexican War. In the autumn of 1854, while in San Francisco enroute back to Washington Territory, Governor Isaac Stevens publicly disputed and chided him at an after-dinner gathering for claiming (perhaps with some justification) that he, rather than General Zachary Taylor, deserved the credit for the U.S. Mexican War victory at Buena Vista, earning the apparent life-long enmity of the feisty 70-year old Department Commander. Wool's scornful and cavalier treatment of Stevens and his refusal to support the territory's citizens in the forthcoming Indian war brought on Stevens's vendetta against him, which probably helped gain him a Congressional censure and to expedite his request for transfer from the Department of the Pacific. General Wool served well in the Civil War, reaching the Regular Army rank of Major General before retiring in 1863 at age 79.

disbanding and prohibiting forces raised strictly for local defense;[1] (2) urged settlers to return in groups to abandoned farms, build protective blockhouses, and cultivate the soil;[2] (3) directed all neutral Indians to move to designated reservations where they would be protected and supported;[3] (4) sent his secretary, Charles Mason, to Washington, D.C. on a successful quest for funds to support neutral Indians; (5) denied the enlistment of friendly North Sound Indians to confine the war to the South, but raised four companies of other friendly Indians who served with distinction, particularly as scouts, guides, messengers, and guardians of neutrals;[4] (6) appealed successfully to Victoria, Portland, and San Francisco for supplies and munitions; (7) created and distributed scrip as legal tender, or promissory notes, to pay the troops and buy munitions and supplies; (8) proclaimed the right of territorial seizure and condemnation of anything essential to prosecute the war, mostly food and work animals; (9) appealed to the staunch patriotism of the white population but served notice that discipline would be enforced and actions detrimental to military needs would be punished.

Even at the peak of opposition to Stevens's policies, he never had less than a two to one majority support from the territorial citizens. His use of Indian allies, roundly criticized, helped to keep more than 9,000 of a total indigenous population of over 21,000 from the warpath. In 20 days, 11 Volunteer companies and two units of Indian auxiliaries were in the field, fully equipped for continuous service.

Governor Stevens's relentless winter campaign, a new war tactic to the Indians, met with success from the beginning. A human dynamo, signing his orders as the Commander-in-Chief, Stevens routinely spent 18- to 20-hour days in the field and office. In less than six months the war in the West was won, and Volunteers not needed for an expedition east of the Cascades were disbanded. A

---

[1]This measure, when enforced against a Seattle company raised and commanded by prominent citizen Arthur Denny specifically and only for the defense of Seattle, earned Stevens the hostility of Denny who later led a successful move in the legislature to censure the Governor for certain arbitrary actions during the war.

[2]Some settlers married to Indian women and Hudson's Bay Company employees and sycophants, safe from Indian depredations, opposed and ignored this program. Any settlers unmolested while others in the area were murdered were to be treated as enemy allies, subject to the rules of war. Farmers suspected of serving as informants for hostile Indians were forcibly removed to settlements or blockhouses or to jail. To prevent their release by habeas corpus, Stevens proclaimed martial law in the counties concerned. The Governor did not believe neutrality was possible in an Indian war. This incident resulted in Stevens arresting and placing in custody Chief Justice Edward Lander for trying to hold court for the arrested farmers, in defiance of the Governor's proclamation. Lander, ruling the proclamation illegal, declared Stevens in contempt of court, but was unable to bring about his arrest. Stevens later paid a $50.00 fine and then pardoned himself. This episode figured prominently in the legislature's later censure of the Governor. President Pierce subsequently reprimanded Stevens for his proclamation though he allowed the Governor's motives were "pure."

[3]Chief Seattle, for one, influenced many Indians to move peacefully to designated reservations. Stevens's success with this program despite some unrest (but no widespread desertions), kept more than 8,500 of nearly 10,000 Indians west of the Cascades loyal or neutral.

[4]Indian volunteers were identified by distinctive, highly-prized deep blue caps with bright red facings, made by territorial ladies led by the First Lady, Mrs. Stevens.

major factor in the successful territorial campaign was the remarkably efficient logistical system which supported the combat troops in the field.

Due to General Wool's orders, United States troops in the territory, under somewhat embarrassed commanders, who later dealt severely with hostile Indians, generally, after early skirmishes, sat with hands tied while the Volunteers prosecuted the war. Regular troop commanders, notably Colonel George Wright (USMA Class of 1822), commanding the Ninth Infantry, and his principal subordinates, Lieutenant Colonel Silas Casey (USMA Class of 1826) and Brevet Lieutenant Colonel Edward J. Steptoe (USMA Class of 1837), influenced by General Wool, appeared to sympathize with the Indians. They often rebuffed the territorial authorities' pleas and requests for support and protection. When Governor Stevens, by direct contact, occasionally gained any obviously needed support from United States commanders, General Wool would promptly rebuke them and reiterate his orders not to cooperate with the Volunteers and their leaders.

Wool avoided direct contact with Stevens, the United States Territorial Governor and Indian Affairs Superintendent, and ignored, misrepresented, or rejected Stevens's letters seeking support and coordinated action in the campaign. In Wool's mind the war was the fault of white speculation, the settlers' greed and brutality; the Indians would be peaceful if left alone and not treated unjustly. He charged that Governor Stevens and other territorials wanted to exterminate the red men, an accusation not borne out by Stevens's directives and actions.

In late 1855 General Wool ordered United States troops in Washington to go on the defensive after learning of the repulse of an initial punitive expedition and other indecisive actions against the hostile Yakimas. He hoped peace would be restored if no major efforts were made against the hostile Indians until spring. He berated Major Gabriel J. Rains (USMA Class of 1827) for calling for and using Volunteer troops, declaring that Regular forces would be sufficient to handle any situation in Washington and Oregon after the arrival of his requested reinforcing regiment. Wool disbanded two companies of Washington Volunteers after they had been mustered into the United States service at Vancouver.[1] One of them had been raised to escort Governor Stevens's party on its return through hostile country from his treaty-making tour east of the Rockies. The General also denounced the successful Oregon Volunteers who had cleared the way for Stevens's safe return. Obviously, unlike Stevens, General Wool had no confidence in and little liking for volunteer troops.

Governor Stevens complained that United States military officers in the territory were trying to make peace with the hostile Indians by restraining the whites instead of punishing guilty Indians, prolonging the war. Further, he thought the conciliatory, passive policy of the Army led the Indians to believe the Volunteers and settlers to be people with ultimate goals different from those of the

---

[1]Early in the war a company of volunteers reinforced the mere 100 regulars at Fort Steilacoom at the request of the post commander. Because of General Wool's action at Vancouver, Stevens refused a later request by the General for reinforcing understrength regulars with volunteer troops to be mustered into the federal service under regular commanders. Despite contrary evidence, Wool later denied that he knew one of the companies he had disbanded had the mission of rescuing the Stevens party in the eastern part of Washington Territory.

Regulars. This disunified front allowed the Indians to exploit the Army against the territorial authorities. Native parleys with United States military officers afforded the aborigines protection against Volunteer attacks, thwarting the Militia's drive for victory.

General Wool's subordinates in Washington did not fully inform Stevens of the General's objectives in the territory; they became clear when his instructions to them were made public after the withdrawal of Volunteer forces to Western Washington following the Second Walla Walla Council in late 1856. The federal forces were to expel the Volunteers from Indian country and disarm them if strong enough to do so (actions that never were attempted). They also were to exclude the Volunteers and American settlers from the region east of the Cascades (in violation of United States law), but were not to interfere with Hudson's Bay Company personnel there. Wool's policy, in effect would make the Cascade Range the frontier to United States settlement from the West Coast, at least until some future time when the eastern Indians agreed to white penetration of their lands. Such a policy hardly harmonized with the plans of Isaac Stevens, most whites in Washington Territory, the United States Government, and Americans in general. Contrary to the reaction of the United States Army's Department of the Pacific to the Northwest Indian War, the few United States Navy and other American vessels on Puget Sound cooperated to the maximum possible extent with Governor Stevens and the Washington Volunteers by providing supporting gunfire and patrolling the Sound. Hudson's Bay Company steamers also patrolled the Sound, effectively tempering Indian activities in the region. American Regular soldiers often rode as guards on patrol and commercial vessels.

Determined to press the war east of the Cascades, and unable to get Colonel Wright's cooperation, Stevens sent Lieutenant Colonel Benjamin Shaw with four companies of Militia through Naches Pass in the summer of 1856 to strike a blow at continuing Indian forays along the Columbia. Shaw moved on a group of Indians in the Grande Rhonde Valley southeast of Walla Walla in July, 1856, dealing them a decisive defeat.[1] The Governor used the victory to call a second Walla Walla council to try to reaffirm the 1855 treaties, confirm Nez Perce friendship, and to restrain doubtful, wavering Indians from joining the hostilities. He also invited hostile tribes to attend, with the proviso that they would submit to United States justice and mercy. He got few takers. Nor did Colonel Wright accept Stevens's invitation to attend the council with a protective force of Regulars. Rather, Wright suggested to Stevens that he rescind the treaties to pacify the region. However, Wright sent Brevet Lieutenant Colonel Steptoe with four companies to begin the long-delayed federal military occupation of the Walla Walla Valley and, despite General Wool's orders, to support Stevens from a distance.

The poorly attended council opened September 11, 1856, and for two fruitless days the representatives of the Cayuse, Walla Walla, and Yakima, and even half of the Nez Perce, denied that they had agreed to sell their lands when they signed the treaties. Many echoed Colonel Wright and asked for the revocation of the treaties

---

[1]Some critics belittle Volunteer victories as atrocities against helpless Indian women, children, and old men, while playing down similar Indian atrocities (and worse) against isolated whites.

and the exclusion of whites from their lands in exchange for keeping the peace. The hostile chiefs spread the idea among wavering leaders that the United States Government, as represented by its Territorial Governor and Superintendent of Indian Affairs, Isaac Stevens, did not have the United States military power behind it.

Though Stevens and his small party were in danger from Indians with concealed arms, Brevet Lieutenant Colonel Steptoe moved his camp farther away when the Governor requested he move closer to the council site and provide a company of dragoons to augment the Governor's security force of a small Militia company and 50 Nez Perce auxiliaries. Eventually Steptoe became aware of the true situation, but with General Wool's policy in mind, instead of complying with Stevens's request, sent a company of dragoons to escort the Governor's party to a camp near his Regulars. The council resumed at Stevens's new camp site and continued with no progress until Stevens closed it on September 17 and departed for The Dalles, escorted by the Militia and Nez Perce security force. Colonel Steptoe then told the Indians that he was there on a peaceful mission, to live among them rather than to fight them, and invited them to a new council at his camp. The hostile Indians, deciding to take advantage of the apparent split in the white ranks, fired the grass at Steptoe's camp to further neutralize him, and fell upon Stevens's party only three miles away. The alert Governor's party moved to good defensive positions and held off the enemy throughout the night. Informing Steptoe of the situation, Stevens advised him that a company of Regular troops would be of service. Steptoe invited the Governor to join him; Stevens made the move before dawn. The war party's attack on the joint camp was beaten off by Army howitzer fire and a charge by the Regulars. The Indians, surprised and incensed at Steptoe's change in attitude, accused him of a breach of faith. At Stevens's suggestion, the joint force built a blockhouse and stockade on the spot; Steptoe left a company to man it, and Steptoe's command and the Militia company escorted the Governor and his party to The Dalles.

Finally, circumstances had forced the Regular Army and the Territorial Governor and his Volunteers to act in common cause. Steptoe's experience led him to recommend to Colonel Wright that United States forces now conduct a vigorous campaign against rebellious Indians. He also confirmed the Governor's report that, despite severe Indian provocation, the Volunteers had committed no atrocities against them nor plundered them in any fashion; they even had returned stray Indian horses and cattle to their indigenous owners. Despite Steptoe's new views and recommendations, General Wool remained adamantly against federal military cooperation with territorial Volunteers and authorities. Wool charged, rather absurdly, that Stevens had called the Second Walla Walla Council only to force a war with the friendly Indians.

Colonel Wright followed these events with his own council, telling several of the hostile chiefs to put past differences behind them, that perfect friendship must exist, and recommending that the treaties never be confirmed. Lieutenant Colonel Steptoe, now in command at the new Fort Walla Walla, chose this opportune time to publish General Wool's earlier order excluding white settlers from Eastern Washington. When Steptoe suggested to Wool that perhaps it would be a good idea to permit "a good industrious colony" to settle in the Walla Walla Valley, Wool retorted that lowering the natural wall of the Cascades between the two races would keep them at war, adding to the protective labors of the Army. He viewed the whole interior as a natural reservation. Amazingly, he considered the whole Oregon Country from the Pacific to the Continental Divide mostly barren, without a navigable river, generally only fit for nomadic tribes who should be allowed to keep it. In his opinion the United States got little of value when it acquired Oregon. That view and the strong protests and recommendations of Stevens and the two Northwest territorial legislatures probably helped inspire General Wool to request reassignment and eased the approval of his request. He was replaced as Commander of the Department of the Pacific by Brevet Brigadier General Newman S. Clarke in May, 1857.

Thwarted in the interior, Superintendent Stevens withdrew his agents from the tribes east of the Cascades, except Bill Craig, assigned to the Nez Perce and married to a woman of that tribe. A quasi-peace between the United States Army and the Indians set in; hostilities between the tribes and the territorials ended.

Upon his return to Olympia after the disastrous Second Walla Walla Council in late 1856, Governor Stevens disbanded the Volunteers and disposed of territorial property acquired during the campaign, including many animals, by public auction, to the advantage of the territorial treasury. A total of 1,896 Volunteers had been mustered, of whom about 1,000 had been in service at any one time. As there were only 1,700 whites in Washington Territory capable of bearing arms during the hostilities, Oregon's contribution of 215 proved invaluable. The Volunteers had built 35 stockades, forts, and blockhouses; settlers constructed 23 and the Regular troops seven. New roads and trails were opened and the few old ones improved. Though the Indians temporarily emerged in control east of the Cascades, most territorial citizens, including the Governor, were proud of the fight they had made to save their homes and principal settlements. Governor Stevens allowed that though he had endeavored to do his duty to the best of his ability for the good of the country, he might have done some things more wisely in light of recent experiences.

The new Commander of the Department of the Pacific, General Clarke, at first followed his predecessor's lead and excluded settlers from Eastern Washington while maintaining garrisons there to protect the Indians. Regardless, many white miners were moving up the Columbia to Colville and Canada, alarming and irritating the Indians. Native depredations and threats, including thefts of Army cattle, prompted Brevet Lieutenant Colonel Steptoe to lead a force from Fort Walla Walla to investigate and redress the abuses. Steptoe, intending to settle the disturbances by peaceful means, set out in May, 1858 with his command poorly armed and equipped for a campaign. Unaware of, or ignoring, the 1855 Spokane Council's indigenous warning for American military forces to remain south of the Snake River, Steptoe crossed to the north side en route to Colville and was struck by a strong force of Spokane, Coeur d'Alene, and Palouse warriors and was forced to withdraw.

Stung by the Steptoe disaster, General Clarke launched an uncoordinated, two-pronged Army invasion of the Indian country east of the Cascades. Colonel

**The Stevens House
Olympia, Washington**

Wright headed a powerful force to crush the Spokane, Coeur d'Alene, and Palouse. Victorious in two pitched battles, he brought the tribes to submission, hanged a number of Indians without trial, burned Indian crops and lodges, and killed many of their horses. Among those hanged (within 15 minutes after surrendering) was the influential, troublesome Yakima war chief Qualchan, alleged perpetrator of many crimes, including the murder of several transient miners. Qualchan's father, Chief Owhi, who had hoped for amnesty, was reported killed while trying to escape from Wright's custody a few days after his son's execution. Upon his return to Walla Walla, Wright executed several of the most troublesome Cayuse and Walla Walla leaders. Colonel George Wright's actions in these circumstances certainly bore no similarity to his refusal only a year earlier to surrender to Governor Stevens for trial native leaders he had taken as hostages.[1]

The second prong was led by Major Robert S. Garnett (USMA Class of 1841) against provocative Yakimas. Though he engaged no large forces of the elusive enemy, in sporadic fighting Garnett captured and executed several Indians deemed involved in killing miners and other depredations, including the murder of Agent Bolon in 1855. Chief Owhi and his son Qualchan had managed to escape from Garnett only to meet their fates at the hands of Wright. Garnett reported that, despite small successes, his foray had been worthwhile, that his "severity" against the Indians had had a "salutary effect" on them.

The belated adoption by the Army of Isaac Stevens's basic views for handling hostile Indians, though with less mercy and greater severity, finally brought peace on the white man's terms to Washington Territory. Steptoe's defeat and Wright's victorious campaign helped bring about the delayed United States Senate ratification of Stevens's much maligned treaties. Had even a milder policy embracing military power been pursued consistently by United States forces, augmented by Volunteers, from the beginning of hostilities, the war could have been ended to white satisfaction, with better Indian results, several years earlier.

In his day as well as today, Isaac Stevens has been a controversial figure, severely criticized, primarily for his Indian policies. The numerous treaties he made with the already simmering, but still peaceful tribes in Washington Territory have been ridiculed as instigating war instead of peace. Such criticism does not give due weight to the main purposes of the treaties — the acquisition of Indian lands by the United States and the confinement, control, and protection of the Indians on designated reservations — objectives that would have aroused the natives no matter who pursued them for the United States. Surely the policy of individual settlers appropriating Indian lands without recognizing Indian claims — the policy under the United States Land Donation Act of 1850 when Stevens arrived on the scene — would not have preserved the peace. Rather, it already had

---

[1] One hostile prisoner held for the Territory by the Army and later released to civilian authorities was the popular Nisqually sub-chief, Leschi, who had opposed the Medicine Creek Treaty. Governor Stevens has been roundly denounced for hanging this influential hostile whom he regarded as a ringleader in the Puget Sound uprising.

raised indigenous alarm and resentment and appeared to be the road to chaos and extermination of the tribes.

Did the situation during the war of 1855-56 call for delay, for temporizing to give the natives time to adjust to their fate, as suggested by the many critics, apparently including General Wool and the United States Army in Washington Territory at the time? Or would suggested delays have given the Indians time to unite in rebellion, to plan and bring on a vastly bloodier, longer, more disastrous war? As previously shown, Stevens's Oregon counterpart in the United States Bureau of Indian Affairs and his co-negotiator at the First Walla Walla Council, Superintendent Joel Palmer, shared and echoed the views of Stevens and their superiors to expedite the agreements. With gold in the Colville area, and the influx of immigrants growing, Stevens's haste to wrap up the treaties reflected his instructions. His arbitrary, patronizing manner of exacting reluctant tribal agreements hardly was a "plus" for the Governor. However, knowing that essentially the terms he proposed would have to be met, and considering the magnitude of the task, Isaac Stevens, true to his nature, hardly was inclined to brook serious opposition or delay. Perhaps the positions of Governor and Superintendent of Indian Affairs should have been separate offices held by different men, though the successful execution of both depended upon working in tandem. And, as indicated earlier, basically what would another Indian Commissioner have done differently within United States policy guidelines? Some type of an official understanding with the tribes seemed essential, or at least desirable before usurping their lands and deeding them to individual settlers. Doubtfully, perhaps another negotiator would have softened the blow to the aborigines. How does one diplomatically tell a mass of people to give up their homelands to him and move to a small, restricted portion of them under his control, and expect the losers to like it? Then too, it probably was a foregone conclusion that Governor Stevens would have dominated or strongly influenced a separate, "independent" Territorial Superintendent of Indian Affairs.

In abstract, the criticism of Stevens and others for encouraging whites to move into lands marked for cession before the treaties became effective has some merit. Apparently the Indians misunderstood or chose to ignore that part of their treaties. It was an important enough point to have been resolved to the satisfaction, or at least complete understanding, of both sides, with no doubt about the other's interpretation of it. Though legal, perhaps such migration should have been delayed until the treaties went into effect. In practice, it probably would have been impossible to enforce. Prompt ratification of the treaties, or prompt rejection with new guidelines by the Senate, might have helped defuse that potentially explosive situation, often cited as the specific cause of the war. Maybe "premature" migration was a short-term cause, but the fact remains, the prospects of land cession and reservation living constituted a double dose of bitter medicine for the Indians — their "handwriting on the wall." Certainly Stevens's treaty policies followed his superiors' instructions and met the approval of a vast majority of territorial citizens and the incoming flood of whites. The prompt extinguishing of Indian titles to the land and the control of the tribes on reservations were the keys to rapid American development of the territory, as demonstrated after the Indians were pacified and the treaties ratified.[1]

For General Wool, Commander of the Department of the Pacific, and his subordinates in Oregon and Washington Territories — all United States officials, instruments rather than makers of American policy — to thwart United States law by interposing the United States Army between the Government's civilian agents in the territories and the Indians, favoring the latter, was an exercise in folly. It tended to encourage the tribes to resist the officially-favored white encroachment with impunity, a course fraught with tremendous danger — the savagery of Indian warfare in the balance. Wool's vision of the worthlessness of the Oregon Country hardly rates accolades for judgment, yet it surely influenced his decisions during the Northwest Indian wars. As a minimum, regardless of personal animosities, the United States Army's Pacific Department Commander and the United States Territorial Governor and Indian Superintendent in Washington should have met and conferred, coordinating actions early in the crisis and periodically during the war. Stevens was eager to do so and made several overtures to that effect. Wool, strangely, rebuffed every move in that direction, even avoided meeting Stevens while visiting military posts in the Territory.

For the American military to encourage the aborigines to disregard the treaties they had signed with the United States civilian representatives in the region was inexcusable. It would have been better for them to have attended and participated in Stevens's councils, as invited to do so by the Superintendent. For Wool to order his troops to have nothing to do with the territorial authorities and Volunteers after hostilities had begun, regardless of their cause, was unbelievable. As Delegate Stevens later pointed out in a speech before the U. S. House of Representatives urging the American Government to pay the territorial war claims:

> . . Well, sir, suppose the treaties did cause the war; suppose we did have vagabonds . . . who committed outrages upon the Indians; suppose some few citizens . . . speculation out of the war; if these things be true, did they make it any less the duty of the people and of the authorities of the territories, a war having come upon them, to protect the settlements? What account would an executive have to render who, when he heard that the Indians were devastating the settlements, burning the houses, and massacring the women and children, had declined to protect those settlements on the ground that here and there a white man had outraged the Indians and had driven them to arms?

---

[1]Presumably, even most critics approve of the treaties' fishing clauses upon which the late U.S. District Court Judge George H. Boldt based his famous and controversial 1974 decision on Indian fishing rights in Northwest waters. Stevens's treaties compare very favorably with others made elsewhere before and after his councils in essential points: longevity and impact on the Indians after becoming effective. Also, Indian realization of the treaties' more favorable terms to them could have begun much sooner, perhaps forestalling early, long-lived Indian fears and some resentment, if Congress had acted decisively on them promptly.

He went on to point out that the treaties were not the doing of the settlers, nor were the convening of the councils, or the appointment of the commissioners and their actions.

Stevens continued:

> Not at all. It was the act of your Government. It was the act of your Congress. It was done under the order of your President. The people of the territories certainly were not responsible, nor were the executives of those people responsible.

After disposing of military administrative matters at the cessation of hostilities in late 1856, Governor Stevens turned his attention to civil matters. When the 1857 legislature convened, opposition he had aroused during the war struck with a vengeance. Led by council member and chairman of the military committee, Arthur Denny of Seattle, the legislators passed a resolution censuring him while failing in an attempt to remove him from office. The lawmakers then passed Stevens's entire legislative program, which dealt with loose ends from previous measures, some interrupted by the war, further territorial improvements, and measures to resolve war claims and other issues brought on by the conflict.

An angry citizenry embarrassed the legislature by electing Stevens Territorial Delegate to Congress by a 986-to-549 vote on July 13, 1857. Accepting the unanimous Democratic nomination, Stevens had stumped all of Western Washington in a five-week campaign, traveling 1,460 miles to speak at 40 meetings. Stevens resigned the governorship August 11. He felt that with the groundwork he had laid, he now could best serve the territory in Congress and in the national capital, where he could use his persuasive powers to push through still pending important measures submitted for territorial development. The new territorial legislature elected with him rebuked its predecessor for its unwarranted resolution against Stevens and declared that the censure did not reflect the majority opinion of the citizens of Washington Territory.

Stevens was reelected to a second two-year term as Delegate to Congress in 1859 by a vote of 1,684 to 1,094. While back in the territory between terms, he strongly influenced the Governor and the commander of the new Military Department of Oregon (comprising most of the Territories of Washington and Oregon), Brigadier General William S. Harney, to maintain a tough stand against British Governor Sir James Douglas's new threat to acquire San Juan Island. By doing so, Stevens helped to keep it and all the San Juans within the dominion of the United States.

During his two terms in Congress Isaac Stevens was a tireless friend of Washington Territory while vindicating his earlier controversial policies as Governor and Superintendent of Indian Affairs. He introduced 63 bills and resolutions, 12 amendments, and two memorials, and made at least nine major speeches. Delegate Stevens's considerable accomplishments included: Senate ratification of all eight of his Indian treaties that were on hold; payment of the Washington and Oregon war debts, overcoming opposition by a New York representative inspired by none other than General John E. Wool; increased territorial mail service; ensured the construction of the Fort Benton-Walla Walla Road, connecting the Missouri and Columbia Rivers, with Lieutenant John Mullan, Jr., Artillery (USMA Class of 1852) confirmed as officer-in-charge (against the opposition of the Army Topographical Engineers).[1] He also urged construction of three transcontinental railroads (pointing out the advantages of the northern route), one of the first, if not the first, to favor publicly such a course. He warned that Canadian efforts to be first to build a railroad to the Pacific Northwest, if successful, might draw Asian trade away from the United States. He won approval for an expanded territorial road net, an armed steamer on Puget Sound, and funds for the Blackfoot farms promised in his 1855 treaty. Washington's delegate proposed a Government-hosted Northwest Indian chief visit to the national capital and got approval for a new land office and district in the southern part of the territory; secured land for a marine hospital, a territorial lunatic asylum, and the erection of other public buildings; and urged a survey of the Oregon-Washington boundary.

At long last, by working on it every morning before breakfast, Stevens completed his monumental Northern Railway Survey Report. It filled 797 pages in two volumes. The Senate and House each published 10,000 copies; to meet the growing demand, Stevens got his old rail-route antagonist, Jefferson Davis, then a senator from Mississippi, to push through a Senate order for 10,000 additional copies. Stevens urged an early detailed railroad survey made, based on his report, which he termed a reconnaissance, prior to construction of the line — a task he estimated would take 10 years to complete. In all departments of government Stevens exerted considerable influence, respected for his promptness and brief, lucid presentations. Again his never-failing courteous, considerate treatment of those at the clerical level paid off in the expeditious handling of his proposals.

In his spare time Stevens, now a national figure, managed to put out a widespread circular letter to people desiring to settle in Washington Territory. Extolling the virtues of the Northwest, it contained a wealth of detailed information on routes, climate, soil, available land, natural resources, waterways, and tips on procedures to follow when encountering Indians. He met with some skepticism in a long major speech delivered in New York City to the American Geographical and Statistical Society effusively praising the wonders and potential of the Great Northwest. However, time and events in great part have borne him out.

Indefatigable, Stevens accepted the chairmanship of the National Democratic Party's National Executive Committee, charged with its organization and with canvassing the nation for its party's 1860 presidential candidate, John C. Breckinridge of Kentucky, later a Confederate General. In one night Stevens wrote the party's address to the nation. Firmly against secession, Stevens believed the best way to save the then shaky Union was to recognize that only the individual

---

[1]Mullan's 624-mile road became a main artery for immigrants into the Northwest until the advent of the Northern Pacific Railroad in 1883. Today's U.S. Highway Interstate 90 closely follows the road's most difficult mountain stretch between Spokane, Washington and Deer Lodge, Montana across the Continental Divide — a tribute to Mullan's choice of routes, confirming Stevens's choice of and faith in Mullan as the builder of the road.

states had the constitutional right to decide for or against slavery within their boundaries. He thought slavery would not be practicable in the territories, and, inasmuch as the territories would become states in a few years, it would not continue to be an issue. He campaigned for Breckinridge believing that the Democratic Party's three-way split, resulting in four major presidential candidates, would throw the election into the House of Representatives where Breckinridge would have an excellent chance to win. When Lincoln became the President-elect and the Southern states began to secede, Stevens called for a convention of all states to restore the Union. When many of his political associates joined the secessionists, Stevens denounced the movement and immediately, permanently broke from them. He tried to get a weak and vacillating President Buchanan to cleanse his cabinet of southerners and take a strong stand in defense of the Government and the country, to include protecting government property and installations being seized by seceding states. He urged Buchanan to sustain Major Robert Anderson (USMA Class of 1825) at Fort Sumter and helped organize a regiment of District of Columbia Militia for the security of the President, the forthcoming presidential inauguration, and the capital itself.

At the end of his second congressional term Stevens returned alone to Olympia where he again denounced secession and worked to strengthen territorial support of the Federal Government. Advocating reorganization and arming of the territorial Militia, he accepted the captaincy of the company of Puget Sound Rifles in Olympia. Though a majority of the delegates elected to the Territorial Democratic Convention were Stevens men, strong opposition, claimed by some to be fed by bribes, put his renomination as a candidate for congressional delegate in doubt. Indignant at such treatment after the benefits he had gained for the Territory, and learning of the Confederate capture of Fort Sumter, Stevens withdrew from the race. He, however, magnanimously supported his successful opponent (who lost the subsequent election) declaring, "The convention's choice is my choice." The day the nominating convention adjourned Stevens tendered his services to the Federal Government "in whatever military position the Government may see fit to employ them."

Back in Washington, D.C., in 1861, private citizen Isaac Stevens suffered the indignity and frustration of not being immediately returned to military service. Though President Lincoln bore no grudge against Stevens for his 1860 election opposition (he actually was impressed by Stevens), there were sufficient influential enemies mustered against him to block temporarily any appointment worthy of his tremendous ability. Despite regaining General Winfield Scott's friendship, several Stephen A. Douglas Democrats who never forgave his former close association with secessionists, to the detriment of their candidate, were able to hold him at bay. Also arrayed against such an obviously needed talent was his old friend and former subordinate, now Major General George B. McClellan, Commander of the Army of the Potomac. Finally, on August 10, 1861 Stevens accepted the colonelcy of the 79th Highlanders, a New York regiment badly cut up at Bull Run and disgruntled at not being returned home to recuperate as promised. Colonel Stevens promptly squelched a budding mutiny and quickly turned the regiment into one of the Army's best, distinguishing itself in subsequent skirmishes. The 79th's new commander early won the endearing affection and respect of the unit's officers and men.

The Commander of the Army of the Potomac, General McClellan, ignored and snubbed Colonel Stevens when in his presence during the general's visits to Stevens's superiors. He continued this childish and petulant behavior even after Stevens gained his first star. Against McClellan's advice, Lincoln made Stevens a brigadier general on September 28, less than two months after he had returned to military service. Aware of McClellan's strong desire to avoid a general engagement and of his preference for the defensive, Stevens predicted the Army of the Potomac was doomed to disaster under "Little Mac." He was glad to escape from McClellan's overall command when he was transferred to brigade command under Major General T.W. Sherman (USMA Class of 1836) to operate along the Southern Coast. When the 79th Highlanders requested reassignment to Brigadier General Stevens's new command, with the concurrence of the new general, McClellan unsuccessfully opposed the move, declaring the regiment to be the best in his army.

General Stevens's energy, demonstrated military skill and judgment, aptitude for command, and especially his aggressive boldness — his eagerness to come to grips with the enemy — must have been a breath of fresh air to Abraham Lincoln at that time. With McClellan temporarily on the sidelines due to his disastrous Peninsula Campaign, Stevens commanded a division in Major General John A. Pope's[1] new Army of Virginia in the Northern Virginia Campaign during the summer of 1862. General Lee decisively defeated Pope's army at the Second Battle of Bull Run. General Stevens's division, as the rear guard, covered Pope's withdrawal. At Chantilly on September 1, 1862, correctly perceiving the beginning of a Confederate flanking movement as a major Jacksonian envelopment, Stevens threw his division against Jackson's[2] much larger command so fiercely that, with support from Major General Philip Kearny's division, he stopped the rebel movement in its tracks, preventing a serious Union disaster. In the heat of the Battle of Chantilly General Stevens ensured the removal from the field of his wounded son and adjutant, Captain Hazard Stevens, then moved on foot to the front of the attack. Recovering the colors of the 79th Highlanders from the dying bearer, he led the charge with the colors aloft. General Isaac Stevens died that day

---

[1]General Pope graduated from West Point in 1842. After his debacle at Second Bull Run, he was sent to Minnesota to fight the Sioux.

[2]Confederate Major General Thomas J. (Stonewall) Jackson (USMA Class of 1846), Robert E. Lee's "right arm," commanded a 20,000-man division at Chantilly; Stevens's division numbered 5,000. The following month Jackson was promoted to Lieutenant General and given command of one of the new corps of the reorganized Army of Northern Virginia. In early May, 1863 he was mistakenly shot by his own troops while returning in early darkness from a reconnaissance of the front during the Battle of Chancellorsville. He was apparently recovering from the amputation of his left arm and other wounds when pneumonia set in, and he died May 10, 1863 at age 39. One of the greatest commanders of the Civil War, General Jackson's stand at First Bull Run earned him his nickname and keyed the Confederate victory there; his spectacular "foot cavalry" campaign in the Shenandoah Valley still is studied as a model of celerity. His move to Pope's rear at Second Bull Run led to that Southern triumph. His brilliant envelopment of the Union Army at Chancellorsville gave Lee his most striking, classic victory.

**Brigadier General of U.S. Volunteers
Isaac Ingalls Stevens
during the Civil War**

[Special Collections Division, University of Washington Libraries]

from Confederate fire on the Chantilly battlefield, the colors still in his grip. He was buried at Newport, Rhode Island, his onetime "hometown," as a Major General, U.S. Volunteers.[1]

The diminutive mental giant, only 44 years old, was struck down in the prime of life, at the peak of his potential. Though he already had accomplished much more than most men in a full lifetime, how much more would Stevens have achieved in the service of his country and his fellow man if he had survived to see his dreams of the Great Northwest unfolding? Who knows what heights he would have reached given more time and opportunities? It is reliably reported that at the time of Stevens's death Abraham Lincoln, with the concurrence of his advisors, and support from the press, was considering putting him in command of all the Union armies in Virginia. Lincoln considered him the fiercest field commander of all his West Point generals. Certainly Stevens was the logical choice, based upon his long-term military seniority and his brilliant record at the time of his death. Without question, if he had lived he would have risen rapidly to high command in the war for the Union. Stevens's untimely death lessened and delayed recognition for the extraordinary service he had performed during his short meteoric rise in public life. Ambitious indeed, but Isaac Stevens's correspondence and actions clearly reveal his willingness to subject his personal ambitions to duty in the service of his country. He never faltered when faced with great odds, difficulties, and risks to his well being, reputation, and record. Isaac Stevens served Washington Territory and his nation well.

Colonel Robert A. Matter
United States Army, Retired
USMA, Class of 1939

---

[1]Stevens's promotion to major general is as controversial as his career. One version simply states that it was effective July 4, 1862, less than a year after he received his first star, and nearly two months before his death. Another depicts the promotion as posthumous, with date of rank retroactive to July 4, 1862.

WILLIAM A. SLAUGHTER:
AN EARLY CASUALTY OF THE INDIAN WAR, 1855-56

During the westward expansion of the nation, the Army played a key role in providing expeditions, topographical surveys, frontier security, protection for settlers, and skills and services not generally available in pioneer settlements. The posts that housed the soldiers performing these duties often were isolated and remote, but symbolically and in practice were centers for the pioneers. Military garrison life in the new territories often was monotonous, and patrols equally so — except during periods of Indian unrest, when field duty could become suddenly violent and dangerous.

This was the pattern of military and pioneer life in the Washington Territory, — officers and men sharing both the daily routine and the occasional hazards, and some paying with their lives. One of these, stationed at Fort Steilacoom, was a young West Point graduate named William Alloway Slaughter.

Slaughter was born in Kentucky in 1827, the first child of Alban and Mary Alloway Slaughter. Shortly after his birth, the family moved to Lafayette, Indiana, where Alban Slaughter served as a Justice of the Peace and Court Administrator. In 1844, young William Slaughter entered West Point, graduating in 1848 after the end of the Mexican War. He received his brevet commission as a second lieutenant, Second Infantry, and reported to Fort Hamilton, New York, awaiting sea transportation to California and his first troop assignment. The voyage became a nightmare since Slaughter was prone to seasickness.

After a miserable, seven-month passage around Cape Horn, he arrived in California to the good news that he had been promoted en route from brevet rank to second lieutenant. The bad news was that his West Coast orders were a mistake; he should have been assigned to the Great Lakes region. Back to the East Coast he went, by the Isthmus of Panama, sick all the way, only to arrive and receive firm orders for a third queasy voyage back to the West Coast.

His duty was largely routine. His most noteworthy assignment was as security escort for the topographical party sent to fix and mark the U.S. border along the Gila River, established by the Treaty of Guadalupe Hidalgo. In 1850, he was indeed transferred to the Great Lakes, assigned to a Fourth Infantry company at Fort Gratiot, Michigan, one of a series of forts controlling the entrances and waterways to the Great Lakes system. There, his military duties were less rigorous than in the West, and his social life became more active, culminating in courtship and marriage to Mary Wells, the only daughter of a local merchant.

Soon afterward, the Fourth Infantry was assembled at Fort Columbus, New York, for assignment to the Department of the Pacific, headquartered in California. Married less than a year, the Slaughters began their long trek, chiefly by water: lake steamer to Buffalo, down the Erie Canal, rail to Albany, Hudson River steamer to New York, where the Regiment assembled some 700 officers, men, wives, and servants and boarded the *U.S.S. Ohio* for Panama. The trip across the Isthmus was typically brutal, with about 15 percent losses to cholera before the California-bound vessel was reached and boarded.

After a brief respite at Benicia Barracks, near San Francisco, Lieutenant Slaughter was assigned in 1852 to Columbia Barracks (Fort Vancouver). After staying there through the following spring, he was transferred to Fort Steilacoom at the same time the Washington Territory was created. His wife followed a few weeks later. Fort Steilacoom was typical of the early frontier posts. It was a focal point in a sparsely settled area, Pierce County having then a population of 513 settlers, not counting women and children. The fort provided shelter, military protection, and key services: it had a church, a doctor, a jail, and the only buildings large enough for community gatherings.

Lieutenant Slaughter and his wife quickly got into the spirit of life at Fort Steilacoom and the local community. She ran the Officers' Mess. He surveyed and platted the Port Steilacoom township for Lafayette Balch, eventually owning 32 lots in the town. A Mason, Slaughter was one of the original group who successfully petitioned to form a lodge in Steilacoom. The lodge was founded in 1854, and Slaughter subsequently was elected Senior Warden. He was Worshipful Master of the Lodge at the time of his death in 1855.

In addition to mixing with locally prominent settlers, Lieutenant Slaughter accompanied Governor Stevens during negotiations with Indians. In March 1854, the Governor and a squad of soldiers under Lieutenant Slaughter sailed north to meet with Chiefs Sealth (Seattle) and Patkanim of the Duwamish and Snoqualmie bands, to settle an incident involving the deaths of two white men and an Indian. At the end of 1854, Lieutenant Slaughter was present at the historic Medicine Creek Council on the Nisqually Flats, seated at the main table with Governor Stevens as the treaty negotiations began — a rare honor for an officer just recently promoted to first lieutenant.

Governor Stevens, charged with the purchase of Indian lands and the creation of reservations, embarked on a whirlwind series of councils to sign treaties in the Washington Territory. While there were multiple causes for the Indian War that was soon to follow in 1855-1856, the dissatisfaction of both settlers and Indian tribes with the treaty provisions figured prominently in the rising pattern of conflict in the Territory. In shortly over two months, from late September to early December 1855, Lieutenant Slaughter took part in the opening action of the Indian War and in a series of sorties on the prairies east of Fort Steilacoom, the last of which ended in his death.

The precipitating incident for the Indian War was the death of Andrew Bolon, the Governor's agent for the tribes between the Cascades and the Bitterroot Mountains, who was killed east of the Cascades by members of the Yakima tribe. His death sparked widespread rumors and fears of an Indian uprising, despite the fact that many of the Indian tribes had peaceful relations with the settlers and never took part in any hostilities. Reports of Bolon's death triggered the Army to send a reconnaissance force to Yakima country. Brevet Major Granville O. Haller, with a force of about 100 soldiers and Indian scouts, left Fort Dalles on October 3, and three days later had a day-and-a-half skirmish at Toppenish Creek with a large band of Yakima warriors. He took up defensive positions on a hill, and withdrew

Lieutenant and Mrs. William A. Slaughter in 1852

[Washington State Historical Society]

at night, fighting sporadically the next day until his force outdistanced the pursuing Yakimas.

On September 24, Acting Governor Charles H. Mason had sent a letter to Captain Maurice Maloney, the Commander at Fort Steilacoom, requesting a detachment of troops be sent to punish the Yakima tribe. Lieutenant Slaughter and about 40 men left on September 27 to go through Naches Pass, intending to join Major Haller. Warned by one of his civilian scouts of Major Haller's defeat and the advance of Yakima warriors into Naches Pass, Lieutenant Slaughter halted his advance and withdrew to the vicinity of the White River.

The news of the abortive reconnaissance expedition raised a storm of civilian and military reaction. Acting Governor Mason declared war on the Indians and authorized the formation of two volunteer companies of Militia. When the word reached the Department of the Pacific, Brigadier General John E. Wool dispatched 70 men to Fort Vancouver and asked for a regiment from the east coast, a request that was granted. Meanwhile sporadic Indian attacks continued. In late October, in several raids and ambushes, Indians killed three families along the White River, two envoys attempting to reach Chief Leschi, and two members of a messenger party from Captain Maloney, who was in the field. Fearful of a general uprising, many settlers left their farms and fled to Fort Steilacoom.

Lieutenant Slaughter and Company C, Fourth Infantry, moved to the Puyallup River and Connell's Prairie to intercept Indian tribes and prevent their joining together. On November 3, after a patrol located a group of Nisqually Indians preparing an ambush along the Green River, Lieutenant Slaughter attacked the Indians, claiming 30 killed. He was unable to cross the river and cut them off; nevertheless, the action was one of the first successful ones in the campaign.

Toward the end of the month, on November 24, Lieutenant Slaughter began a reconnaissance in force from Camp Montgomery, a supply base near the Puyallup River, toward the White River. Not making contact by the end of the day, he made camp, with the uneasy premonition that the rainy weather would bring fog and increased chances of an Indian raid. He was correct. His position was fired on during the night, and — despite doubled sentries — about 40 horses were stolen.

The next day, Lieutenant Slaughter's command was augmented by a detachment of 25 men from Company M, Third Artillery, who had arrived as reinforcements from San Francisco. The next several days were spent in search of hostile Indians, but without success. On December 3, Lieutenant Slaughter was joined by Captain Gilmore Hays and a detachment of Washington Militia, with instructions to rendezvous at the junction of the White and Green Rivers with another small force of Volunteers led by Captain C. C. Hewitt. The next day, after a long march in the rain, the joint force set up camp. That evening, the position was fired upon by Indians, and Lieutenant Slaughter was killed by a musket shot as he was conducting a planning meeting with the other commanders. Two other men, Corporal Ganett L. Barry of the Regulars and Corporal Julian Clarendon of the Militia, were killed, and five were wounded. Mortally wounded, Private John Cullum of the Regulars died the next day.

The death of Lieutenant Slaughter was widely mourned. The Legislature passed a resolution of condolence and adjourned for the day as a mark of respect. Newspapers published laudatory articles. He was buried at Fort Steilacoom with full military and Masonic honors in a ceremony attended by Acting Governor Mason, Lafayette Balch, and other prominent citizens. As a final note of respect, when Mrs. Slaughter later returned to the east coast, she was accompanied by Acting Governor Mason.

In 1892, when the Army disbanded Fort Steilacoom, Lieutenant Slaughter's remains were reinterred in the military cemetery at the Presidio of San Francisco. However, the state of Washington did not forget him. When the area near the place of his death became a city, it was initially named Slaughter, before it came to be known by its present name, Auburn. The site was further honored in 1919 in a ceremony attended by hundreds when a permanent monument was erected in honor of Lieutenant Slaughter and Corporals Barry and Clarendon.

The Washington post at which Lieutenant Slaughter served likewise has not been forgotten. After the Army's departure, Fort Steilacoom eventually passed into the hands of the state as a mental hospital. Today, on the grounds of Western State Hospital, four buildings remain of the fort. Earlier, in a move to prevent their destruction, a citizens' group successfully had the buildings placed on the National Register of Historic Places.

More recently, as a project to celebrate the Washington State Centennial in 1989, the buildings were restored by a non-profit organization, Historic Fort Steilacoom. By being returned to public use, the buildings are, in a very real sense, a permanent remembrance of Lieutenant William Slaughter and the other soldiers who gave their lives to protect the Washington Territory.

Colonel Robert L. Bradley[1]
U.S. Army, Retired
USMA Class of 1949

---

[1]For some research material, the author gratefully acknowledges Joseph Koch of Auburn, Wash.

AUGUST V. KAUTZ:
SOLDIER, BUILDER, EXPLORER

A day or two after my arrival I went down to the mouth of the creek which gives its name (Steilacoom) to the post and the location, and had my first sight of the Sound. Two gentlemen from the post were with me, and I could not control my admiration at the beauty of the scene. The tide was flood and the limpid waters reproduced the fir-clad shores. The snow-clad Olympics were in full view, and the clear air enabled us to see far into the Narrows.

August V. Kautz

This 1853 diary entry makes it clear why August Kautz, then a brevet second lieutenant of infantry, formed such a lasting bond with Puget Sound and the Northwest.

August Valentine Kautz was born January 5, 1828, at Ispringen, Baden, Germany, the first of seven children of George and Doratha Lawing Kautz. That same year his parents immigrated to the United States and, after living three years in Baltimore, Maryland, settled in Brown County, Ohio.

George Kautz was a close friend of Jesse R. Grant, father of Ulysses S. Grant (USMA Class of 1843),[1] a future general and 18th President of the United States. Although not a classmate of Ulysses (who was six years his senior), August Kautz was strongly influenced by the same stern schoolmaster in the same two-room schoolhouse.

Influenced also by the lesson of the Alamo and the fervent patriotism of rural Ohio, August Kautz developed a strong, precocious patriotism that never slackened the rest of his life. On June 8, 1846, one month after war was declared on Mexico, he enlisted as a private in the First Ohio Volunteer Infantry. He fought in the Battle of Monterey and was mustered out at the end of his enlistment on June 14, 1847.

In June 1848, he entered the United States Military Academy as a member of the Class of 1852. At West Point he was one of many men who later rose to prominence during the Civil War. After graduating in June, 1852, he was assigned to Fort Columbus, Governors Island, New York, with a brevet commission as a second lieutenant in the Fourth Infantry — then stationed on the West Coast.

---

[1]As a brevet captain, Grant served in the Territory of Washington at Columbia Barracks (Fort Vancouver) as Quartermaster of the Fourth Infantry Regiment, arriving with the Regiment in September, 1852, and departed a year later for an assignment in California. Brevet Captain Grant and Second Lieutenant Kautz were both on duty at Columbia Barracks in 1853.

Charles B. Hall New York

**Major General of U.S. Volunteers
August Valentine Kautz
during the Civil War**

[Special Collections Division, United States Military Academy Library]

In December, 1853, after a grueling passage that included crossing the Nicaraguan Isthmus by barge and mule, Lieutenant Kautz arrived in San Francisco. There he received orders to report to the Fourth Infantry headquarters at Columbia Barracks (later Fort Vancouver) across the Columbia River from the future city of Portland.

In March, 1853, Congress formed the Territory of Washington out of the northern half of the Oregon Territory. Simultaneously, Lieutenant Kautz was ordered to join Company C, Fourth Infantry at the Puget Sound outpost, Fort Steilacoom. He would remain on duty in the Territory for the next eight years, except for a one-year sabbatical to Europe in 1859.

From his every diary entry it is clear that the Washington Territory was etching an indelible impression on him. There were, of course, the frustrations and rigors of frontier duty and the elements of danger and excitement of encounters with hostile Indians. The diary is replete with accounts of the tedium of isolated garrison living and the often oppressive weather. Yet, through all of the recounted travails, there appears a growing enchantment with the beauty and majesty of the forest, the Sound, and the mountains. His optimism is perhaps best shown by his early and frequent investment in parcels of land — a practice apparently uncommon among his fellow officers.

His very first mission, shortly after his arrival at Fort Steilacoom, was to lead a small detachment to investigate the sale of liquor to the Indians. These sales were a frequent source of trouble, and in this instance led to the disappearance and presumed death of several white settlers along the lower Sound. In May of 1853, with an open ship's launch, a sergeant, 10 men, a guide, and a month's supplies, Kautz set out to conduct an expedition to "intimidate the Indians." In his words, "When the strength of my command is considered in connection with the hordes of Indians then to be found along the shores of Puget Sound, the absurdity of this order becomes apparent." The expedition, which Kautz viewed as less than fully successful, lasted almost a month and resulted in several arrests and a reasonable amount of excitement. During this, his first independent mission as an officer, he got an extensive and accelerated introduction to Puget Sound, the local Indians, and their customs; and he made the acquaintance of many of the early settlers.

His first tour of duty at Fort Steilacoom was to be brief, for during the summer of 1853, trouble intensified between the white settlers and the Indians in the valley of the Rogue River in southern Oregon. The discovery of gold in 1851 and the continued prospecting had made the clash inevitable. Lieutenant Kautz was sent first to Fort Vancouver and then, with a small howitzer and six men of the Third Artillery, was ordered to Fort Orford in southern Oregon to protect the settlers and the miners. For over a year, peace was maintained. It wasn't until 1855 that he undertook his major campaign of the war in Oregon, during which he was to be wounded for the first time.

Meanwhile, in the Washington Territory, relationships among the settlers, the Army, the Indians, and the territorial officials deteriorated into open warfare. Indians had attacked and killed settlers in the White River Valley, had infested the village of Seattle, and had forced a general evacuation of all the settlers from the Puyallup Valley. During the latter campaign, Lieutenant William Slaughter, one of

Lieutenant Kautz's friends at Fort Steilacoom, was killed. Kautz was promoted to First Lieutenant and ordered back to Fort Steilacoom as Slaughter's replacement. For the next year and a half Kautz was involved in the war west of the Cascades, where he was again wounded and wrote much in his diary of the time he called "rough field service."

Following the active campaign, Lieutenant Kautz settled into this duties as Quartermaster and Commissary Officer at Fort Steilacoom. It was during this period that he undertook the climbing of Mount Rainier. On July 16, 1857, after a difficult and perilous climb and some unseasonably cold and stormy weather, Kautz left the last remaining members of his party to attempt by himself the final ascent. The severe cold and the violent winds forced him to abort the climb about 400 feet from the summit. The expedition, out of provisions and exhausted, was forced to return to Fort Steilacoom. Following his recovery from the climb, Lieutenant Kautz settled into the major task of reconstructing Fort Steilacoom. He completed a design, secured the lumber, fired the bricks, and supervised the construction of the new fort buildings, some of which still stand today. During this period he found time to do some local mapping and survey work and to become an integral member of the greater Steilacoom community.

In the autumn of 1858, he was assigned to Camp Semiahmoo as escort for the U.S.-Canada Border Commission. The winter of 1858-59 found the members of the commission visiting elsewhere, his commanding officer on leave, and Lieutenant Kautz left in command of the camp. In February he received word that his application for a leave of absence had been approved, and in April he departed for a short visit home to Ohio and a one-year tour of Europe. Following his stay in Europe, he expected to return to the Northwest via ship, crossing the isthmus as he had done the first time. However, he was ordered to report to Jefferson Barracks, Missouri, where he joined the Blake Expedition with instructions to lead 150 recruits across the country to Oregon. Following completion of his mission to deliver the recruits to the newly established Fort Colville, he would be free to join the troops at his new duty station, Camp Chehalis.

While Kautz was stationed at Camp Chehalis, the Southern states moved rapidly toward secession. As officers of Southern sentiments one by one resigned, and the Southern states began to secede, Kautz was ordered to report for duty in the East. He would not return for many years. First, he had to fight his share of the Civil War, attaining the rank of Major General of Volunteers; serve on the military court that tried the Lincoln assassination conspirators; command troops in the Midwest; and pursue Indians in the Southwest.

In 1891, almost 39 years after he commenced his career, Kautz returned to the Northwest. He was promoted to brigadier general and assigned to Vancouver Barracks as Commander of the Department of the Columbia. On January 5, 1892, pursuant to law, he was retired at his 64th birthday. Kautz settled permanently in Seattle, were he died on September 5, 1895.

Major General Thomas F. Cole
U.S. Army, Retired
USMA Class of 1952

SILAS CASEY:
COMPASSIONATE WARRIOR

Silas Casey, lieutenant colonel of the Fourth Infantry Regiment, came to the Puget Sound District of the Washington Territory already an experienced Indian-fighter and military commander. These attributes he brought to bear on putting an end to the Indian War west of the Cascades. At the same time, he was a compassionate leader who understood the plight of the native Americans, realizing that the Indian Wars of the 1850s stemmed from longstanding differences between dissimilar cultures. Through more than five years' service in the Puget Sound area, he was a moderating force in the many conflicts between the Indians and the land-hungry white settlers.

A graduate of West Point's Class of 1826, Casey drew frontier duty on his first assignment, and engaged hostile Indians for the first time in September 1828. Later he served against the Seminoles in Florida between 1837 and 1842, and the Coquille Indians in Oregon during the fall of 1851.

In 1855 the Indians on Puget Sound joined with other tribes throughout the Territory in what became, for the tribes west of the mountains, the last great attempt to resist the white man. Indian discontent was engendered by the uncompensated taking of their lands, for which payment had been promised in treaties made in good faith with the United States. Further, their lands were being taken by settlers, their hunting grounds destroyed, their ancient burial grounds desecrated.

War began in mid-September 1855, prompted by Indian killings of a number of miners in eastern Washington Territory and the slaying of the Indian agent who went to investigate the killings. Reinforcements from the Puget Sound District were called east of the Cascades, but returned to face mounting hostility from local Indians in the District. On October 31 messengers on their way to Fort Steilacoom were ambushed and killed. Fearing the hostile Indians, most of the settlers from the surrounding area fled to the fort for protection. In November the main body of troops from the fort skirmished north of the Puyallup Valley, and several running battles ensued.

Lieutenant Colonel Casey arrived by steamer with two companies of the Ninth U.S. Infantry, and took command of Fort Steilacoom and the Puget Sound District on January 17, 1856. In February, Casey joined elements of the Fourth Infantry and Third Artillery already in the field, marched a force into the White River Valley, and dealt a series of defeats to the Indians.

In March 1856, the decisive battle west of the Cascades was fought at Connell's Prairie. A force of 110 volunteers was attacked by 150 Indian warriors. After an all-day battle, the Indians were routed. The defeated Indians broke into small bands, never again to assemble into forces large enough to carry out any major operations. On May 19, Lieutenant Colonel Casey was able to report that the war west of the mountains was at an end.

Major General of U.S. Volunteers
Silas Casey
during the Civil War

[Special Collections Division, United States Military Academy Library]

Casey's Puget Sound service and the 1856 Indian campaign were complicated by the conflict between the Army and Territorial Governor Isaac I. Stevens over war strategy and policy toward the Indians. Stevens had graduated at the top of the 1839 class at West Point. He was independent and ambitious, and though he had resigned from the Army to accept the governorship, he continued to operate in a manner that suggested military command.

At the general outbreak of hostilities, Stevens immediately urged vigorous action, recommending a winter campaign to break the will of the hostile Indians and to destroy their provisions and livestock. Brevet Major General John E. Wool, Commander of the Department of the Pacific, a veteran of the Mexican War and War of 1812, with 44 years of service, planned to proceed slowly until the extent of the hostilities could be determined and necessary reinforcements moved to areas of hostilities. He ruled out a winter campaign, but assured the Governor that the Army would pursue the war with promptness and vigor when the situation was right.

General Wool insisted throughout the winter that future hostilities would be more the fault of the whites than the Indians. Ironically, from the beginning of the war, the Army represented the voice of compromise and moderation, while the Governor, as the leader of the white settlers, took the position that the war would be prosecuted until the last hostile Indian was eliminated.

Stevens countered Army inaction by calling out Volunteers, speaking of a spirit of cooperation with the Regulars, but also insisting that *he* would be issuing the orders and formulating campaign policy. Ignoring Wool, he began urging his policies on the Regular Army commanders, particularly on Lieutenant Colonel Casey.

Blocked in his desire for a winter campaign east of the Cascades, the Governor determined to seal off the mountain passes, therefore, isolating the Puget Sound Indians during the winter. Since the Volunteers could not seal all the passes, Stevens attempted to use Casey's command to supplement the Militia. Casey countered by requesting that two companies of Volunteers be placed with the Army, enabling the Army alone to protect the frontier. Stevens refused to give up control of the Volunteers, insisting that the Governor become the final authority in an emergency, thereby ignoring tradition.

A second area of dispute for Casey and Stevens was policy towards the friendly Indians. Casey assumed that the Army would deal with the hostile Indians and conceded that since the Governor was also Superintendent of Indian Affairs, Stevens was responsible for the friendlies. But as to the hostiles, Casey informed the Governor that he was sending troops to check on the status of Indians at the Black River and would consider it inappropriate for Stevens to order Volunteers to take action against these Indians. Stevens's heated response was that all Indians had been ordered out of the area and that any who remained were subject to punishment.

Animosity between Stevens and the Army did not end with the termination of the war. A prime bone of contention involved Indian leaders who had been captured or who had surrendered. Stevens had insisted from the beginning that the instigators of the war would suffer.

Stevens had assumed that he and Colonel Wright, Commander, Ninth Infantry, were agreed to accept only unconditional surrender and to bring alleged murderers to trial. But after forging a truce east of the Cascades, Wright felt it would be unwise, if they wished for peace, to punish any Indians for acts committed during the war. The Governor insisted on trials even if they caused renewed Indian unrest. Casey, supporting Wright's position, met Stevens's order to turn certain Indians over to him, but suggested that the better way would be to consider that they had been at war with the Indians but now were at peace.

Among the Indian leaders that Stevens especially wanted punished was Leschi, who, while not a chief, was one of the leaders in the Nisqually and was influential and universally liked. He had always maintained friendly relations with the whites and was well known to Silas Casey.

Leschi was accused of being involved in the murder of A. Benton Moses near Connell's Prairie in October 1855. While a fugitive, Leschi offered to surrender to Casey, but Casey suggested that he hide until favorable negotiations could be made. Soon thereafter, however, Leschi's nephew betrayed him to territorial authorities.

Captured on November 13, 1856, Leschi went on trial November 16, but because of legal maneuvering to try to free him, he was not sentenced until December 1857. Through further legal and non-legal actions the date of execution was delayed until February 19, 1858.

Most of the actions to free Leschi were carried out by Casey's officers, especially Lieutenant August V. Kautz, and had Casey's wholehearted approval. At this time, Leschi was confined at Fort Steilacoom, which facilitated maneuvers to delay final action on Leschi. Casey, as Commander of Fort Steilacoom, played the principal role in these instances.

Casey exhausted all options in his efforts to save Leschi. When asked by Leschi defenders simply to retain the prisoner and prevent the execution, Casey had to face up to his duty. He knew he had no right to retain the prisoner because he was merely holding Leschi at the request of the court. To the surprise of many in the Steilacoom area, Casey released Leschi to the sheriff in charge of the hanging party, but refused permission for the hanging to take place on military property.

Lieutenant Colonel Silas Casey lived the Regular Army's policy of compromise and moderation in dealing with the Indians and the settlers. By resisting the Territorial Governor's urging to deal in a heavy-handed manner with the Indians, he persuaded most natives west of the Cascades to refrain from open warfare.

He was often severely criticized by the white settlers, even to the point of being hanged in effigy during the delay in Leschi's conviction. But with war's end west of the mountains, the settlers soon realized that they could safely return to their land. Casey always responded quickly with troops to the few minor Indian attacks that occurred. The Puget Sound area had been made free for settlers to live in relative harmony with the Indians.

Brigadier General Vasco J. Fenili
U.S. Army, Retired
USMA Class of January, 1943

GEORGE WRIGHT:
PEACEMAKER IN EASTERN WASHINGTON'S
CLASH OF CULTURES

George Wright was born in Norwich, Vermont, in 1803. His uncle John Wright, Jr. had graduated from West Point in 1814, and young George was also drawn to a military career. When he was barely 15 years old, he sought an appointment to the Academy, and was admitted as a cadet in September, 1817 — the year that Brevet Major Sylvanus Thayer became the Superintendent of the United Sates Military Academy and began the sweeping changes into a technically-oriented curriculum that earned him the soubriquet "The Father of the Military Academy."

Cadet Wright was graduated in 1822, the Academy's 309th graduate, and was posted as a second lieutenant to the Third Infantry Regiment, stationed at Fort Howard, Wisconsin. In 1826 the Third Infantry was transferred down the Mississippi to Jefferson Barracks, near St. Louis. Though still a second lieutenant, Wright was selected to serve occasionally as Regimental Adjutant. He was promoted to first lieutenant in September, 1827.

About the time of his promotion, George Wright and Margaret Wallace Foster were married. She was the youngest of 11 children of a prominent, elite Pennsylvania family. Five of the six daughters who reached maturity married military men. The Wrights had three children: two sons and a daughter.

The Pawnee Indians, some 150 miles to the north of Jefferson Barracks, had become troublesome, threatening the white settlers. It was decided to send a small force to visit the Pawnee villages to ascertain their degree of hostility and their intentions. First Lieutenant Wright's reputation as an intelligent, dependable young officer led to his selection for this risky operation. He visited all five Pawnee villages, and made the 500-mile circuit without incident. His report covered the Indian grievances, as well as his own assessment of the situation.

In 1831, Brevet Brigadier General Henry Leavenworth appointed Lieutenant Wright to the position of Regimental Adjutant, a duty he held for five years. When the post commander was absent, Wright acted in that capacity. During this time, mounting tensions along the Mexican border caused the Regiment to be moved into Louisiana, on the Sabine River, bordering Texas.

In 1836, after 14 years of service, Wright was promoted to captain, and placed on recruiting duty. About this time a Canadian insurrectionist group calling themselves "The Patriots" planned a revolution, with the aim of establishing a Republic of Canada. Captain Wright, who was recruiting in northern New York State, became aware of the movements of both the Patriots and the Canadian armed forces, which he dutifully reported to the Army's Adjutant General. The Patriots' base of operation was on an island in the Niagara River, and a U.S. flagged steamer was used to transport their arms. In pursuing the rebels, Canadian forces trespassed on U.S. territory, a matter that caused the U.S. forces considerable concern.

George Wright

[Special Collections Division, United States Military Academy Library]

Finally, the Patriots landed an armed force on Canadian soil, were defeated, and dispersed. However these events caused Congress to authorize another regiment, the Eighth Infantry, to thwart any further border crossings. Colonel William J. Worth, who had been Commandant of Cadets while Wright was a cadet, was placed in command, and Captain Wright was assigned to the regiment. The regiment was moved from Troy, New York to the newly-created post of Madison Barracks on Lake Ontario. Captain Wright was placed in command of Company F. In April, 1840 the Regiment was sent to operate against the Winnebago Indians in Wisconsin, after which the Regiment was moved south to Jefferson Barracks, Missouri.

The Seminole Indians in Florida had been attacking, killing, and robbing white settlers even before Florida was ceded to the United States. The Army tried, without success, to curtail their depredations. All Army units were committed at one time or another in a series of small, bloody battles, involving both Regulars and Volunteer units, over a period of seven years. By 1840, the War Department directed Colonel Worth to take command of all armed forces operating in Florida, including some naval units, to end the war. Colonel Worth discharged the Volunteers, and organized the 5,000 Regulars into small guerrilla-type bands, which operated continuously throughout the affected areas.

Captain Wright, who had been absent on sick leave, returned to participate in a number of scouting expeditions. On one of these, he led a force of six officers and 102 enlisted men in canoes for 24 days without losing a single man due to sickness or action. Despite persistent efforts, the results were disappointingly small. Finally, after two years of continuous operations, Colonel Worth believed that only a few Indians survived, and declared that the Indians left were insignificant, and that the war was over. A grateful President John Tyler gave Colonel Worth a brevet to brigadier general. Worth in turn ordered Captain Wright brevetted to major for "meritorious conduct, zeal, energy, and perseverance."

In 1845, when Texas was admitted to the Union, Mexico declared war on the United States. Captain Wright, who had been placed on recruiting duty, hastened to rejoin his regiment, which, by the time he caught up with it, had landed at Vera Cruz, Mexico. The first major engagement came when Brevet Brigadier General Worth's division was ordered to take Churubusco. The initial assault was repulsed by enemy fire. Captain Wright led the Eighth Infantry by way of corn fields and irrigation ditches to take the critical position with a bayonet charge. In the final assault, Wright, the second-in-command, kept the charge going by rallying the troops to where they were most needed. For his aggressive action, Wright received a brevet to lieutenant colonel for this action. But victory did not come cheaply: Of the 2,600 Americans who fought the 7,000 Mexicans for two and a half hours in hand-to-hand combat, over half became casualties, with 133 killed; the Mexicans lost a full third of their army.

The next day, the Commander-in-Chief, Major General Scott, ordered General Worth to take Molino del Rey, thinking that it was lightly defended. But the Mexicans considered it the gateway to their capital, and had it heavily defended. General Worth directed Captain Wright to lead the assault with 500 picked officers and men, and to capture the center, where the artillery was. The attack succeeded, but at heavy cost. The Mexican artillery fired both grape and shot over level ground, while their infantry poured musket rounds from the flanks. Once the Mexican infantry realized that the Americans who had driven them out at bayonet point were a smaller force than theirs, they returned and made a desperate rally firing from housetops. It was then that Wright was struck down, along with two other officers, sustaining a shoulder wound. Twenty-seven men were killed. It took the action of another brigade to finally force the Mexicans back. Lieutenant Issac I. Stevens (USMA Class of 1839), later the first Governor of Washington Territory, helped the wounded Wright off the field of battle. For his bravery, Wright was brevetted to Colonel.

After 26 years of service, Captain Wright was promoted to Major of the Fourth Infantry Regiment. At the time he was on sick leave recovering from his shoulder wound, but by October, 1848, he had joined the regiment for duty as the Post Commander at Fort Ontario in New York State. The regiment was stationed at border posts around the Great Lakes until 1852, when it was assembled at Governors Island in New York Harbor for deployment to the West Coast, by way of Panama. The Regimental Lieutenant Colonel, B. L. E. Bonneville (USMA Class of 1815) was in command while the Regimental Colonel went on sick leave instead of deploying to the West Coast. Although some dependents accompanied the Regiment, Major Wright's family remained in New York. Crossing the Isthmus of Panama was very difficult: The new railway was not completed, so part of the journey had to be made by flatboat and mule-back. Cholera broke out, causing over a hundred deaths among soldiers and dependents.

At the Pacific Division Headquarters in Benicia, California, Major Wright, as the senior regimental major, was assigned to command the Northern California District, serving in his brevet lieutenant colonel rank, with Companies B, D, and F assigned. Lieutenant Colonel Bonneville and the remainder of the Fourth Infantry continued on to Columbia Barracks (Fort Vancouver). Company E was later sent to Brevet Lieutenant Colonel Wright from Columbia Barracks. The Northern California District was at Fort Reading, which had been constructed by Company E, Second Infantry. Elements of the First Dragoons and Third Artillery were also assigned to Fort Reading. Subordinate posts included Fort Humboldt and Fort Jones.

The two and a half years he spent in California were probably the most frustrating in Wright's career. Like the Seminoles in Florida, hostile Indians operated in small bands, with complete familiarity with the terrain, stealing from, and sometimes murdering, white settlers; settlers in turn took their wrath out on peaceful Indians. Brevet Lieutenant Colonel Wright was criticized in the press for defending any Indians, regardless of the circumstances.

In 1855, after 33 years of service, Brevet Lieutenant Colonel Wright was promoted to Lieutenant Colonel in the Fourth Infantry. His promotion to full Colonel came exactly one month later, to fill the colonelcy in the newly-reactivated Ninth Infantry, one of four regiments authorized by Congress to meet the needs of the expanding country. The Ninth Infantry was destined to be stationed in the Pacific Northwest.

Colonel Wright left Fort Reading on May 9, 1855 and took command of his new regiment on July 3 at Fort Monroe, Virginia. The companies were recruited on the East Coast and assembled at Fort Monroe for training. The Regiment embarked with accompanying dependents on the steamship _St. Louis_ on December 15. With the isthmus railway completed, the Ninth crossed the isthmus in a four-hour train ride, without exposure to tropical sickness. The Regiment left Panama in two ships, arriving at Fort Vancouver on January 21 and 22.

The settlers of the Pacific Northwest were in conflict with the Indians, who opposed white intrusion onto tribal lands. The most open opposition came from the Yakima Tribes. The year before, two companies of Colonel Wright's previous regiment, the Fourth Infantry, under a seasoned Brevet Major Granville O. Haller, had been badly mauled in Yakima country, with five dead and 17 wounded. Afterward, a punitive force under command of Major Gabriel Rains (USMA Class of 1827), consisting of 750 soldiers from the Fourth Infantry, Third Artillery, First Dragoons, and Oregon Territorial Volunteers, failed to engage the Yakimas, who chose not to give battle. A lack of aggressive leadership was alleged afterwards in charges and counter-charges, all dismissed by the Pacific Department Commander. In any case, the Yakimas remained defiant, and their defiance spread to the Puget Sound and to the Walla Walla Valley, and would soon engulf the entire Columbia River Plateau.

In addition to the military challenge, Colonel Wright found himself in a political battle as well. Congress had created the Washington Territory in March, 1853. Its first Governor was the same Isaac I. Stevens who had assisted Colonel Wright off the Mexican War battlefield. Governor Stevens was also the territory's Superintendent of Indian Affairs, and had led the survey for the northern railroad route from Saint Paul, Minnesota to Puget Sound. As both Governor and Superintendent of Indian Affairs, Isaac Stevens made treaties with the Indians as far east as Montana, with the objective of confining the tribes to reservations. This would free former tribal lands for white settlement and for the northern railway route. The Indian uprisings were a direct result of the treaties, which the Indians felt were forced upon them.

Opposing this unfair treatment of the Indians was Colonel Wright's immediate superior, Brevet Major General John E. Wool, Commander of the Department of the Pacific. The defeat of Brevet Major Haller by the Yakimas had brought the general from his Benicia, California headquarters to Fort Vancouver on November 15. A righteous aristocrat, he believed in his decisions and could not tolerate others with dissenting views. General Wool in public severely chastised the Territorial Governors for their treaties, and their Territorial Militias for their inhumane treatment of the Indians. This placed Colonel Wright in an awkward position with the Territorial Governments.

General Wool departed Fort Vancouver three days before Colonel Wright arrived. In addition to leaving antagonism for Colonel Wright to face, the General left instructions for Colonel Wright to command the Columbia River District, which generally stretched from the Pacific Coast to the Continental Divide, except for the Puget Sound area. His command included — besides most of his Ninth Infantry — companies of the Fourth Infantry, the Third Artillery, and the First

Dragoons stationed at Fort Vancouver and Fort Dalles, the only posts located in the district. Lieutenant Colonel Silas Casey (USMA Class of 1826), the regimental second-in-command, was ordered to continue on to Fort Steilacoom with two companies of the Ninth Infantry to command the Puget Sound District. At that time the Fourth Infantry and Third Artillery companies stationed at Fort Steilacoom were in the field operating against the Indian bands rebelling against Governor Stevens's treaties. At Fort Vancouver, Colonel Wright was to prepare for operations while awaiting further instructions from General Wool.

Most Regimental Colonels in the early 1800s were on detached service from their regiments, serving in brevet ranks at higher headquarters or commanding posts far removed from their unit of assignment. Field command was left to the regimental lieutenant colonel. Colonel Wright did not follow this mold. He stayed with his regiment, commanding forces in the field while fulfilling area and post command assignments at the same time.

General Wool arrived in early March to lay out his operations plan. Two companies under the regimental junior major, Robert S. Garnett (USMA Class of 1841), were sent to reinforce the Puget Sound District, while one Fourth Infantry company was reassigned to the Northern California District. Colonel Wright retained six of his Ninth Regiment's companies and two Fourth Infantry companies, plus a company from the Dragoons and the Third Artillery, for operations in the Columbia River District. General Wool directed Colonel Wright to establish two new military posts: one in the Walla Walla area, the other in Yakima country.

On March 8, Colonel Wright began moving troops and supplies up the Columbia River by steamer to Fort Dalles, which was to be his new headquarters and supply base. General Wool wanted Colonel Wright to move elements of his force both to the Walla Walla Valley and into Yakima country, so that a simultaneous operation in each hostile area could protect supply lines to the other. Colonel Wright chose not to divide his force, and planned to establish the post in the Walla Walla Valley before moving against the Yakimas. This decision caused General Wool to accuse the Colonel of being influenced by Governor Stevens.

The move from Fort Dalles to the Walla Walla Valley began on March 26, with the first night's camp about five miles from Fort Dalles. Before midnight a messenger arrived from the Fort Dalles post commander, Brevet Major Haller, informing Colonel Wright that Yakima, Klickitat, and Cascade Indians had attacked the civilian settlements at Fort Cascades — where operational commitments had reduced the garrison to nine soldiers, with a cannon at the "Middle Blockhouse." The two river steamers operating on the Columbia above the cascades, *Mary* and *Wasco*, had escaped when the attack started at the upper landing, and lay at Fort Dalles awaiting instructions.

At daybreak the next morning, Colonel Wright marched his command back to The Dalles and embarked 250 soldiers on the two steamers. A howitzer was mounted on each steamer. The Dragoon horses were loaded on barges to be towed by the boats. With this load the 60 mile journey down the river was tedious. The *Mary* had mechanical difficulties, and the river currents caused a continually dangerous situation for the heavily-laden boats. Colonel Wright stopped the

**A blockhouse at Fort Cascades
of the type besieged in the
"Cascades Massacre"**

[Pemco Webster & Stevens Collection, Washington State Museum of History & Industry]

movement at night, requiring the steamers to tie up at shore.

Fort Cascades consisted of three separated sites (upper, middle, and lower), located along 12 miles of turbulent water, where fortifications had been erected on the north or Washington side of the river to protect the portage trans-shipment sites. Civilian communities had sprung up adjacent to the military facilities. All Colonel Wright knew of the situation at Fort Cascades was the steamer crews' report of an attack by numerous Indians on the civilian settlement at the upper landing site. He assumed that the other sites had been attacked as well.

Slamming ashore at the upper landing, Colonel Wright's soldiers charged the Indians, who were besieging settlers defending from a large log store building. Then a task force under Brevet Lieutenant Colonel Edward J. Steptoe (USMA Class of 1837) consisting of two infantry companies, dragoons, and artillery, continued down the portage road on the Washington side of the river to relieve the siege of the soldiers and civilians at the "Middle Blockhouse."

From Fort Vancouver, Second Lieutenant Philip E. Sheridan (USMA Class of 1853, and a future Commanding General of the Army), commanding a force of 40 dragoons, had cleared the lower landing site of hostile Indians. One dragoon was killed. This task force then crossed to the Oregon side to escape detection, moved up to a point opposite the "Middle Blockhouse," and recrossed the river in preparation to relieve the blockhouse. With the two Army forces approaching, the Yakima and Klickitat warriors melted away into the forested terrain, leaving behind the Cascade Indians who disappeared into their hiding place.

Fourteen civilians and three soldiers were killed, and 12 civilians were wounded in this unprovoked attack on Fort Cascades. Colonel Wright's force lost two men. Three Indians were known to have been killed by the relief force. (Indians customarily carried off their dead and wounded, preventing an accurate account of their casualties.)

During his maneuver from the lower to the middle landing, Lieutenant Sheridan had discovered the hiding place of the Cascade Indians who had participated in the attack. He took a force there to apprehend participants, who were identified by determining which rifles had been fired. Thirteen were arrested for participating in the attack. After the trial, Colonel Wright approved the sentences for nine to be hanged and the others to be jailed at Fort Vancouver.

After the "Cascades Massacre," General Wool directed Colonel Wright to postpone establishing the Walla Walla post, and to move against the Yakimas. His mission was to demonstrate the Army's capability and to force the Indians to sue for peace. Colonel Wright began the move north from Fort Dalles at the end of April, with two companies of the Ninth, one of the Fourth, one of dragoons, and one of artillery, following the same route that Haller had taken the previous fall when he was defeated by the Yakimas. They were not opposed, and the force moved beyond the previous battleground to the Naches River, where they established Fort Naches as an operational base. The river was too high from spring rains to be crossed, so the command had to wait until the river lowered sufficiently.

In late May there was an indication that the Yakimas were preparing to give battle, so Colonel Wright brought from Fort Dalles Brevet Lieutenant Colonel

Steptoe, the regiment's senior major, with his command of three Ninth Infantry and one Fourth Infantry companies. In addition, Major Garnett and two Ninth Infantry companies were released from the Puget Sound District and moved to Fort Naches as further reinforcement.

While this Army force was assembling, Chief Owhi and Chief Teias came to Fort Naches to talk, but the principal agitator, Chief Kamiakin, remained on the far side of the river. He had been the chief instigator of resistance and refused to talk peace. Chiefs Owhi and Teias professed that they would fight no more and were all of one mind for peace. They told Colonel Wright that the treaties Governor Stevens had forced upon them were the cause of the conflict. Colonel Wright was conciliatory, but made it clear that they must lay down their arms and become peaceful. The chiefs promised to return in five days with all stolen goods and to comply with Colonel Wright's demands. Instead, they vanished. It was reported that Chief Kamiakin and his followers had gone east to the area of the Spokane tribe.

Colonel Wright realized that he had to drive a wedge between the belligerent Kamiakin and the chiefs who wanted peace. The Yakima victories of last year must be erased. Leaving Brevet Lieutenant Colonel Steptoe and three companies at Fort Naches to protect the operational base, Colonel Wright set out on June 17 with a force of about 450 men in six infantry companies and one each of dragoons and artillery to make a show of force penetrating into the Yakima heartland.

The command moved up the Yakima River towards Snoqualmie Pass and then generally east across the mountains into the Wenatchee Valley. Father Marie Charles Pandosy, who had spent many years with the Yakimas, brought some of the Indian chiefs in for conference with Colonel Wright, who learned that the Indians were busy fishing the early summer run and wanted to collect an adequate supply of salmon before leaving this productive fishing area. After the salmon supply was assured, they would follow Colonel Wright's wishes. To insure that they would do so, Colonel Wright took into custody Chief Teias and his family as hostages. Teias was the brother of Owhi and the father-in-law of Kamiakin.

On July 9, Colonel Wright's command broke camp and went down the Wenatchee River to the Columbia, then on across the Kittitas Valley to Fort Naches. Father Pandosy had persuaded the Indians of the virtues of peace and the wisdom of trusting Colonel Wright. Under the priest's influence, about 500 Indian men, women, and children, along with their livestock, accompanied the Army column. Some stolen horses and mules were returned to the Army. Colonel Wright gave credit in his dispatches to Father Pandosy for persuading these Indians to comply with his demands.

The command reached Fort Naches on July 21 and rested two days. They had traveled over 300 miles through rugged country not visited before by white man, where the Indian had felt hidden from the power of the Army. (The route taken by Colonel Wright is depicted on the map entitled "Colonel Wright's 1856 Operations in Yakima Country," page 148.) To consolidate this gain, Colonel Wright left a force to operate in the Kittitas Valley through the summer, and directed Major

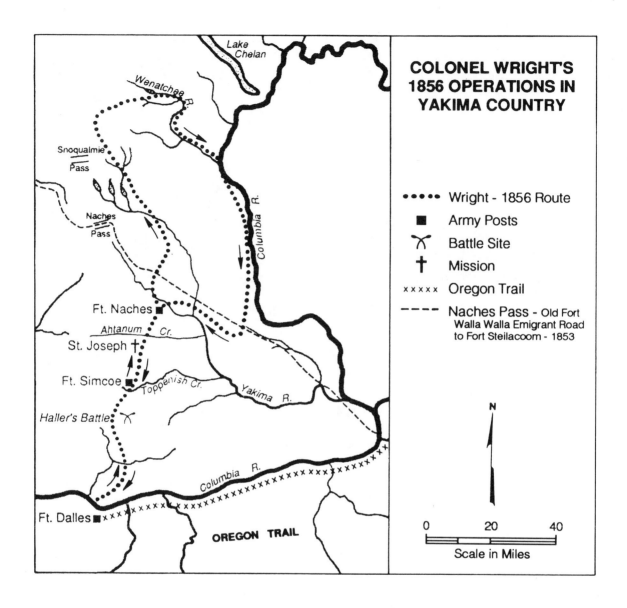

COLONEL WRIGHT'S 1856 OPERATIONS IN YAKIMA COUNTRY

Garnett to establish Fort Simcoe as one of the two posts ordered by General Wool. Fort Simcoe would garrison four companies in the Yakima tribal area, and would be available for rapid response to disturbances. Colonel Wright abandoned Fort Naches as no longer needed. With Chief Kamiakin and his followers gone from the area, Colonel Wright had effectively ended conflicts in Yakima country.

With the Yakima campaign coming to a close, Colonel Wright sent Brevet Lieutenant Colonel Steptoe and four companies to the Walla Walla Valley to select a site for and construct the second post ordered by General Wool. About this time Governor Stevens decided to hold another council with the Indians in the Walla Walla area. General Wool refused to honor the Governor's request for an escort to protect his pack train. However, Colonel Wright traveled with the Governor from Fort Vancouver as far as Fort Dalles, and told the Governor that Brevet Lieutenant Colonel Steptoe would provide him protection at Walla Walla. This caused the Governor to release all but one of his Territorial Volunteer Militia companies and to cancel the call for additional volunteers.

Governor Stevens held council for six days, but the Indians were seething at the slaughter of women, children, and old men by Washington Territorial Volunteers at a village in the Grande Rhonde Valley. Few of the major chiefs attended, making the session unsuccessful. The Stevens party set out for The Dalles, but was attacked by Indians from many tribes. Brevet Lieutenant Colonel Steptoe had to rescue them and escort the Governor and his party to The Dalles.

Colonel Wright had two concerns at Walla Walla: getting the barracks constructed before winter set in, and controlling the Indians' unrest. Intending to resolve the differences with the Indians, Colonel Wright left Fort Dalles with Company A and Brevet Lieutenant Colonel Steptoe's command on October 5 for a 12-day march to the Walla Walla Valley. He summoned tribal chiefs for a new conference, but only a few local chiefs responded. He assured those in attendance that he understood their grievance against the Governor and that the settlers would be kept out of their land until after the treaties were ratified by Congress. He had the area commander, Brevet Lieutenant Colonel Steptoe, issue a proclamation barring the country east of the Cascades to all whites except missionaries, Hudson's Bay employees, and Colville miners. Colonel Wright, escorted by Company A, returned to Fort Dalles on November 12.

For Colonel Wright, 1856 had been a successful year. It ended with an unusually cold winter. Both Fort Simcoe and Fort Walla Walla were under construction and had progressed sufficiently to give the soldiers and their dependents protection from the elements. The Yakima tribe had been subdued, and a major building program was underway at Fort Dalles.

The spring of 1857 brought a new commanding general to the Department of the Pacific: Brevet Brigadier General Newman S. Clarke replaced General Wool. General Clarke initially continued the policies of his predecessor, but exercised diplomacy in the political arena. The Army's exclusion policy of preventing settlers from moving into the interior remained under attack by the Washington Territorial Legislature.

General Clarke came to Colonel Wright's headquarters in June, 1857. Although he said nothing at the time, he later criticized Fort Dalles as too extravagant (although less had been spent there than at either Fort Vancouver or the Presidio of San Francisco). The General issued an order that all future non-permanent posts would be of the simplest construction required to protect the troops from undue exposure. He also ordered an end to construction at Fort Dalles, which prevented building an adequate hospital and a water system for fire control. The General's criticisms included the size and design of Colonel Wright's quarters — although the house did double duty as headquarters offices, and was shared with his adjutant and son-in-law, Lieutenant Philip A. Owen, and his wife.

At Fort Simcoe all was quiet, with Chief Kamiakin's brother Skloom returning livestock stolen by some young warriors during the harsh winter. In the Walla Walla area, the Nez Perce, Walla Wallas, and other locals remained friendly. To the north, other tribes were considered friendly or at least neutral, but the Palouse there were menacing, and raided the Walla Walla Valley, stealing livestock — including 13 government head.

Early in January, 1858 Brevet Lieutenant Colonel Steptoe was alerted at Fort Walla Walla to prepare for operations in the spring, upon the return of the dragoon horses, which had been taken to Fort Vancouver where there was adequate fodder. Original instructions were to go east into the Shoshoni Indian area along the Oregon Trail. When rumors that two miners had been killed in the Colville area were followed by a petition for Army protection, signed by 40 Colville citizens, Steptoe decided to make a reconnaissance in force north to the Spokane River and Colville area. The force would consist of Troops C, E, and H of the First Dragoons and part of Company E, Ninth Infantry, manning two howitzers. He reported this to Colonel Wright and the Pacific Division Headquarters.

The force of five officers and 152 men departed Fort Walla Walla on May 6, not anticipating that they would meet any sizable force of hostiles. On the tenth day out, they suddenly encountered an overwhelming force of Indians that blocked any further advance. Steptoe wanted to avoid combat and started to withdraw. This the Indians took as a sign of weakness. The Indians harassed the soldiers, resulting in combat between the moving Army column and the warriors. While protecting the flanks, Brevet Captain Oliver Taylor (USMA Class of 1846) was mortally wounded and Second Lieutenant William Gaston (USMA Class of 1856) was killed. Three soldiers, a civilian, and two Nez Perce scouts were also killed. After dark, while the Indians withdrew to sleep, the force conducted an orderly night withdrawal, guided by the Nez Perce Chief, Timothy. After 70 miles they reached the Snake River and safety.

Colonel Wright learned of the route of the reconnaissance force on May 22 and forwarded Steptoe's report to General Clarke at Benicia, California, on the 23rd. He believed that the hostilities had been caused by the plan to build the Mullan Road from Fort Walla Walla to Fort Benton through the Spokane and Coeur d'Alene areas. This project was immediately delayed.

Evidently the relative calm in the Walla Walla area caused the Colonel to lose sight of the Indian opposition to Governor Stevens's treaties and the entry of white settlers into their areas. Now his main concern was assembling and supporting a force to strike back as soon as possible and defeat the Indians before there was general war in the Pacific Northwest.

Word of Steptoe's defeat reached the Army's headquarters in New York and the Government in Washington, D.C. in July. Although Colonel Wright was not singled out, ex-Governor Stevens — now the Territorial Delegate in Congress — used the defeat as proof of the failure of the Army policy towards the Indians, pointing out that the senior officers involved over the past years had lost whatever reputation they ever had. For the Commander-in-Chief of the Army, Major General Winfield Scott, this was the second defeat of his Regulars in less than three years; positive action was needed to restore their reputation. In the years to come General Scott would prevent Colonel Wright from progressing in rank; historians have pondered the reasons. In 1855 the General had promoted Wright to the colonelcy of the Ninth Infantry, but after this latest incident, he blocked opportunities for promotion even when they became readily available with the Army's expansion for the Civil War.

General Clarke arrived at Fort Vancouver to take personal charge of the plans, and summoned Colonel Wright and his two subordinates, Brevet Lieutenant Colonel Steptoe and Major Garnett, for conference. He sent to Father Joseph Joset — the Jesuit missionary to the Coeur d'Alenes — conditions that had to be met by the Indians. The missionary sent back the tribal reply: No white settlers could stay in their country; they would not permit a road to be built through it; they would not permit troops to pass through to Colville; and they had joined the Spokanes and Chief Kamiakin's followers to resist white encroachment. Elated by their defeat of the Army troops under Brevet Lieutenant Colonel Steptoe, the Indian leaders declined to meet with General Clarke or his representatives.

The campaign plan was completed by July 4, placing Colonel Wright in command of a force of over 600 to move north from Fort Walla Walla against the Indians in early August. Colonel Wright was to have four companies of the First Dragoons, six companies of the Third Artillery, and two companies of his Ninth Infantry. Steptoe was to remain behind with a garrison to protect Fort Walla Walla. From Fort Simcoe, Major Garnett was to conduct a secondary thrust with four companies from the Fourth and Ninth Infantries, leaving a fifth company behind to protect the fort and rear area.

Colonel Wright moved his headquarters to Fort Walla Walla and began the detailed plans in preparation for the operation. First, the colonel made a treaty with the Nez Perce to insure their support. In the treaty Colonel Wright specified that when the Nez Perce helped the United States, the government would provide arms, ammunition, and other supplies and would pay for anything provided by the Nez Perce. For any misunderstandings the treaty specified that a council of chiefs would consider the circumstances. For the coming operation, the Nez Perce would provide a mounted force of 30 scouts to be outfitted in U.S. Army uniforms for easy identification. Colonel Wright's treaty with the Nez Perce served to protect the rear area during the coming operations.

This was to be the largest operation ever conducted in the Pacific Northwest: 30,000 rations for 38 days of operations had to be assembled, ammunition brought in, and fodder obtained for the 600 animals of the dragoons and the pack train. In addition, 100 civilian packers and herders had to be found, along with a sizable herd of cattle for rations. Artillery companies were sent from California to be riflemen. The soldiers had to be trained to use the new longer-ranged rifles then being issued, while the dragoons were issued a new breech-loading carbine.

Colonel Wright was thorough and demanding, earning the respect and admiration of the officers, noncommissioned officers, and soldiers. He carefully planned every aspect of the expedition, and the preparations, both in training and in logistical support, were meticulously worked out. All units were vigorously drilled and trained to use their weapons effectively.

As the supporting campaign to Colonel Wright's main effort, Major Garnett moved out from Fort Simcoe toward the juncture of the Okanogan and Columbia Rivers on August 10. There were nine officers and 306 men in four infantry companies outfitted for a 50-day campaign. He was supported by 50 civilian packers and herders handling a pack train and a herd of about 225 animals. Part of the Fort Simcoe mission was to cause the Indians to move into the path of the main effort.

Colonel Wright's first elements left Fort Walla Walla on August 7, and moved north to the mouth of the Tucannon on the Snake River, where they constructed Fort Taylor, named for the Brevet Captain Taylor killed in the Steptoe expedition. The expedition crossed the Snake on August 25 and 26. It consisted of 570 Regulars and 30 Nez Perce scouts. The units involved were Companies C, E, H and I of the First Dragoons; Companies B and E of the Ninth Infantry; and companies A, B, C, K, and M of the Third Artillery with two howitzers. Brevet Major Francis O. Wyse (USMA Class of 1837) and his Company D, Third Artillery, remained at Fort Taylor to secure the crossing site, boats and supplies. (Routes taken by Brevet Lieutenant Colonel Steptoe, Major Garnett, and Colonel Wright are depicted on the map entitled "Operations in 1858," page 153.)

Colonel Wright was a strict disciplinarian. Each day's regimen was scheduled to ensure that the command operated with smooth military precision. At reveille and retreat all arms and ammunition were inspected. Men slept with their ammunition belts on and arms stacked in their immediate area. One company guarded the bivouac at night while reduced noise and light discipline were strictly enforced.

Colonel Wright had received word that a large number of Indians were gathering in the vicinity of Spokane Falls, so he took the trail that led directly to that area. On August 30, Indians were observed on the hills ahead, but they withdrew when the dragoons advanced towards them. They appeared again the next day, apparently trying to decoy the troops towards the ground the Indians had chosen for battle. Just before camp was made on the 31st, the Indians initiated contact by attacking the supply train commanded by the Quartermaster, Captain Ralph W. Kirkham (USMA Class of 1842), but were driven off by three companies of riflemen.

The Battle of Four Lakes began the next day. At daylight the Indians were observed on a high hill about two miles northeast of the Army camp. Colonel Wright took about two hours to observe and plan. Just after nine, he deployed two dragoon companies as skirmishers up the north side of the hill to fix the Indians' position. Led by the Nez Perce scouts, Colonel Wright took six companies to the east and up where the ascent was easier, driving the Indians down to the foot. The Indians gathered below in a pine woods and on the plain.

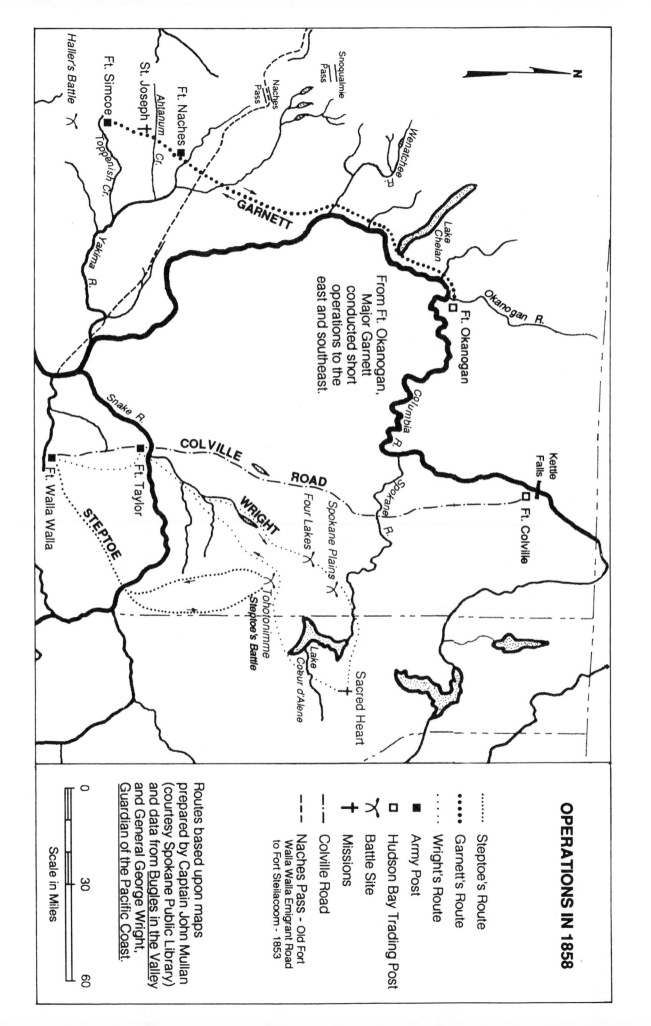

OPERATIONS IN 1858

N

From Ft. Okanogan, Major Garnett conducted short operations to the east and southeast.

Snoqualmie Pass

Naches Pass

Wenatchee R.

Lake Chelan

Ft. Okanogan

Okanogan R.

GARNETT

Columbia R.

Kettle Falls

Ft. Colville

Spokane R.

COLVILLE ROAD

Snake R.

WRIGHT

Four Lakes

Spokane Plains

Ft. Taylor

STEPTOE

Ft. Walla Walla

Tohotonimme
Steptoe's Battle

Lake Coeur d'Alene

Sacred Heart

Haller's Battle

Ft. Simcoe

St. Joseph

Ahtanum Cr.

Ft. Naches

Toppenish Cr.

Yakima R.

Legend:
.... Steptoe's Route
•••••• Garnett's Route
••••• Wright's Route
■ Army Post
□ Hudson Bay Trading Post
⚔ Battle Site
✝ Missions
–·–·– Colville Road
– – – Naches Pass - Old Fort
Walla Walla Emigrant Road
to Fort Steilacoom - 1853

Routes based upon maps prepared by Captain John Mullan (courtesy Spokane Public Library) and data from Bugles in the Valley and General George Wright, Guardian of the Pacific Coast.

Scale in Miles
0   30   60

Colonel Wright sent three rifle companies and the howitzer to flush the woods, while the remaining rifle units came down the hill and on to the plain in a skirmish line, followed by the dragoons leading their horses. The Indians tactics were to ride towards the skirmish line, fire their weapons, and ride away. The skirmishers kept advancing, taking a toll of the hostile Indians by well-aimed fire. When the colonel observed that the Indians were confused, he sent the dragoons through the infantry to attack the warriors. This pattern was repeated. With heavy losses, the Indians retreated from the battlefield, followed for about 10 miles by the Nez Perce scouts. The battle lasted less than four hours. Colonel Wright's command had not suffered a single casualty.

Soldiers and horses were fatigued from the long march and the battle. Colonel Wright made camp for a three-day rest and to make preparations to continue the campaign. He wrote by hand his official report, addressed to General Clarke's adjutant, Brevet Major William W. Mackall (USMA Class of 1837) at the Department of the Pacific's forward headquarters at Fort Vancouver:

Four Lakes, W. T., Lat. 47 32 deg. North, Long. 118, 29 deg. West. September 2d, 1858.

Sir: I have the honor to submit the following report of the battle of the "Four Lakes," fought, and won by the troops under my command, on the first inst. Our enemies were the Spokane, Couer d'Alene, and Palouse Indians.

Early in the morning of the 1st, I observed the Indians collecting on the summit of a high hill, about two miles distant, and immediately ordered the troops under arms, with a view of driving the enemy from his position, and making a reconnaissance of the country in advance.

At half-past 9 a.m. I marched from my camp with two squadrons of the First Dragoons, commanded by Brevet Major W. N. Grier,[1] four companies of the Third Artillery armed with muskets, commanded by Captain E. D. Keyes;[2] and the rifle battalion of the 9th Infantry, commanded by Captain F. T. Dent;[3] and one mountain howitzer, under command of Lieut. J. L. White,[4] Third Artillery, and thirty friendly Nez Perce, under the command of Lieut. John Mullan,[5] Second Artillery. I left in camp all equipage and supplies, strongly guarded by Lieutenants H. G. Gibson[6] and G. B. Dandy;[7] a mountain howitzer, manned, and, in addition, a guard of fifty-five men under Lieut. H. B. Lyon,[8] the whole commanded by Capt. J. A. Hardie,[9] the field officer of the day.

I ordered Brevet Major Grier to advance to the north and circle around the base of the hill, in order to gain a position occupied by the Indians with a view of to intercepting the retreat when driven from the summit by the foot troops. I marched

[1]Brevet Major William N. Grier (USMA Class of 1835).
[2]Captain Erasmus D. Keyes (USMA Class of 1832).
[3]Captain Frederick T. Dent (USMA Class of 1843).
[4]Lieutenant James L. White (USMA Class of 1853).
[5]Lieutenant John Mullan, Jr. (USMA Class of 1852).
[6]Lieutenant Horatio G. Gibson (USMA Class of 1847).
[7]Lieutenant George B. Dandy (USMA Cadet, 1849-52; did not graduate).
[8]Lieutenant Hylan B. Lyon (USMA Class of 1856).
[9]Captain James A. Hardie (USMA Class of 1843).

with the artillery and rifle battalion and Nez Perce to the right of the hill, in order to gain a position where the ascent was more easy, and also to push the Indians in the direction of the dragoons. Arriving within 600 yards of the Indians I ordered Captain Keyes to advance a company of his battalion deployed and drive the Indians from the hill. This service was gallantly accomplished by Captain Ord[1] and Lieut. Morgan,[2] with Company K, Third Artillery, in cooperation with the 2nd Squadron of Dragoons under Lieutenant Davidson.[3] The Indians were driven to the foot of the hill, and there rallied under the cover of ravines, rocks and bushes.

On reaching the crest of the hill I saw at once that the Indians were determined to measure their strength against us, showing no disposition to avoid a combat, and firmly maintaining their position at the base of the hill, keeping up a constant fire on the squadron of dragoons, who were awaiting the arrival of the infantry troops. In front of us lay a vast plain, with some 400 to 500 mounted warriors, rushing to and fro, wild with excitement, apparently eager for the fray; to the right, at the foot of the hill in the pine forest, the Indians were also seen in large numbers.

With all I have described, in plain view, a tyro in the art of war could not hesitate a moment as to the plan of battle.

Captain Keyes, with two companies of his battalion,[4] commanded by Lieutenants Ransome[5] and Ihrie,[6] with Lieutenant Howard, were ordered to deploy along the crest of the hill, in view of the dragoons and facing the plain.

The rifle battalion under Captain Dent, composed of two companies of the Ninth Infantry under Captain Winder[7] and Lieutenant Fleming,[8] was ordered to move to the right and deploy in front of the pine forest; and the howitzer under Lieutenant White, supported by a company of artillery under Lieutenant Tyler,[9] was advanced to a lower plateau, in order to gain a position where it could be fired with effect.

In five minutes the troops were deployed. I ordered the advance. Captain Keyes moved steadily down the long slope, passed the dragoons, and opened a sharp, well directed fire, which drove the Indians to the plains and the pine forest. At the same time Captain Dent with the rifle battalion, Lieutenant White with the howitzer and Lieutenant Tyler with his company, were hotly engaged with the Indians in the pine forest, constantly increasing by fugitives from the left.

Captain Keyes continued the advance, the Indians retiring slowly; Major Grier, with both squadrons, quietly leading their horses in the rear. At a signal they mounted, they rush with lightening speed through the intervals of the skirmishers, and charge the Indians on the plain, overwhelm them entirely, kill many, disperse all and in five minutes not a hostile Indian was to be seen on the plain. While this scene was enacting, Dent, Winder and Fleming, with the rifle battalion, and Tyler and White with Company A and the Howitzer, had pushed rapidly forward and driven the Indians out of the forest beyond view.

---

[1]Captain Edward O.C. Ord (USMA Class of 1839).

[2]Lieutenant Michael R. Morgan (USMA Class of 1854).

[3]Second Lieutenant Henry B. Davidson (USMA Class of 1853).

[4]Not mentioned: Lieutenant Lawrence Kip (USMA Cadet, 1853-54; did not graduate) was Captain Keyes's Battalion Adjutant.

[5]Lieutenant Dunbar R. Ransome (USMA Cadet, 1847-50; did not graduate).

[6]Lieutenant George P. Ihrie (USMA Cadet, 1845-47; did not graduate).

[7]Captain Charles S. Winder (USMA Class of 1850).

[8]Lieutenant Hugh B. Fleming (USMA Class of 1852).

[9]Lieutenant Robert O. Tyler (USMA Class of 1853).

After the charge of the dragoons and pursuit for a mile on the hills they were halted, their horses were completely exhausted, and the foot troops again passed through them for about a thousand yards; but finding only a few Indians in front of us on remote hill tops, I would not pursue them with my tired soldiers, a couple of shots from the howitzer sent them out of sight. The battle was won. I sounded recall, assembled the troops, and returned to camp at 2 p.m.

It affords me the highest gratification to report that we did not lose a single man either killed or wounded during the action, I doubt not, in great measure, to the fact that our long range rifles can reach the enemy, where he cannot reach us. The enemy lost eighteen or twenty killed and as many wounded. I take great pleasure in commending to the Department the coolness and gallantry displayed by every officer and soldier engaged in the battle.

Very respectfully, your obedient servt.,

G. Wright
Col. 9th Infy., Commanding

Colonel Wright, his command now rested after the long march and battle, resumed the advance on September 5, proceeding northward towards the Spokane River. After moving about five miles, the force sighted Indians some three miles ahead. The colonel stopped to close up the pack train and to prepare for what became the decisive Battle of Spokane Plains. Two companies of infantry and one of dragoons were assigned to guard the pack train, and four artillery companies were placed on a skirmish line about a mile long.

The Indians had set fire to the grass. Colonel Wright ordered the skirmish line, dragoons, and howitzer to advance through the flames, driving the enemy in front of them. Whenever the Indians gathered, the howitzer fired on them. Whenever an open space in the generally wooded terrain was reached, the dragoons passed through the foot troops attacking the enemy, then fell behind the foot troops when the terrain favored infantry deployment. Colonel Wright kept the pack train close to the main body, preventing Indian attempts to capture the supplies and to scatter the animals.

Colonel Wright pushed forward 25 miles, fighting the Indians for 14 of those miles. Indian losses were heavy, including two chiefs; Kamiakin was injured by a tree limb felled by a cannon shot.

The Spokane Plains Battle dismayed the Indians and made them despondent. The warriors were dispersed, their spirits broken. It was evident that the Indians were now ready to make peace. Colonel Wright had organized, trained, and deployed his soldiers for outstanding performance at Four Lakes and Spokane Plains. His officers who wrote of the battles in letters and publications did so without a single word of criticism; to the contrary, they praised their Colonel's conduct of the operations. As for the Indians, their confederation was broken; there would be no more wars with the whites, or with other tribes in the Washington Territory.

As with the previous battle, Colonel Wright wrote a report to Brevet Major Mackall at the forward headquarters of the Department of the Pacific. Colonel

Wright again lauded the performance of his officers and men in a handwritten report sent to the Department Headquarters:

> Headquarters, Expedition Against Northern Indians, Camp on Spokane River, W.T., 1 1/2 miles below the falls, September 6, 1858.
>
> Sir: I have the honor to submit the following report of the battle of the Spokane Indians, fought by the troops under my command on the 5th inst. Our enemies were the Spokanes, Coeur d'Alenes, Palouses, and Pend d'Oreilles, numbering five to seven hundred warriors.
>
> Leaving my camp at "Four Lakes" at 6 1/2 a.m. on the 5th our route lay along the margin of a lake about three miles, and thence for about two miles over a broken country thinly scattered with pines, when emerging on to the open prairie, the hostile Indians were discovered about three miles to our right and in advance, moving rapidly along the skirt of woods and apparently with a view of intercepting our line of march before we should reach the timbers.
>
> After halting to close up our long pack train, I moved forward and soon found that the Indians were setting fire to the grass at various points and on my right flank. Captain Keyes was now directed to advance three of his companies, deployed as skirmishers, to the front and right. This order was promptly obeyed and Captain Ord with Company K, Lieut. Gibson with Company M, and Lieutenant Tyler with Company A, 3rd Artillery, were thrown forward. At the same time Capt. Hardie, Company G, 3rd Artillery, was deployed to the left, and the howitzer under Lieutenant White supported by Company E, 9th Infantry, were advanced to the line of skirmishers. The firing now became brisk on both sides, the Indians attacking us on the front and on both flanks. The fires on the prairie nearly enveloped us, and were rapidly approaching the troops and the pack train. Not a moment was to be lost. I ordered the advance. The skirmishers, the howitzer, and the first squadron of dragoons under Major Grier, dashed gallantly through the burning flames and the Indians were driven back to seek shelter in the rocks. As soon as a suitable position could be obtained the howitzer under White opened fire with shell. The Indians were again routed from their cover, closely pursued by our skirmishers and followed by Grier, with his squadron leading.
>
> All of this time our pack train was concentrated as much as possible, and guarded by Capt. Dent, 9th Infantry, with his Company B, Lieutenant Davidson, 1st Dragoons, with his Company E, and Lieutenant Ihrie, 3rd Artillery, with his Company B, advancing. The line bore off to the right, which threw Ord and Taylor with skirmishers to the left. A heavy body of Indians had concentrated on our left, when our line moved quickly forward and the firing became general throughout the front, occupied by Ord, Hardie, and Tyler, and the howitzer under White, supported by Winder with Gregg's troop of dragoons following in the rear, waiting for a favorable opportunity to make a dash. At the same time, Gibson, with Company M, 3rd Artillery, drove the Indians on the right; an open plain intervening, Major Grier passed the skirmishers with his own and Lieutenant Pender's[1] troops, and charged the Indians, killing two and wounding three.
>
> Our whole line and train advanced steadily, driving the Indians over rocks and through ravines.
>
> Our point of direction having been changed to the right, Capt. Ord found himself alone with his company on the extreme left of the skirmishers and open to a large body of enemy.

---

[1]Lieutenant William D. Pender (USMA Class of 1854).

They were gallantly charged by Captain Ord and driven successfully from the high table rocks, where they had taken refuge. Captain Ord pursued the Indians, until, approaching the train, he occupied the left flank.

Moving forward toward the Spokane river, the Indians still in front, Lieutenants Ihrie and Howard, with Company B, 3rd Artillery, were thrown out on the right flank and instantly cleared the way. After a continuous fight for over seven hours, over a distance of over fourteen miles, we encamped on the banks of the Spokane river — the troops exhausted by a long and fatiguing march, twenty-five miles, without water and for two-thirds of the distance under fire.

The battle was won, two chiefs and two brothers of the Chief Garry killed, besides many of lesser note either killed or wounded. (Since the battle we learned that Kam-i-a-ken, war chief of the Yakimas, was nearly killed by a shell.) A kind Providence again protected us, although at many times the balls flew thick and fast through our ranks, yet we had but one man slightly wounded.

The friendly Nez Perces were employed chiefly as spies and guides, as well as guards to the pack train. As usual they behaved well.

Respectfully, etc.,
G. Wright
9th Inf'y, Com'g

Colonel Wright allowed his command one day to recuperate from the battle before beginning the search for more hostile Indians to complete his mission. Some appeared across the Spokane River during that day, indicating a desire to talk. The next day, September 7, Colonel Wright proceeded up the Spokane River, two miles above the falls, where Chief Garry crossed over to the south side to meet with the colonel. Chief Garry came to plead for peace for the Spokanes. Garry said that he opposed war, but that other chiefs and the younger warriors refused to listen and follow his council. Colonel Wright was stern with Chief Garry, sending him back to his tribe with a demand for unconditional surrender and the threat of extermination as the alternative.

Later that day Pohlatkin, a Spokane war chief, and nine of his warriors came into the soldier camp. Colonel Wright detained the chief for his past defiance of authority and for leading the attacks against Brevet Lieutenant Colonel Steptoe as well as for the recent attacks. One of the warriors, a Palouse, was identified as the murderer of a miner. After he was tried and found guilty, Colonel Wright approved the proceedings, and directed execution of the sentence by hanging.

On September 8, the command continued marching on the grassy plain along the south side of the river. Two of chief Pohlatkin's sons appeared on the opposite bank demanding the release of their father, but Colonel Wright had not completed his investigation and refused.

After marching about eight miles, the force came in sight of an extensive dust cloud, determined to be caused by a large herd of horses and cattle being driven south. The dragoons and the Nez Perce scouts captured the entire herd of about 800 horses, but the cattle were too wild to corral. It was conjectured that the horses belonged to a Palouse Chief and troublemaker named Tilcoax.

At first Colonel Wright was disposed to keep the horses; but there was concern that the Indians would stampede them along the march, which could cause the loss of government stock as well. Captain E. D. Keyes, the expedition second-in-command and artillery battalion commander, was appointed by Colonel

Wright as president of a board of officers to recommend what should be done with the horses. The colonel approved of the board's recommendation to allow the officers and the quartermaster to select one or two each; the remainder were to be destroyed. It took two days for two companies to shoot the remaining 690 horses, giving the name of "Horse Slaughter Camp" to the location. Most of those retained were too wild and had to be destroyed eventually. Later, the colonel learned that the Indians were not overly concerned when the horses were captured, believing that they could get them back, but their destruction dismayed the Indians and added to their humiliation and defeat.

In the meanwhile, Father Joset send a messenger from the Coeur d'Alene Mission with a letter to Colonel Wright explaining that the Indians knew they were beaten and had asked Father Joset to be their intercessor for peace. Also, those who had not joined in the hostilities were delighted with the soldier victories, since they had been threatened for not joining the others. Colonel Wright sent back a stern reply that all who had taken part in the war must come in with their guns, families, and possessions. He also gave assurances that no sentences of hanging would be given for acts of war. At the same time, two Indians came in under a white flag representing Chief Big Star, who said he wished to surrender but could not catch up because his followers had lost all their horses. This may have been a ploy to get the colonel to give them some of the captured horses.

Colonel Wright and his command reached the Coeur d'Alene Mission late on September 13. A wagon and some artillery limbers left behind because of the ruggedness of the terrain were burned by dissident Indians who were tailing the column. Father Joset and his assistants, helped by Chief Vincent, lived up to their roles as intermediaries, inducing hostile Indians to surrender and to return stolen horses and mules.

Colonel Wright held a council on September 17 with 95 chiefs and other head men present. The Indians admitted their guilt, expressed contrition, and agreed to all demands of the government. This included the surrender of men who started the attack on Brevet Lieutenant Colonel Steptoe, as well as giving Indian hostages to the government, all to be returned after one year. Although General Clarke later criticized the leniency of the treaty, Chiefs Pohlatkin and Vincent were pleased and both signed the treaty. Chief Pohlatkin was then released to return to the Spokanes to prepare for the next conference.

The next day Colonel Wright began moving the command and the hostages west towards Spokane country. On the 21st, a group of Palouse Indians came into camp claiming to be Coeur d'Alenes, wanting to learn if they could get the same surrender terms as the Coeur d'Alenes. Colonel Wright answered affirmatively.

Father Joset had assembled over a hundred chiefs and members of the Spokane tribe at Latah Creek, about 15 miles south of today's Spokane, for a conference with Colonel Wright on September 23. Chiefs Kamiakin and Tilcoax, the reported owner of the destroyed horses, came in the night before the conference was to be held, but left before Colonel Wright's arrival. The colonel sent Chiefs Garry and Big Star to persuade Kamiakin to come in, but he refused for fear of being taken to Walla Walla as a prisoner. After this the wounded Kamiakin fled to Canada.

Colonel Wright prevailed at the council, making the same demands as he had to the Coeur d'Alenes. The Indians made long speeches characterized by humility, acknowledging their guilt. Also attending was Coeur d'Alene Chief Milkapsi, who had missed the Couer d'Alene Council. He had been instrumental in getting his people to attack the Steptoe force. The Chief admitted his guilt and asked to sign his tribe's treaty. The colonel allowed this after giving the chief a stern lecture. Representatives of smaller tribes were told to consider themselves part of the Spokane Treaty as long as they conformed to the treaty's terms.

Other situations also required Colonel Wright's firm execution of justice. At sunset on the day of the Spokane council, the Yakima Chief Owhi, brother-in-law of Kamiakin, rode into the soldier camp alone, saying that he wanted peace. Colonel Wright reminded Owhi that he had already deceived Colonel Wright in 1856 during the Yakima Campaign by promising to bring all of his people into the Colonel's camp, but instead vanished. After requiring Owhi to send for his son Qualchan, a notorious Yakima war chief, Colonel Wright had Owhi placed in chains.

Two days later, Chief Qualchan rode into the soldiers' camp, accompanied by his wife and his brother. They rode up to Colonel Wright's tent and dismounted. Captain Keyes, informed Colonel Wright that he had important visitors. After recognizing Qualchan, Colonel Wright released his wife and brother and had the war chief hanged. A few days later, Owhi was shot and killed in an escape attempt.

That evening many Palouse Indians came in, saying that Kamiakin had fled north, and that they had seceded from his band. Wright had previously warned these Indians of severe punishment for participating in hostilities. He had arrested 15 of the warriors known to have participated in the war against the Army, including two who had stolen government livestock in the Walla Walla Valley. Colonel Wright directed that six deemed to be the most notorious be hanged, and the others placed in irons for the march to Fort Walla Walla.

Chief Slowiathy of the Palouse Tribe met the column four days later on the Palouse River, with nearly all of the tribe who had remained in the area. This chief had not participated in hostilities, and the tribal leaders now turned to him for leadership. Colonel Wright held council on September 30 pointing out that there was justification to hang all of them. He did not make a treaty with them, but told them that they would be exterminated if they did not stay in their own country and keep out troublemakers. Colonel Wright demanded the surrender of those who had murdered miners, and the six braves who had stolen Army cattle. One murderer came forward, but the others could not be found. When the Army column started for Fort Walla Walla, Colonel Wright called for the six cattle rustlers. They were immediately surrendered. The murderer and three of those recognized as notorious marauders were hanged at the council site. The usual number of hostages, one chief and four men with their families, were taken along.

Major Garnett's force from Fort Simcoe reached the Hudson's Bay Fort Okanogan on September 7 and conducted search operations to the east. The two forces were never less than 100 miles apart. Upon learning of Colonel Wright's victories at Four Lakes and Spokane Plains, Major Garnett began the return march to Fort Simcoe. The men's shoes were worn out and supplies were low. They had captured and punished some fugitives from justice, but had not had any battles or significant skirmishes. One West Pointer, Second Lieutenant Jesse K. Allen (USMA Class of 1856), was killed in action, and Private William Liche of Company C, Ninth Regiment straggled behind on a march and was found dead the next morning. The initial elements reached Fort Simcoe on September 23.

When the command reached Fort Walla Walla on October 5, Army Inspector General Colonel Joseph K. F. Mansfield, a West Point classmate of Colonel Wright, was inspecting the post. Colonel Wright formed the dirty and unshaven troops on the parade ground as they arrived. Colonel Mansfield complimented the troops on the condition of their equipment and the cleanliness of their arms, directly reflecting on the command policies of Colonel Wright.

Four days later council was held with the Walla Walla and Cayuse Indians. Chiefs Lawyer and Looking Glass and some friendly Nez Perce also attended. After indicting the Walla Wallas and Cayuse, Colonel Wright directed all who had taken part in recent hostilities to stand up. Thirty-five stood up. In this group were three Walla Wallas who had murdered whites. Another had failed to deliver a message from Brevet Lieutenant Colonel Steptoe to Fort Walla Walla, and instead attempted to organize local Indians to attack Fort Walla Walla while the troops were away. Colonel Wright ordered these four to be hanged.

Thus ended the campaign. A total of 16 Indians had been executed; with few exceptions, these had surrendered voluntarily, or had been turned over by members of their tribes, in full expectation of punishment. Colonel Wright had not only won the war but also consolidated the victory by remaining firm and providing fair terms and treatment to the vanquished.

Some contemporary readers may consider Colonel Wright's methods harsh, but the Indians themselves regarded them as just. Colonel Wright had brought a lasting peace to Washington Territory that continued after statehood. Indian Wars occurred later in Oregon and Idaho, but never again in Washington.

Although he was quite satisfied with the military outcome, General Clarke expressed to the Army Commander-in-Chief, Major General Scott, some dissatisfaction with the treaties. General Clarke had told Colonel Wright that the treaties should specify as a _right_ the passage of soldiers and citizens through Indian lands. In language less stringent than Clarke had wished, the treaties provided that all white persons _could_ travel throughout unmolested. Nevertheless, both generals highly commended Colonel Wright in their official reports.

However, Colonel Wright and other military leaders could no longer protect the Indian from white intrusion. General Clarke and the Army headquarters in New York changed their position to favor ratification of the treaties. In September, 1858 the Army opened up the interior of Washington to settlers, although the Senate did not ratify the Governor Stevens Treaties until March 9, 1859, and even then the treaties were not to be effective until the following March.

The defeat of Brevet Lieutenant Colonel Steptoe resulted in the creation of a new command, separating the Pacific Northwest from California: The new Department of Oregon embraced both Oregon and Washington Territories. Brigadier General William S. Harney arrived in September, 1858 to command the new Department, expecting to find ongoing hostilities instead of peace. The general had a reputation for Indian fighting. His tactics had earned him the title of "Squaw Killer." He down-played Colonel Wright's victories as minor skirmishes, pointing out that only one soldier had been wounded, and looked for ways to initiate further campaigns against the Indians in Eastern Washington.

In 1859, General Harney shifted the concentration of Colonel Wright's forces farther east by closing Fort Simcoe in May, and establishing Harney's Depot — later called Fort Colville — in Spokane country in June. He moved Colonel Wright's headquarters from Fort Dalles to Fort Walla Walla in July.

The next year, General Harney was relieved from command for defying the Army Commander-in-Chief's orders by continuing the confrontation with the British over ownership of the San Juan Islands. Colonel Wright replaced General Harney as Commander, Department of Oregon on July 5, 1860, and moved his headquarters, both Regimental and District, to Fort Vancouver.

In the spring of 1861, the outbreak of the Civil War caused Regular Army units to be moved east and the Army to reorganize its command structures. Colonel Wright left Fort Vancouver on September 13, 1861 and on October 20 was appointed Commander, Department of the Pacific, with headquarters in San Francisco, California. His command included all of the states west of the Continental Divide, except for today's New Mexico and Arizona. Colonel Wright was appointed a Brigadier General of Volunteers, but retained his position as Colonel, Ninth Infantry. As a senior Regular Army colonel at the time, Colonel Wright should have been appointed to major general, the grade called for by the level of responsibility.

For over three years General Wright managed his command with the efficiency, competence and firmness he had displayed throughout his career. He was an ideal superior, granting his district commanders measures of autonomy, but continuing to exercise leadership and providing them full support. Although there were no major Civil War battles fought west of the Rockies, the Confederate Army invaded and captured Santa Fe, Albuquerque, and Tucson, necessitating sending Volunteer units to drive them out. There were secessionist movements, particularly in southern California, and with the crucial presidential election of 1864 approaching, military detachments were sent to many towns to assist civil authorities in preventing trouble on election day. Indian attacks along the Oregon Trail, concerns about French and Confederate influence just across the border in Mexico, Mormon resistance to the federally-appointed governor and judiciary, the defense of western seaports from attack by a Confederate warship, and protection of the transcontinental telegraph line were among the many problems General Wright had to contend with. Unlike other commanders west of the Mississippi River, General Wright seldom bothered the War Department with problems, showing an understanding of the priorities of the Army in fighting the Civil War.

By 1863, General Wright was recognized as an influential figure in California, with newspapers and periodicals giving him considerable attention. While most Union-oriented newspapers were supportive, some editors attacked his policies of suppressing disloyalty. Based partly on this press coverage, Secretary of War Edwin M. Stanton decided to replace Brigadier General Wright with Major General Irvin McDowell (USMA Class of 1838), who had lost the First Battle of Manassas in 1861.

For whatever reason, a major general was replacing a perfectly competent brigadier general, who was now moved to a subordinate command — the District of California, with headquarters in Sacramento. This relief by an officer with 16 years less service, who had himself been relieved for failure on the battlefield, must have been a disappointment to Brigadier General Wright; but he accepted it with characteristic obedience. In his year in Sacramento, General Wright continued to demonstrate his honesty and his implacability to political pressure. While Commander of the Department of the Pacific, he had done an outstanding job in most difficult situations. He had less pressure in Sacramento, but still maintained his level of performance.

His brevet promotion to Brigadier General was dated December 19, 1864. This recognition for long, faithful and meritorious service meant that in the postwar years he could retain the colonelcy of the Ninth Infantry, but be posted to assignments calling for a brigadier general and serve in that rank. With the Civil War ended, the Army reorganized in June of 1865 into five divisions and 18 departments. Department 17 was the Department of the Columbia, with headquarters at Fort Vancouver, which included the state of Oregon and the territories of Washington and Idaho. General Wright was assigned by the Secretary of War to that command, the area of his pre-Civil War successes. He never arrived.

Brevet Brigadier General George Wright set sail from San Francisco on July 28, 1865 for the journey to Fort Vancouver aboard the steamship _Brother Jonathan_ with his wife, Margaret, aide-de-camp Lieutenant Edward Waite, orderly Leach, horse, and Newfoundland dog. Overloaded and struggling in a storm, the ship turned south to take shelter at Crescent City, California. Just before one in the afternoon on July 30, 1865, the steamship struck a reef and sank. Only one lifeboat was launched, with 16 survivors aboard. It is generally accepted that Margaret Wright refused to leave in a lifeboat without her husband, and the General and his wife of over 44 years stood embracing on the quarter-deck near the ship's captain as the ship went down.

The United States Military Academy Association of Graduates biography of General George Wright ends with this epitaph:

> Rest, white haired veteran, 'neath the murmuring waves;
> No more the sounds of war disturb thy sleep;
> Our land, all strewn with patriot-warriors' graves,
> Give one proud conquest to the mighty deep!

The remains of General Wright and his wife were eventually recovered and taken to San Francisco for transportation east for burial. However, citizens of Sacramento made representations to General McDowell persuading him that the interment should be where they considered their home, in Sacramento.

Full military services were held in San Francisco on October 21, 1865. The coffins were then transported by steamer to Sacramento where all city flags were flown at half-mast. The following day the coffins were taken in a procession to the Congressional Church, where a brief service was held. Interment was in the old Sacramento City Cemetery. In 1872, the remains of General Wright and his wife were reinterred in the plot of the Judge Samuel Cross family where a prominent monument was erected with the inscription:

> Gen. George Wright, U.S.A.
> and his wife
> died
> July 30, 1865
> Lovely and pleasant in their lives,
> and in their death they
> were not divided

Another inscription on plaque at the base of the monument summarizes the life of General George Wright, albeit somewhat inaccurately.

After General George Wright's death, there were numerous tributes given written and orally to this soldier. The *Oregon Reporter* contained a long article that was typical:

> The cause of civil order, private and public life have lost a noble and most gallant friend, at a time when excitement, violence and a spell of maddening fanaticism rules the hour. General Wright held the supreme military command on the coast . . . The influence of prominent politicians, the frenzied clamor of a licentious press, and a prostituted pulpit were powerless in swerving him from the path of duty which he had chosen. . . . His prudence, foresight, firmness and wisdom spared the Pacific Coast from Civil War.

Many of his subordinates wrote about this great soldier, describing his command qualities and stating their admiration. Major General E. D. Keyes, the second-in-comand for the 1858 campaign in Eastern Washington Territory, comments in his book, *Fifty Years' Observation of Men and Events, Civil and Military*:

> The commander of our expedition, Colonel George Wright, a native of Vermont and a graduate of the Military academy of the class of 1822, was every inch a soldier and gentleman. In the year 1838 I heard Colonel Worth say of Wright, who was then a major, that he was entitled by his soldierly qualities to be advanced two grades. . . .My position of second in command was one the difficulties of which have always been recognized by military men. The chief sometimes dislikes or envies his junior, and the latter discovers faults that he, if in command, would have avoided. From the commencement of the campaign my relations with Colonel Wright were confidential and cordial, and if I were to give expressions of admiration and respect for that gallant soldier and gentleman, I fear my style would appear more flowery than the rules of rhetoric prescribe for a narrative of facts. The discipline he enforced was extremely rigid and severe. After crossing into hostile country, reveille was at three o'clock a.m., and the hour of march generally five o'clock.
>   . . . Nothing in his conduct indicated that an acknowledgment of my deserts would dwarf his fame, and his order after the battle of the Spokane plain was profuse in the praise of the conduct of others, while it was silent in regard to his own.

As to his soldierly qualities, Brigadier General George B. Dandy, one of the Third Artillery Lieutenants on the 1858 campaign as a subaltern of General Keyes, wrote while still a Lieutenant that he considered Colonel Wright to be the best commanding officer under whom he had ever served.

Father Joset, after the battle of Spokane Plains, wrote:

> From the first, the Colonel knew how to disable them that, by their own admission, they cannot war anymore . . . he has terrified the bad Indians by his severity as much as he won the hearts of the good ones by his clemency.

General George Wright numbers among the heroes of Washington State to both the white and Indian cultures. He was a devoted husband and father while following the demands of a profession that demands first priority. This leader was admired by his subordinates and highly respected by his peers and superiors. He was a West Pointer who brought a lasting peace to Washington.

Brigadier General C. Coburn Smith
U.S. Army, Retired
USMA Class of 1931

EDWARD JEVNOR STEPTOE:
CARETAKER OF THE PALOUSE HILLS

Look closely at a detailed map of the State of Washington, and along the eastern edge of the state you will see the name "Steptoe" in three places: the Town of Steptoe, Steptoe Butte State Park, and Steptoe Memorial State Park. You might also know that the original name for the first civilian settlement of what is now Walla Walla, Washington was "Steptoeville." This "Steptoe" must have been highly respected, at least by the local population; perhaps an Indian Chief? However, if you by chance have a certain historic map of the United States[1] you might notice in the same area the legend: "Steptoe's Defeat." Perhaps not so glorious a leader, after all, you conclude. In fact, all of these locations are named for Edward Jevnor Steptoe (USMA Class of 1837) who had a considerable impact on early Washington Territory, particularly the eastern part, during the short time he served there as a United States Army officer. Should he be remembered for his "defeat," as Custer was? And was he really "defeated?" Before considering these questions, and the part Steptoe played in the development of Washington, let us follow briefly his path from birth until he arrived in Washington Territory in early 1856.

Edward Jevnor Steptoe was born in Bedford County, Virginia, in 1816, into one of the prominent early families of Virginia, one that had had ties with George Washington's family. He grew up in Virginia, but attended Chapel Hill University in North Carolina, graduating at the age of 17. Becoming interested in a military career, like many of his fellow Virginians, he sought an appointment to the United States Military Academy at West Point, New York, and was successful, thanks to the influence of an uncle. In 1837 he was commissioned a second lieutenant in the artillery, graduating 34th in a class of 50 cadets, many of whom were later to play prominent roles in the Civil War.

Steptoe's first duty assignment was in Florida, where he saw action against the Seminole Indians, doing mostly patrols and "pacifying" duty with infrequent engagements. In 1846, when the War with Mexico broke out, Steptoe was a First Lieutenant (but soon to be Captain) in command of an Artillery Company[2] that fought with distinction in several battles, becoming known as "Steptoe's Battery." For "gallant and meritorious conduct" he was made a Brevet Major after the Battle of Cerro Gordo, and later, in September, 1847, for "gallant and meritorious conduct" at the Battle of Chapultepec, he became a Brevet Lieutenant Colonel. Also of note is the fact that during the War with Mexico, Steptoe became a good friend of General Franklin Pierce, a future President who was to have some impact on Steptoe's career.

Steptoe's next assignment of note came in September, 1854 when, as a "permanent" captain in the Third Artillery he was put in command of a force at

---

[1]National Geographic Society, *Historical Atlas of the U.S.*, p. 46.
[2]Artillery units were not officially called "batteries" until 1883.

Edward Jevnor Steptoe

[Special Collections Division, University of Washington Libraries]

Salt Lake City, Utah Territory, with a mapping and reconnaissance mission to Fort Lane, Oregon. However, Steptoe's departure was delayed until early 1855 by problems that developed between the federal government and the Mormons — in particular their leader Brigham Young, who had been appointed Governor of the Territory by President Pierce's predecessor President Fillmore. President Franklin Pierce (Steptoe's friend from Mexican War days) decided to remove Brigham Young and to appoint Steptoe in his place as Governor of the Utah Territory. In fact, the Senate had confirmed the appointment before Steptoe was informed. President Pierce wrote to Steptoe telling him of the proposal and action, but stated that it would be necessary for Steptoe to resign his commission from the Army if he accepted, and asked if he would be willing to accept under this condition. Steptoe "respectfully declined," stating that he preferred to stay in the Army as a career. He was not eager to get into politics. He completed his mission in the West and returned to his home in Virginia. In March, 1855, he was promoted to "permanent" Major in the Ninth Infantry and became one of the senior officers assigned to staff the newly organized Regiment at Fortress Monroe, Virginia. Colonel George Wright (USMA Class of 1822) was its commander.

After a recruitment and training program, the Ninth Infantry sailed from Fortress Monroe for the Northwest via the Isthmus of Panama on December 15, 1855. At Panama, the Regiment was divided into two groups for the trip north, Steptoe sailing with Colonel Wright and six companies on the *Golden Age*. They landed at Fort Vancouver, Washington Territory on January 21, 1856. The remaining four companies arrived a day later; two went on to the Puget Sound District at Fort Steilacoom, while the other two remained with Colonel Wright. Brevet Major General John E. Wool, Commander of the Department of the Pacific, assigned Colonel Wright to the command of the Columbia River District, ordered him to establish a headquarters at Fort Dalles, and directed him to establish two forts in the area, one to be in the Walla Walla Valley.

Colonel Wright, with Steptoe[1] as his second-in-command, had under his command eight Ninth Infantry companies and those companies of the Fourth Infantry, the Third Artillery (primarily employed as infantry), and the First Dragoons (Calvary) that were already stationed in the Columbia River District. In addition to the Regular Army units, there were various local Militia or "Volunteer" units in action. Since the Whitman Massacre in November, 1847 near Walla Walla, the local governments and population had intensified efforts to control and confine the various Indian tribes by the time the Ninth arrived. In fact, in December, 1855, a battle of some magnitude (sometimes referred to as the "Frenchtown Fight") took place in the Walla Walla Valley between Oregon Territorial Militia troops and the Walla Walla Indians, the Indians finally withdrawing. The Militia troops remained in the area throughout the winter,

---

[1]In various writings Steptoe is referred to as "Major," "Lieutenant Colonel," or "Brevet Lieutenant Colonel." His "permanent" or "pay" rank was that of Major in the Ninth Infantry; however, when he was acting as Colonel Wright's second-in-command, post commander, or a separate commander, he was entitled to use his brevet rank of lieutenant colonel. In this monograph we try to avoid confusion by referring to him simply by his surname.

establishing Fort Bennett. (The Hudson's Bay Company had abandoned its Fort Walla Walla because of Indian unrest.) The Militia withdrew to Fort Dalles in March, 1856, leaving the Walla Walla Valley without a fort.

Who were these Indian peoples with whom Steptoe was about to become involved? Some were peaceful, others belligerent and predatory. The Yakimas, located east of the Cascades in the Columbia River Valley, were causing trouble at the time Steptoe arrived. The Nez Perce Indians, living in the Walla Walla Valley and to its east, were generally considered to be highly developed and cooperative with the Army. The Walla Walla Tribe was also in the Walla Walla Valley area. To their south were the Cayuse and Umatilla Tribes and to the north their allies the Palouse. The Palouse were considered troublemakers and undependable. To their north were the Spokanes and the Coeur d'Alenes. One of the primary foods of the Indians in this area was the camas plant (its root or bulb), which grew naturally there. The Indians considered its growing fields to be vital to them.

In March, 1856 Colonel Wright began to move his force to Fort Dalles in compliance with General Wool's order. This required movement of a large amount of supplies up the Columbia River and portage for several miles at the Cascades, where there were blockhouses for protection. Civilian communities grew up near the blockhouses. On March 29, Yakimas, Klickitats, and some local warriors attacked and laid siege to one of the blockhouses, manned by soldiers, and a two-story log store where settlers had sought shelter. Several soldiers and settlers were killed. On learning of the attack, Colonel Wright took a force from Fort Dalles by two river steamers down the Columbia to counterattack. When ashore, the Colonel dispatched Steptoe with a force of two companies of the Ninth Infantry, a detachment of Dragoons and a howitzer to relieve the situation at the "middle" site. At the same time a force under the command of Lieutenant Philip E. Sheridan (USMA Class of 1853) approached from Fort Vancouver in the west. With Steptoe's forces closing in from the north and east and Sheridan's force coming from the south and west, the Indians were apparently trapped. However, they escaped before the forces could close on them. One story has it that a bugle in Steptoe's command sounded, and the Indians vanished. This was Steptoe's "baptism of fire" in the Pacific Northwest. Steptoe rejoined Colonel Wright's forces and in May, 1856, moved north from Fort Dalles into Yakima country, Colonel Wright having decided that this area needed immediate attention. A supply depot, Fort Naches, was built, and Steptoe was left there with three companies in support of the main force which moved on north and eventually caused many of the Yakimas to seek peace.

It was now August, 1856. In September, a force under Steptoe's command moved east to establish the fort in the Walla Walla Valley. The force consisted of a company of the Fourth Infantry and one of the Ninth Infantry, a company of the Third Artillery, and a company of Dragoons. While Wright and Steptoe were operating against the Yakimas, The Washington Territorial Governor and Superintendent of Indian Affairs, Isaac I. Stevens (USMA Class of 1839), sent Washington Territorial Militia to "pacify" the Indians in southeastern Washington Territory (Cayuse, Walla Walla, and Umatilla). After some fighting during July in the Grande Rhonde Valley of Oregon Territory, Governor Stevens called the Indian Chiefs to a meeting (to become known as the "Second Walla Walla Council") with their unconditional surrender in mind. At about that time, most of the Volunteer troops who had been fighting there completed their "term" and left for home, leaving Stevens with only a small military escort. (In accordance with General Wool's policy, Wright had refused to give Stevens any assistance.) The meeting with the Indians failed, so Stevens decided to return to The Dalles.

Steptoe and his force of four companies were camped only a few miles away. Stevens was attacked several times, but was eventually saved when Steptoe sent some troops to his assistance. (It was reported that General Wool reprimanded Steptoe for giving this assistance.)[1] Leaving one company in the area, Steptoe and the balance of his command returned to The Dalles with Governor Stevens. Incensed over what he deemed interference with the Army's operations by the Governor and his Volunteers, General Wool admonished Colonel Wright for not going to the Walla Walla Valley, and for allowing Governor Stevens to "treat with the Indians you [Wright] have been ordered to subdue."[2]

Steptoe and his men then returned to the Valley and by mid-November had established an encampment or cantonment. It stood on the bank of Mill Creek near the Nez Perce Trail, and six miles from its junction with the Walla Walla River. It was called Fort Walla Walla.[3] While Steptoe was establishing the fort, Colonel Wright went to the Valley and called a council with the Indians in the area. However, only three Cayuse and two Nez Perce chiefs attended. Nevertheless, Wright said he was satisfied that the Indians wanted peace, and he was opposed to any implementation of the treaties that Stevens had negotiated with the Indians until ratified by the U.S. Government. He felt that the treaties were the cause of all the trouble in the area.

The winter of 1856-57 was relatively peaceful in the Walla Walla Valley area, and a small settlement grew up around the military base. The people began to call it "Steptoeville" (in 1859 it officially became Walla Walla). In the spring of 1857 a better site was selected just west of the initial site and on higher ground. A survey was made and approval received for the new location. Construction began there with the arrival of Company E, Ninth Infantry and a sawmill. This permanent site was occupied in 1858.

In June 1857, Brevet Brigadier General Newman Clarke replaced General Wool as Commander of the Department of the Pacific. Steptoe's forces were changed and augmented so that by 1858 he had under his command at Fort Walla Walla Companies B and E of the Ninth Infantry and Companies C, E, H and I of the First Dragoons.[4] Steptoe also had a number of "mountain" or "pack" howitzers, which were manned by the Ninth Infantry troops. No military action of

[1]Glassley, R. H., *Indian Wars of the Pacific Northwest* (Portland, Oregon: Binfords & Mort, 1972), p. 141.

[2]H. Dean Guie, *Bugles in the Valley* (Yakima, Wash.: Republic Press, 1956), p. 52.

[3]The former Fort Walla Walla, at the juncture of the Columbia and Walla Walla Rivers, was established by the British in 1818 as Fort Nez Perce. The name was changed to Fort Walla Walla in 1821. Hudson's Bay Company operated it as a trading post until abandoning it in 1856.

[4] The First Dragoons eventually became the First Cavalry in 1861.

Above: **Fort Walla Walla in 1857.**

Below: **City of Walla Walla and Fort Walla Walla, 1862.**

[Both photos: Special Collections Division, University of Washington Libraries]

MILITARY POST & CITY OF WALLA-WALLA, W.T. IN 1862.

consequence took place in 1857 in Steptoe's area, but problems were developing with the Indians as a result of an influx of prospectors to the newly discovered gold field in the Colville vicinity (180 miles to the north of Fort Walla Walla). In addition, there was confusion over what actions were to be taken to implement Governor Stevens's 1855 treaties with the Indians, which were still not ratified by the U.S. Government. General Clarke instructed his military commanders that no action should be taken to implement the provisions of the treaties until ratified by Congress, and that the Indians should be so informed.

In October 1857, an incident occurred that caused Steptoe to write to General Clarke.[1]

> Fort Walla Walla
> October 19, 1857
>
> Sir: It is my duty to inform the general that Mr. J. Ross Brown, acting, I believe, as an agent of the Indian bureau, did, in a recent conversation with 'Lawyer,' the Nez Perces' chief, assert that Governor Stevens' treaty of Walla Walla would certainly be ratified and enforced.
>
> Mr. William Craig, who acted as interpreter on the occasion, gives me this information.
>
> Considering that this statement is in direct opposition to what the Indians have been told by us, and to what as I believe nearly all of them desire, it seems to me in very bad taste, to say the least of it. Mr. Brown could not possibly have known that the treaty will be ratified, and even if he had, the proper time to enlighten the Indians on the subject is obviously after it shall have become a law of the land. He had no right to unsettle the Indian minds on a point respecting which his convictions are probably no stronger than the opposite belief of many others in daily intercourse with them.
>
> I will simply add that in my opinion any attempt to enforce that treaty will be followed by immediate hostilities with most of the tribes in this part of the country; for which reason it does appear to me greatly desirable that a new commission be appointed, and a new treaty made, thoroughly digested and accepted by both sides.
>
> Very respectfully, your obedient servant,
>
> E. J. Steptoe,
> Brevet Lieutenant Colonel USA,
> Commanding Post

General Clarke forwarded Steptoe's letter to the War Department, indicated his concern, and stated that "I believe the present treaties can only be enforced by war, and hope this will be avoided by a new commission."[2] In addition, General Clarke and his predecessor, General Wool, promoted the policy that during this time no further settlers should be allowed in the area until the matter was

---

[1]This letter and the other items of official U.S. Army correspondence used in this monograph are excerpted from B. F. Manring, *Conquest of the Coeur d'Alenes, Spokanes and Palouses*, initially published in 1912, republished in 1975 by Ye Galleon Press, Fairfield, Washington.

[2]Manring, *Conquest of the Coeur d'Alenes*, p. 249.

resolved. However, incoming settlers complained to the Washington Territorial Government, which issued the following resolution:

> Whereas certain officers of the United States Army, commanding in the county of Walla Walla, have unlawfully assumed to issue orders prohibiting citizens of this Territory from settling in certain portions thereof, and in accordance with said orders have driven citizens and settlers from their claims and homes acquired under the laws of the United States, to their great injury —
>
> Therefore be it resolved by the legislative assembly of the Territory of Washington that, in our opinion, the said orders are without the authority of law, and that the acts done under said orders are a high handed outrage upon the rights and liberties of the American people.
>
> Resolved, That the Governor be required to give the proper authorities at Washington all necessary information on the subject of the outrageous usurpation of the military over the civil authority.
>
> Resolved, That we believe the above usurpation to be the very worst form of martial law, proclaimed by tyrants not having feeling in common with us, nor interests identified with ours.
>
> Resolved, That a copy of the above resolutions be forwarded to our delegate in Congress, and that he be requested to represent the matter to the proper department of Washington city, to the end that the evil be corrected.
>
> Passed January 15, 1858.
>
> J. S. Vancleave,
>
> Speaker House Representatives
>
> C. C. Pagett,
>
> President of the Council

The Washington Territorial Legislature's resolution was sent to the War Department, but it did not result in any change in policy — the War Department's or General Clarke's. At the same time, problems were developing in other areas so that on January 12, 1858 General Clarke gave Steptoe the following instructions:

> Headquarters, Department of the Pacific,
> San Francisco, California, January 12, 1858
>
> Sir: Brigadier General Clarke directs me to say that he desires you to recall your dragoons and horses as early as the state of the roads and the grass, or your supply of forage will permit.[1]
>
> He wishes your command to be in a state of full efficiency at the earliest possible day. Lieutenant Gregg,[2] First Dragoons, will be directed to join you with his company as soon as the order for the return of your detachment reaches Vancouver, and to guard your horses in the march.
>
> The general wishes you to be deeply impressed with the importance of obtaining early and full information in relation to the Indian tribes in your vicinity, and south and east towards Fort Hall and the Salmon river.

---

[1]The horses had been sent to Fort Vancouver for the winter because of the lack of forage at Fort Walla Walla.

[2]Second Lieutenant David McM. Gregg (USMA Class of 1855), commanding Company H, First Dragoons.

Information from various sources and points on the frontier leads him to the conclusion that through the Mormons the Indians are being inclined to hostility, and that a conflict in Utah may be the signal for trouble on the frontier, and it is not improbable that the Mormons may move north.

He wishes you to be prepared in advance for either contingency. Full and prompt report of all information, and your opinion founded thereon, is desired. I am, sir, very respectfully, your obedient servant,

W. W. Mackall
Assistant Adjutant General

As a result of General Clarke's "alert," Steptoe began to accumulate such "intelligence" of the Indian situation as he could. He became aware of a number of problem areas to his north where the Palouse and Spokanes were, and, on April 17, in a letter to General Clarke, announced his intention of making an expedition there as soon as the dragoon horses — which Brevet Captain O. H. P. Taylor (USMA Class of 1846), the commanding Company C, First Dragoons, had taken to Fort Vancouver for the winter — returned to Fort Walla Walla.

Fort Walla Walla, April 17th, 1858

Sir: There appears to be so much excitement amongst the Palouse and Spokane Indians as to make an expedition to the north advisable, if not necessary; I shall accordingly start with three companies of dragoons in that direction as soon as possible after the arrival of Brevet Captain Taylor.

Some forty persons living at Colville recently petitioned for the presence of troops at that place, as they believed their lives and property to be in danger from hostile Indians. I cannot tell at this distance whether they are needlessly alarmed, but shall visit Colville before returning.

Two white men are reported to have been killed recently near Palouse river on their way to Colville. An Indian gave me today the names of the Palouse Indians said to be implicated. I am inclined to think the rumor is correct, but will investigate the matter thoroughly during my trip.

A few nights ago a party of the same tribe made a foray into this valley and carried off horses and cattle belonging to various persons, both whites and Indians, and thirteen head of beef cattle, the property of the commissary department. It is my impression that they did not suppose these animals to be in our charge or they would not probably have taken them. However, it is very necessary to check their thieving, or of course worse trouble will grow out.

I have the honor to be, very respectfully, your obedient servant,
E. J. Steptoe

During April the dragoon horses, escorted by Brevet Captain Taylor and the newly-assigned Company H, First Dragoons, arrived at Fort Walla Walla. On May 2, Steptoe wrote to General Clarke that there appeared to be considerable disturbance among the Indian tribes, so he planned to take a force north in hopes of checking it. On May 6, 1858 Steptoe and his force departed on their fateful expedition. The best description of what took place is found in Steptoe's own "after action" report:

Fort Walla Walla, May 23, 1858

Major: On the 2nd instant I informed you of my intention to move northward with a part of my command. Accordingly, on the 6th I left here with C, E, and H, First dragoons, and E, Ninth infantry; in all, five company officers and one hundred and fifty-two enlisted men. Hearing that the hostile Palouses were near Al-pon-on-we, in the Nez Perces' land, I moved to that point, and was ferried across Snake river by Timothy, a Nez Perce chief. The enemy fled towards the north, and I followed leisurely on the road to Colville. On Sunday morning, the 16th, when near the To-hoto-nim-me in the Spokane country, we found ourselves suddenly in the presence of ten or twelve hundred Indians of various tribes — Spokanes, Palouses, Coeur d'Alenes, Yakimas, and some others — all armed, painted, and defiant. I moved slowly on until just about to enter a ravine that wound along the bases of several hills, which were all crowned by the excited savages. Perceiving that it was their purpose to attack us in this dangerous place, I turned aside and encamped, the whole wild, frenzied mass moving parallel to us, and, by yells, taunts, and menaces, apparently trying to drive us to some initiatory act of violence. Towards night a number of chiefs rode up to talk with me, and inquired what were our motives to this intrusion upon them. I answered that we were passing on to Colville, and had no hostile intentions toward the Spokanes, who had always been our friends, nor towards any other tribes who were friendly; that my chief aim in coming so far was to see the Indians and the white people at Colville, and, by friendly discussion with both, endeavor to strengthen their good feelings for each other. They expressed themselves satisfied, but would not consent to let me have canoes, without which it would be impossible to cross the Spokane river. I concluded, for this reason, to retrace my steps at once, and the next morning (17th) turned back towards this post. We had not marched three miles when the Indians, who had gathered on the hills adjoining the line of march, began an attack upon the rear guard, and immediately the fight became general. We labored under the great disadvantage of having to defend the pack-train while in motion and in a rolling country peculiarly favorable to the Indian mode of warfare. We had only a small quantity of ammunition, but, in their excitement, the soldiers could not be restrained from firing it in the wildest manner. They did, however, under the leading of their respective commanders, sustain well the reputation of the army for some hours, charging the enemy repeatedly with gallantry and success. The difficult and dangerous duty of flanking the column was assigned to Brevet Captain Taylor and Lieutenant Gaston,[1] to both of whom it proved fatal. The latter fell about twelve o'clock, and the enemy soon after charging formally upon his company, it fell back in confusion and could not be rallied. About a half hour after this Captain Taylor was brought in mortally wounded, upon which I immediately took possession of a convenient height and halted. The fight continued here with unabated activity, the Indians occupying neighboring heights and working themselves along to pick off our men. The wounded increased in number continually. Twice the enemy gave unmistakable evidence of a design to carry our position by assault, and their number and desperate courage caused me to fear the most serious consequences to us from such an attempt on their part. It was manifest that the loss of their officers and comrades began to tell upon the spirit of the soldiers; that they were becoming discouraged, and not to be relied upon with confidence. Some of them were recruits but recently joined; two of the companies had musketoons, which were utterly worthless in our present condition; and, what was most alarming, only two or three rounds of cartridges remained to some of the men, and but few to any of them. It was

---

[1] Second Lieutenant William Gaston (USMA Class of 1856), commanding Company E, First Dragoons.

plain that the enemy would give the troops no rest during the night, and they would be still further disqualified for stout resistance on the morrow, while the number of enemies would certainly be increased. I determined, for these reasons, to make a forced march to Snake River, about eighty-five miles distant, and secure the canoes in advance of the Indians, who had already threatened to do the same by us. After consulting with the officers, all of whom urged me to the step as the only means in their opinion of securing the safety of the command, I concluded to abandon every thing that might impede our march. Accordingly we set out about ten o"clock in perfectly good order, leaving the disabled animals and such as were not in condition to travel so far and so fast, and, with deep pain I have to add, the two howitzers. The necessity for this last measure will give you, as well as many words, a conception of the strait to which we believe ourselves to be reduced. Not an officer of the command doubted that we would be overwhelmed with the first rush of the enemy upon our position in the morning; to retreat further by day, with our wounded men and property, was out of the question; to retreat slowly by night equally so, as we could not then be in condition to fight all next day; it was therefore necessary to relieve ourselves to all encumbrances and to fly. We had no horses able to carry the guns over 80 miles without resting, and if the enemy should attack us en route, as, from their ferocity, we certainly expected they would, not a soldier could be spared for any other duty than skirmishing. For these reasons, which I own candidly seemed to me more cogent at the time than they do now. I resolved to bury the howitzers. What distresses me is that no attempt was made to bring them off; and all I can add is that if this was an error of judgment it was committed after the calmest discussion of the matter, in which, I believe, every officer agreed with me.

Enclosed is a list of the killed and wounded. The enemy acknowledge a loss of 9 killed and 40 or 50 wounded, many of them mortally. It is known to us that this is an underestimate, for one of the officers informs me that on a single spot where Lieutenants Gregg and Gaston met in a joint charge twelve dead Indians were counted. Many others were seen to fall.

I cannot do justice, in this communication, to the conduct of the officers throughout the affair. The gallant bearing of each and all was accompanied by an admirable coolness and sound judgment. To the skill and promptness of Assistant Surgeon Randolph[1] the wounded are deeply indebted.

Be pleased to excuse the hasty appearance of this letter; I am anxious to get it off and have not time to have it transcribed.

I have the honor to be, very respectfully, your obedient servant,

E. J. Steptoe
Brevet Lieutenant Colonel United States Army

Some comments on the expedition and on Steptoe's report are in order. Steptoe was apparently unaware of the extent of the unrest among the Indian tribes to his north (Palouse, Spokane and Coeur d'Alene). They were upset by the growing number of settlers and prospectors coming into or through their areas, by the rumors that they had heard concerning plans by the U.S. Government to build a road through their area,[2] and by the threat to their camas growing fields. Another problem was that, though some of their chiefs may have been or seemed to be

---

[1]Assistant Surgeon John F. Randolph.
[2]Lieutenant John Mullan (USMA Class of 1852) had conducted a survey for that road. Mullan's work is recounted in one of the monographs in this book.

cooperative with the settlers and the government, the chiefs did not hold "absolute rule;" the tribal "rank and file" often acted independently (as in the attack on Steptoe).

There is a popular misconception as to the location of the hill on which Steptoe took his stand that night of May 17, 1858, before escaping to the south. That hill is often incorrectly identified as "Steptoe Butte." This hill, or butte, actually called "Pyramid Peak" at the time, was several miles south of the hill that Steptoe's forces actually occupied — a hill near the present town of Rosalia, Washington. The hill had at its base a creek that the Indians called Ingossomen or Tohotonimme. The battle took its name from the Nez Perce name for the creek. Evidently Pyramid Peak began to be called "Steptoe Butte" as a result of "tall tales" and misinformation about the fight, and the misnomer stuck.

Steptoe's casualty report listed seven killed or mortally wounded, 13 wounded, and one missing. The "missing" was First Sergeant Edward Ball, who as a member of the liquor-destroying detail (prior to the retreat) apparently destroyed some of the liquor by personally consuming it, "went to sleep" in the nearby brush, and missed the silent departure formation. Miraculously, he was able to make his way alone back to Fort Walla Walla. The two officers who were killed were Brevet Captain O. H. P. Taylor (USMA Class of 1846) and Lieutenant William Gaston (USMA Class of 1856). Their remains were eventually buried side-by-side at West Point.

**Graves of Brevet Captain Taylor and Lieutenant Gaston
Cemetery, United States Military Academy,
West Point, New York**

[Brigadier General C. Coburn Smith]

Steptoe's "defeat" and casualties caused repercussions in the "high command" in the area and in Washington, D.C. In June, 1858 General Clarke, the top commander in the Northwest, held a conference with his officers, Colonel Wright and Steptoe included. General Clarke decided that decisive action against the Indian tribes in the eastern Washington area was required, and ordered a large force organized. The major part of it was gathered and trained at Fort Walla Walla under Colonel Wright; a second force was gathered at Fort Simcoe under Major Robert S. Garnett (USMA Class of 1841). Wright's force decisively defeated the Indians in that area, and they accepted Colonel Wright's peace terms, putting an end to extensive military operations in eastern Washington.

Steptoe was not made part of the attacking force, but was left in command at Fort Walla Walla. He was reportedly "unhappy" at being excluded and not given a chance to "recoup" from his ill-fated military operation. However, he had developed some health problems in the last year or so, including a form of recurrent partial paralysis. It was also a logical command decision to leave the "second-in-command" behind at the main base when the commander "went off to battle." Whatever the reasons for Steptoe's exclusion from further combat may have been, he gave his poor health as the reason for requesting an extensive furlough to return to his home in Virginia in early 1859. The request was approved.

In Virginia he became engaged to Mary R. Claytor, and they were married the following year. He and his bride spent the winter of 1860-61 in Cuba but returned to Virginia in the spring, at which time he suffered a recurrence of his paralysis. Steptoe was nonetheless able to maintain his position in the Army, and in September, 1861 was promoted to "permanent" Lieutenant Colonel of the Tenth Infantry. Two months later in November, 1861, he resigned due to his poor health. He was considerably upset by the outbreak of the Civil War, but in spite of his sympathy for his home state of Virginia, he remained loyal to the Federal Government. However, he stayed inactive. He died at the age of 49 on April 6, 1865, survived only by his wife. Their one child, a daughter, had died a year earlier. The inscription on his monument in the Lynchburg, Virginia cemetery reads:

Sacred by this Monument to the Memory of
Edward J. Steptoe,
Late Lieut. Colonel in the Army of the United
States, who was born in Bedford County, Va.,
1816 & died 1865.

A soldier by avocation and profession, he was sans peur et sans reproche. A grateful Government testified its sense of the value of his services by advancing him through various gradations to the elevated rank he held in its military service, where he had reached the high noon of existence; crowning all with the graceful tender, through an Executive who had been his companion in arms, in a foreign land, of exalted civil position, which he declined.

Religion and Patriotism were beautifully blended in the character of him who sleeps beneath, for he was not less a soldier of Christ than of his country. Like the Captain of his salvation, he was "made perfect through suffering" and hath now entered into the joy of his Lord.

**Monument commemorating the Battle of Tohotonimme
near Rosalia, Washington**

[Colonel Ernest J. Whitaker]

Should Edward Steptoe be remembered by historians only for his "defeat," and the derogatory connotation that entails? The fact that so many locations were and still are named for him suggests that he left a very favorable impression on the local population, at least. Apparently these people considered his action in the "Palouse Hills" to be commendable, and would regard him as the "Caretaker of the Palouse Hills." But was Steptoe's engagement with the Indians in May, 1858 truly a "military defeat" in the first place? He embarked on his mission of "reconnaissance" with no intent of doing battle with the Indians; in fact, when confronted by them he attempted to secure peace or "non-conflict." When he learned of the superior force confronting him and realized the danger, was it not prudent to withdraw as he did? Historian B. F. Manring states: "The escape of Colonel Steptoe from an army of savages sufficiently numerous to overwhelm his own force, and who possessed every advantage which the situation could offer, with no force that could attempt a rescue within a hundred miles, has not a parallel in the history of American Indian Warfare."[1] In a report written on June 27, 1858, Father Joset, a Catholic priest in charge of the Coeur d'Alene Mission at the time, said, "What breaks my heart, is to see Colonel Steptoe, the zealous protector of Indians, exposed to blame which ordinarily attaches itself to bad success; however, in the eyes of reflecting men, who know his situation, his retreat will do him infinite honor."

It is left to the reader to judge Edward Steptoe's proper place in history.

Ernest J. Whitaker
Colonel, U.S. Army, Retired
USMA Class of 1941

---

[1]Manring, *Conquest of the Coeur d'Alenes*, pp. 125-6.

GEORGE EDWARD PICKETT:
DEFENDER OF THE SAN JUANS

George Edward Pickett, like fellow West Pointer George A. Custer, is remembered in American history for a courageous but disastrous military engagement. But unlike Custer, he lived to fight again — for the Confederacy, until the end of the Civil War. The order to "charge" up Cemetery Ridge at Gettysburg on July 3, 1863 was actually given by General Robert E. Lee, but the plan was only half-heartedly supported by Pickett's commander and old friend, General James Longstreet. Pickett carried out the order to the best of his ability and nearly accomplished the mission. He is reported to have said (to Longstreet): "Then I shall lead my division forward, sir."[1]

During the Civil War Pickett wooed and married LaSalle Corbell of Richmond, Virginia, a woman half his age who later wrote his biography, *Pickett and His Men*.[2] Strangely, she does not mention the wooing and marriage in her book; but they apparently took place while Pickett was recovering from a serious wound received at the Battle of Gaines Mills in 1862, when LaSalle was a young nurse in Richmond. They were married by the time the battle of Gettysburg took place. An earlier wife, Sallie Minge, also of Richmond, died the same year they were married (1851), but writings make little mention of her.

Pickett's military career after Gettysburg was rather erratic. Historian D. S. Freeman writes, "neither he nor his division is ever the same again;"[3] and his health was not the best. After the war Pickett reportedly turned down an offer by General Ulysses S. Grant to be U.S. Marshal for Virginia, believing it would be a betrayal of his fellow Virginians. Instead, he established himself as an insurance agent in Norfolk, Virginia. He died there at the age of 50 in 1875.

Less noted, though of more interest to the present topic, is what George Pickett did *before* the Civil War, in Washington Territory, as a captain in the U.S. Army. Had the Civil War not occurred, Pickett might have been remembered in history for an altogether different type of military action — in defense of the Union rather than in attack upon it — as "Defender of the San Juans."

Little information is available about George Pickett's early life before he went to West Point. He was born in Richmond, Virginia in 1825, and remained a loyal Virginian until his death. He first appears on the national scene as a cadet at the United States Military Academy. His widow wrote that Pickett's uncle, a lawyer, had an Illinois lawyer friend named Abraham Lincoln, who was able to get Pickett an appointment from that state to West Point in 1842. His career at the Academy was less than noteworthy: Like Custer, he graduated at the bottom of his class

---

[1]The Civil War generals named here all graduated from West Point: Lee, 1829; Longstreet, 1842; Custer, 1861.

[2]LaSalle Corbell (Mrs. George E.) Pickett, *Pickett and His Men*.(Philadelphia: J. B. Lippincott & Co., 1913).

[3]Douglas Southall Freeman, *Lee's Lieutenants*, Vols. I, II, and III (New York: Charles Scribner's Sons, 1945).

Captain George E. Pickett

academically. This did not mean that he lacked in military ability, as he proved in the Mexican War some five years after his graduation. He distinguished himself in several military engagements, particularly at Chapultepec in September, 1847, where he participated in the assault and capture of the city and was made brevet captain for gallantry in action.

After the Mexican War, Pickett served principally in the Southwest, particularly in Texas. He was stationed at Fort Bliss, Texas from 1854 to 1855, and it was here that he became close friends with James Longstreet, with whom he had served in Mexico, and who was to have considerable influence on his later career. In the summer of 1855 Pickett reported to Fortress Monroe, Virginia, to command Company D of the newly organized Ninth U.S. Infantry. The Ninth was scheduled for duty in Washington Territory. Brevet Major General John E. Wool, Commander of the Department of the Pacific, had been given the task of subduing the Indians in the territory, and he felt he could do this only with additional Regular troops. The Washington Territorial Governor, Isaac Stevens, had signed a number of treaties with Indian tribes in the Territory, and many of the Indians were in rebellion because of the terms of the treaties.

So, in December 1855, the Ninth Infantry sailed for the Pacific Northwest from Fortress Monroe, going by way of Panama, across the isthmus by rail, and then up the West Coast by ship. For the trip up the West Coast, the Ninth was divided into two groups: Company D was in the second group commanded by Lieutenant Colonel Silas Casey. It eventually arrived at Fort Vancouver, Washington Territory on January 22, 1856, and Casey with Companies D and H moved on to Fort Steilacoom. The two companies then began operations against the Indians. Pickett was on court-martial duty in Florida from November 1855 to March 1856, so did not make the trip with his company, but joined it later at Fort Steilacoom. He was to remain in the Washington Territory until June 1861 when he resigned to join the "rebellion against the United States" (as stated on his official record). His wife states in her book that arrest orders were issued for him by the military command on the Pacific Coast, but he eluded capture and made his way to Virginia to join the Confederate Army.

In the late 1840s and early 1850s, the United States Government's greatest concerns were with Great Britain and Mexico, since these countries and the United States had forced all other powers out of North America except the Russians in Alaska. The problems with Mexico were closer to home, more immediate, and led to war. The problems with Great Britain were longstanding and related to claims to the Pacific Northwest (or the Oregon Country) and boundary lines between Canada and the United States. The Oregon Country claims resulted from earlier explorations. In 1800, Spain ceded to France its claim to the vast Great Plains of today's United States, covering most of the land west of the Mississippi River and drained by the Mississippi-Missouri River system. In 1803, France sold these lands to the United States in the "Louisiana Purchase," and President Thomas Jefferson, sent Captains Meriwether Lewis and William Clark to explore the northern tier of the Louisiana Purchase and the Oregon Country from the Continental Divide to the Pacific Ocean. South to north, the Oregon Country stretched from the 42nd parallel to the 54°40' parallel, bordering Russian Alaska.

The British, meanwhile, were exploring the Oregon Country, coming from eastern Canada, and were expanding their interests, principally through the Hudson's Bay Company. During the War of 1812, United States interests were pushed out, but in 1818, Britain and the United States agreed to joint occupancy of the Oregon Country. It gave both nations the right to occupy and use the Oregon Country, but denied either the right to possess it. This concept of "joint occupancy" continued to be applied as years passed and the boundary dispute could not be settled. Nevertheless, in 1824, the U.S. signed a treaty with Russia fixing the northern boundary of the Oregon Country as the 54°40' parallel.

In the late 1840s the concept of "Manifest Destiny" ("to overspread and to possess the whole of the continent which Providence has given us," according to a New York editor of the time) swept the country, and its "Fifty-four-forty or fight" slogan was used by James Polk in his campaign for the Presidency. He won the election and became President in 1845, making James Buchanan his Secretary of State. Polk soon became deeply involved in problems closer to home (the Mexican War) and wanted to avoid any conflict with the British. In 1846 Buchanan negotiated the Treaty of Washington with the British Minister to the United States, Richard Packenham, making the 49th parallel the boundary between Canada and the United States in the Oregon Country, except that the British retained the whole of Vancouver Island, which extends more than 50 miles south of the 49th parallel. This presumably solved the problem. In 1848 the Oregon Territory was officially established by the United States, and in 1852 the Territorial Legislature included the San Juan Islands in one of its counties.

Domestically, the most pressing problem facing the United States was slavery. But in the Northwest, the principal problems were three: the influx of settlers (the result of the opening of the Oregon Trail, and of the glowing reports sent back by missionaries who had gone west to minister to the Indians); maintaining peace with the various Indian tribes; and territorial disputes with the British (principally the Hudson's Bay Company). The flow of settlers, including gold seekers, reached the mouth of the Columbia River and spread north and south. The area to the north of the Columbia River sought independence from the dictates of the Territorial Government, and was established as the Territory of Washington in 1853. Early the next year, the Washington Territorial Legislature made the San Juan Islands a part of Whatcom County.

In late 1854, following the Federal Government's new Indian policy of concentration — calling for tribes to be restricted to areas that the white man promised never to violate — Governor Stevens began negotiating treaties throughout the territory. However, in some cases the treaties created more problems than they solved, and difficulties with the Indians continued. In the Puget Sound region, the problems were caused primarily by raids from tribes such as the Haida and Tlingit coming down from Vancouver Island and Alaska. The settlers were concerned that these Indians would ally themselves with local tribes. A decisive engagement was fought in the summer of 1856 by the steamer *Massachusetts* with a band of Stikine Indians of the Tlingit tribe, then encamped at Port Gamble. An Indian defeat in this battle diminished the Indians' desire for major confrontation.

The problems with the British arose from the fact that the Treaty of 1846 stated only that the boundary between Vancouver Island and the U.S. would be "the middle of the channel which separates the continent from Vancouver Island," and ignored or overlooked the fact that there were some islands there (see map, "San Juan Islands," page 189). The U.S. position was that the channel referred to in the treaty was the Strait (or "canal" or "channel") of Haro between San Juan and Vancouver Islands; the British position was that it was the Strait of Rosario, east of the island group.

In 1850, the Hudson's Bay Company, with headquarters at Victoria on Vancouver Island, had established a post on San Juan Island as a fishing station, and in 1853 began to raise sheep there. They called the island "Bellevue." In 1854 a U.S. customs agent claimed that the sheep were being raised on American soil; the British countered with a warrant for his arrest, which he evaded by threatening to shoot the British constable; the officer withdrew. In 1855, the sheriff of Whatcom County tried to collect taxes from the Hudson's Bay Company for the sheep; failing to get payment, he seized about 30 sheep. The British protested, saying the island was under their jurisdiction. When the U.S. Government in Washington, D.C. learned of all this, Secretary of State William Marcy instructed Governor Stevens to have his territorial officers abstain from all acts on the disputed grounds that were calculated to provoke any conflict, but at the same time, not to concede to the British "exclusive rights over the premises."

It was against this background that Captain George Pickett arrived in the Washington Territory in mid-1856, at the head of Company D of the Ninth U.S. Infantry. Just what sort of a man was the George Pickett who was shortly to make his mark on Washington territorial history? That he was courageous is evident from his actions in the Mexican War and, later, in the Civil War. His class standing at West Point indicates a lack of interest in or understanding of academic matters. A portrait of him at the time indicates that he was of medium build with long black hair and a mustache in the fashion of the day. Freeman describes him: "In the spring of 1863 when Pickett goes to Southside, Virginia he is 38 years old, but has the good fortune of being near the home of a vivacious girl not half his age who thinks him the greatest of cavaliers. She sees nothing but romance in those long ringlets of his that his brother officers consider odd."[1] However, Longstreet, in 1898, wrote: "In memory I can see him, of medium height, of graceful build, dark glossy hair worn almost to his shoulders in curly waves, of wondrous pulchritude and magnetic presence, as he gallantly rode from me that memorable 3rd of July, 1863."[2]

This was the Pickett who, during the early summer of 1856, led his company primarily in scouting (pacifying) missions among the Indians. They operated out of Fort Steilacoom, the headquarters of Lieutenant Colonel Silas Casey, who had military responsibility for western Washington. In August, 1856, as a result of the growing number of settlers in the Puget Sound area, the problems with the Northern Indians, and the dispute with the British over the San Juans, it was

---

[1]Freeman, *Lee's Lieutenants.*
[2]Pickett, *Pickett and His Men.*

decided to establish a military fort on Bellingham Bay in Whatcom County, where a small coal mining community was in need of protection. Pickett and his company sailed from Fort Steilacoom on August 21 aboard the brig *George Emery*, and established Fort Bellingham on August 26, 1856. Fort Townsend — with Company I, Fourth Infantry under Major Granville O. Haller — was established about two months later on the other side of Puget Sound.

At Bellingham Bay, a neutral meeting ground for the various tribes, George Pickett was kept busy maintaining peace with the Indians. Pickett's wife, LaSalle, wrote in her book that Pickett became quite friendly with the Indians — particularly the Nootkas and Chinooks — and even translated a version of the Lord's Prayer into an Indian language. She does not, however, mention Pickett's marriage to an Indian "Princess" (as Pickett called her) of the Haida tribe. Pickett first met the woman at Semiahmoo, later again at Fort Bellingham. After a short courtship, they were married in both tribal and U.S. civil ceremonies, and took up residence in a house in Bellingham. On December 31, 1857, a son, James Tilton Pickett, was born; the mother died soon after the boy's birth. Because Pickett realized he could not properly care for the child, he arranged in December, 1859, for William Collins and his wife, of Mason County, to care for young Jimmie. With occasional financial support from his father, Jimmie was raised by Mrs. Collins (later Mrs. Walter). He attended the Union Academy in Olympia and an art school in California, leading to a position as an artist for the *Seattle Post-Intelligencer* and later for the *Portland Oregonian*. He died of an illness in Portland in 1889, having known of his father and his career, but never having known him personally.

In 1857, Britain and the United States created a commission to delineate the boundary, and the work began near Semiahmoo, about 25 miles north of Fort Bellingham, with a joint survey party moving east, surveying, clearing, and marking the boundary along the 49th parallel. This commission did not look into the San Juan Island controversy.

The San Juan Island situation came to a boil in June, 1859. The first (and last and only) shot of what was to become known as the "Pig War" was fired. One of the American settlers who came to the island was a young man named Lyman Cutler, who took out a claim on land near the Hudson's Bay Company's headquarters. He proceeded to fence it in and to plant a garden. A magistrate of the Company had some pigs, one of which knocked down the fence and rooted up Cutler's potatoes. On June 15 Cutler got his rifle and shot the pig. Company officials went after Cutler, threatening arrest and trial in Victoria. Cutler countered by saying he was on American soil, but offered to pay for the pig. The British chose to make an incident out of it and sent an official to arrest him; Cutler got his gun and the official departed. At about this time, Brigadier General William S. Harney, Commander of the Department of Oregon, was inspecting the American forts on Puget Sound on the steamer *Massachusetts*. After calling on Pickett at Fort Bellingham, he visited Victoria, Vancouver Island, and then San Juan Island.

Here he found about 25 settlers who had just celebrated the Fourth of July, and who petitioned him for protection from the British and the Northern Indians.

In response to this petition, on July 18, 1859, General Harney issued the following instructions[1] to Captain Pickett to establish a post on San Juan Island (he envisioned a possible four- to six-company deployment):

Headquarters Department of Oregon, Fort Vancouver, W.T., July 18, 1859.

Captain: By Special Orders No. 72, a copy of which is inclosed, you are directed to establish your company on Bellevue or San Juan Island, in some suitable position near the harbor at the southeastern extremity. The general commanding instructs me to say the object to be attained in placing you thus is twofold, viz:

First. To protect the inhabitants of the island from the incursions of the northern Indians of British Columbia and the Russian possessions. You will not permit any force of these Indians to visit San Juan Island or the waters of Puget Sound in that vicinity over which the United States have any jurisdiction. Should these Indians appear peaceable you will warn them in a quiet but firm manner to return to their own country and not visit in future the territory of the United States; and in the event of any opposition being offered to your demands, you will use the most decisive measures to enforce them, to which end the commander of the troops stationed on the steamer Massachusetts will be instructed to render every assistance and co-operation that will be necessary to enable your command to fulfill the tenor of these instructions.

Second. Another serious and important duty will devolve upon you in the occupation of San Juan Island, arising from the American citizens and the Hudson's Bay Company establishment at that point. This duty is to afford adequate protection to the American citizens in their rights as such, and to resist all attempts at interference by the British authorities residing on Vancouver Island, by intimidation or force, in the controversies of the above-mentioned parties.

This protection has been called for in consequence of the chief factor of the Hudson's Bay Company, Mr. Dallas, having recently visited San Juan Island with a British sloop of war, and threatened to take an American citizen by force to Victoria for trial by British laws. It is hoped a second attempt of this kind will not be made, but to ensure the safety of our citizens the general commanding directs you to meet the authorities from Victoria at once, on a second arrival, and inform them they can not be permitted to interfere with our citizens in any way. Any grievances they may allege as requiring redress can only be examined under our own laws, to which they must submit their claims in proper form.

The steamer Massachusetts will be directed to transport your command, stores, etc., to San Juan Island, where you are authorized to construct such temporary shelter as the necessities of the service may demand.

Any materials, such as doors, window-sash, flooring, etc. that can be rendered available will be taken with you from Fort Bellingham. To secure to your command the vegetables of your garden, a small detachment will be left to gather them when grown.

The general commanding is fully satisfied, from the varied experience and judgment displayed by you in your present command, that your selection to the

---

[1]The official U.S. Army correspondence here and throughout this monograph are reprinted from the book *Pickett and His Men*, and are also referred to in David Richardson, *Pig War Islands*. (Eastwood, Washington: Orcas Publishing Co., 1971). They are included in their entirety to give the reader a feeling of the reality of the situation.

duties with which you are now charged will advance the interests of the service, and that your disposition of the subjects coming within your supervision and action will enhance your reputation as a commander.

In your selection of a position, take into consideration that future contingencies may require an establishment of from four to six companies retaining the command of the San Juan harbor.

I am, Captain, very respectfully, your obedient servant,

A. Pleasanton,

Captain Second Dragoons, Acting Assistant Adjutant-General

Captain George Pickett, Commanding Company D, Ninth Infantry,
Fort Bellingham, Puget Sound.

In response to this letter, on the night of July 26, Pickett and 60-70 men of Company D sailed from Fort Bellingham and established a post in southeastern San Juan Island on Griffin Bay the next day. Pickett issued a proclamation that San Juan Island was U.S. territory, and was immediately confronted by three British ships, among them the *Tribune*, a 30-gun frigate, whose captain, Geoffrey Phipps Hornby, demanded that he leave. Pickett declined, saying he would fight to the last man if attacked. The British deferred. On July 30, Pickett informed Lieutenant Colonel Casey of the situation as follows:

Military Camp,
San Juan Island, W.T., July 30, 1859

My Dear Colonel: I have the honor to enclose you some notes which passed this morning between the Hudson's Bay authorities and myself. From the threatening attitude of affairs at present, I deem it my duty to request that the Massachusetts may be sent at once to this point. I do not know that any actual collision will take place, but it is not comfortable to be lying within range of a couple of war-steamers. The Tribune, a thirty-gun frigate, is lying broadside to our camp, and from present indications everything leads me to suppose that they will attempt to prevent my carrying out my instructions.

If you have any boats to spare I shall be happy to get one at least. The only whale-boat we had was, most unfortunately, staved on the day of our departure.

We will be very much in want of some tools and camp equipage. I have not the time, Colonel, to make out the proper requisition, but if your quartermaster can send us some of these articles they will be of great service.

I am, sir, in haste, very truly, your obedient servant,

G. E. Pickett,

Captain Ninth Infantry.

Lieutenant-Colonel S. Casey,
Ninth Infantry, Commanding Fort Steilacoom, W.T.

P.S. — The Shubrick has rendered us every assistance in her power, and I am much indebted for the kindness of officers.

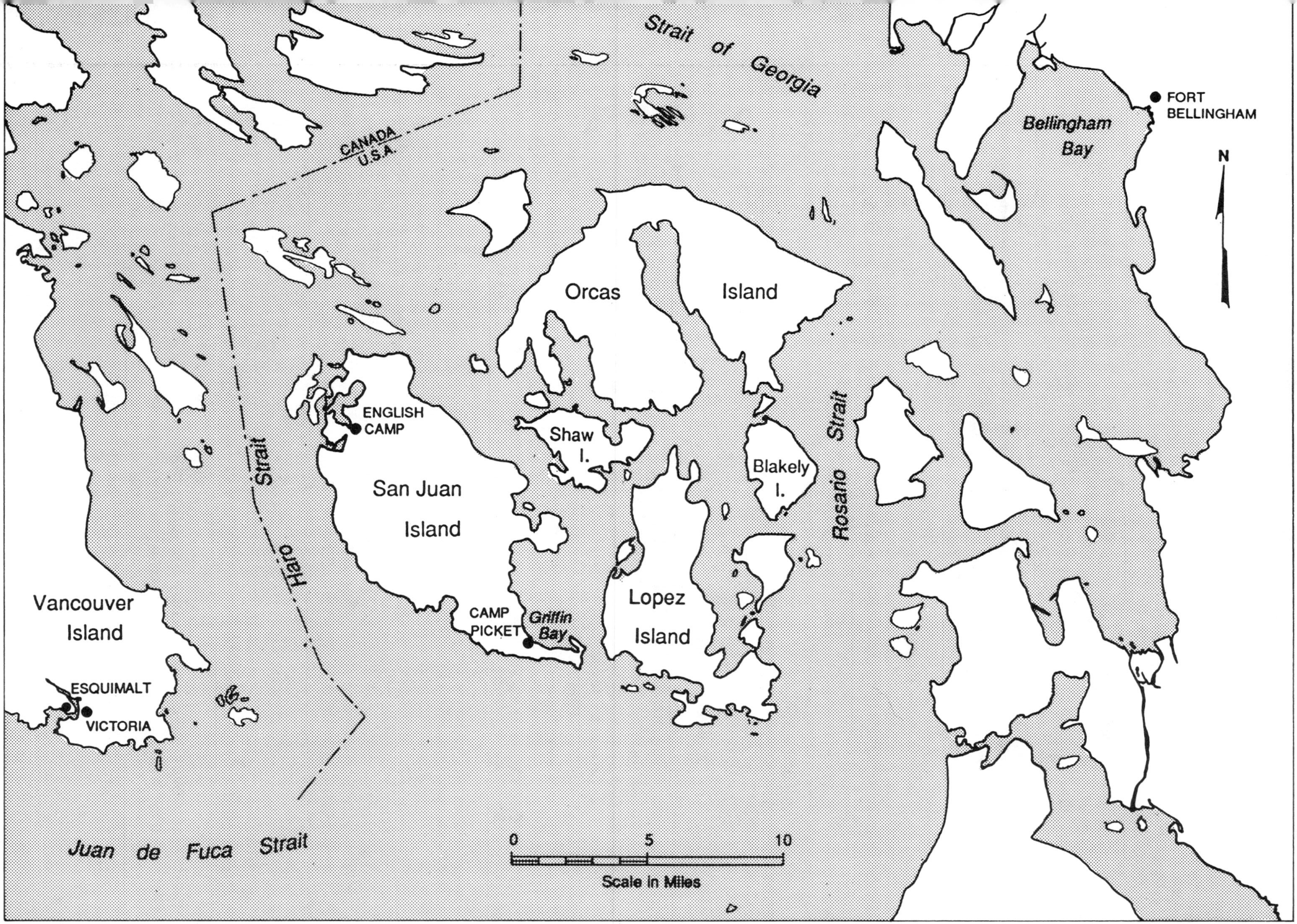

N

FORT
BELLINGHAM

Bellingham
Bay

Strait of Georgia

Rosario Strait

Blakely I.

Orcas
Island

Island

Shaw I.

Lopez
Island

ENGLISH
CAMP

San Juan
Island

CAMP
PICKET

Griffin
Bay

CANADA
U.S.A.

Haro
Strait

Vancouver
Island

ESQUIMALT
VICTORIA

Juan de Fuca Strait

0   5   10
Scale in Miles

SAN JUAN ISLANDS

The "notes" to which Pickett referred are these:

> Bellevue Farm, San Juan, July 30, 1859.
>
> Sir: I have the honor to inform you that the Island of San Juan, on which your camp is pitched, is the property and in the occupation of the Hudson's Bay Company, and to request that you and the whole of the party who have landed from the American vessels will immediately cease to occupy the same. Should you be unwilling to comply with my request, I feel bound to apply to the civil authorities.
>> Awaiting your reply I have the honor to be, sir, your obedient servant,
>> Chas. Jno. Griffin,
>> Agent Hudson's Bay Company
>
> Captain Pickett, Commanding Company D, Ninth Infantry, Island of San Juan

> Military Camp,
> San Juan, W.T., July 30, 1859
>
> Sir: Your communication of this instant has been received. I have to state in reply that I do not acknowledge the right of the Hudson's Bay Company to dictate my course of action. I am here by virtue of an order from my government, and shall remain till recalled by the same authority.
>> I am, sir, very respectfully, your obedient servant.
>
>> George E. Pickett,
>> Captain Ninth United States Infantry, Commanding
>> Island of San Juan
>
> Mr. Charles J. Griffin
> Agent Hudson's Bay Company,
> San Juan Island, W.T.

Casey responded by sending to Pickett's aid the *Massachusetts*, which Pickett had requested. Aboard were Major Haller and his company from Fort Townsend. But when they arrived, Pickett apparently declined the support, and the *Massachusetts*, with Haller and his company, sailed to Semiahmoo.

During the following period, Pickett had several meetings with Captain Hornby of the *Tribune*. Hornby was apparently impressed by Pickett, writing to his wife that Pickett "speaks more like a Devonshire man than a Yankee." However, they confronted each other with "no give" positions: Pickett to resist, and Hornby to land. Pickett is quoted as telling his troops that: "We will make a Bunker Hill of it." However, he asked Hornby for more time, and Hornby held off.

On August 3, Pickett wrote to inform General Harney of this situation, indicating that the British had proposed a "conjoint occupation" of the island, and that Pickett needed further guidance.

Military Post,
San Juan, W.T. August 3, 10 p.m.

Captain: I have the honor to report the following circumstances: The British ships the Tribune, the Plumper, the Satelite are lying here in a menacing attitude. I have been warned off by the Hudson's Bay agent; then a summons was sent to me to appear before a Mr. DeCourcey, an official of her Britianic Majesty. To-day I received the inclosed communications, and I also inclose my answer to same.

I had to deal with three captains, and I thought it better to take the brunt of it. They have a force so much superior to mine that it will be merely a mouthful for them; still I have informed them that I am here by order of my commanding general, and will maintain my position if possible.

They wish to have a conjoint occupation of the island; I decline anything of that kind. They can, if they choose, land at almost any point on the island, and I can not prevent them. I have used the utmost courtesy and delicacy in my intercourse and, if it is possible, please inform me at such an early hour as to prevent a collision.

The utmost I could expect to-day was to suspend any proceeding till they have time to digest a pill which I gave them. They wish to throw the onus on me, because I refuse to allow them to land an equal force, and each of us to have military occupation, thereby wiping out both civil authorities.

I say I can not do so until I hear from the general.

I have endeavored to impress them with the idea that my authority comes directly through you from Washington.

The Pleiades left this morning for San Francisco with Colonel Hawkins.

The excitement in Victoria and here is tremendous. I suppose some five hundred people have visited us. I have had to use a great deal of peace-making disposition in order to restrain some of the sovereigns.

Please excuse this hasty and, I am afraid, almost unintelligible letter, but the steamer is waiting, and I have been writing under the most unfavorable circumstances. I must add that they seem to doubt the authority of the general commanding, and do not wish to acknowledge his right to occupy this island, which they say is in dispute, unless the United States government has decided the question with Great Britain. I have so far staved them off by saying that the two governments have undoubtedly settled this affair, but this state of affairs can not last, and therefore I most respectfully ask that an express be sent me immediately for my future guidance. I do not think there are any moments to waste. In order to maintain our dignity we must occupy in force, or allow them to land an equal force, which they can do now, and possibly will do in spite of my diplomacy.

I have the honor to inclose all the correspondence which has taken place. Hoping that my course of action will meet with the approval of the general commanding, and that I may hear from him in regard to my future course at once, I remain, Captain, your obedient servant.

G. E. Pickett,
Captain Ninth Infantry, Commanding Post

Captain A. Pleasonton,
Mounted Dragoons, Adjutant-General,
Department of Oregon, Fort Vancouver, W.T.

In the communications to which Pickett refers in his August 3 report, Hornby indicates that a joint military occupation is the only remaining feasible course of action likely to prevent a "collision" between opposing forces. He regrets that Pickett was unable to agree, and states: "The responsibility of any such catastrophe does not, I feel, rest on me or her Majesty's representative at Vancouver Island." Pickett's reply states that he cannot agree to any joint occupation until so ordered by his commanding general, and that if Hornby acts he "will then be the person who will bring a most disastrous difficulty, and not the United States officials."

General Harney, in his reply to Pickett, asserts that "no joint occupancy will be permitted," and that he is instructing Lieutenant Colonel Casey to reinforce him. (What the unfortunate Lieutenant Howard did is not recorded).

> Headquarters Department of Oregon,
> Fort Vancouver, W.T., August 6, 1859
>
> Captain: The general commanding instructs me to inform you of the receipt of Governor Douglas's protest to the occupation of San Juan Island, and directs me to inclose a communication, which you will request Captain Hornby, of her Majesty's ship Tribune, to transmit to Governor Douglas with all convenient dispatch.
>
> The general approves the course you have pursued, and further directs that no joint occupation or any civil jurisdiction will be permitted on San Juan Island by the British authorities under any circumstances.
>
> Lieutenant-Colonel Casey is ordered to reinforce you with his command as soon as possible.
>
> Send Lieutenant Howard to Fort Steilacoom in arrest.
>
> I am, Captain, very respectfully, your obedient servant.
>
> A. Pleasanton,
> Captain Second Dragoons, Acting Assistant Adjutant-General
>
> Captain George Pickett,
> Ninth Infantry Commanding on San Juan Island,
> Puget Sound, W.T.

Casey responded by sailing with all available troops and landing in a fog the night of August 9-10 at Griffin Bay, literally under the guns of the British ships, and assumed command. By mid-August he had a total of five infantry and four artillery companies (from the U.S. Fourth and Ninth Infantry and Third Artillery) — a force of about 450 men. The British had available on board ship or nearby a force of about 1,940 men (according to *Pig War Islands*).[1] Fortunately, both sides refrained from "firing the first shot," and at this point, apparently, negotiation and diplomacy took over.

Before long Washington, D.C. learned of the situation. James Buchanan — negotiator of the Treaty of 1846 — was now President and not eager to start a war with Britain, particularly over what some referred to as "a few paltry islands." Although he told Harney that he believed the Strait of Haro to be the proper

---

[1]Richardson, *Pig War Islands*.

boundary line, he did not expect Harney to take possession of the San Juans. The Secretary of War sent the Commander-in-Chief of the Army, Major General Winfield Scott (of Mexican War fame), to straighten things out, telling him that the President's main objective was to preserve the peace and prevent conflict until the title question could be resolved by the two governments.

Scott arrived at the entrance of the Columbia River on October 20, 1859. He told Harney (who came down from Fort Vancouver) that a joint military occupation of the San Juans would be proposed, and then sailed from Puget Sound to get the British agreement. This was not easy; but eventually the British (through Governor Douglas of British Columbia) agreed to a reduced force of about 100 men on each side (Scott had planned to leave Pickett in charge, but Douglas is said to have written a confidential note to Scott saying: "any company except Captain Pickett's"). On November 7, Lieutenant Colonel Casey received orders from Scott that all troops on San Juan Island should be returned to their forts, except one commanded by Captain Lewis C. Hunt, Fourth Infantry, from Fort Steilacoom. Thus George Pickett and his company returned to Fort Bellingham. However, the camp he left on San Juan became known as "Camp Pickett."

Now, for a period of time, Pickett was back to his old duties of patrolling the Bellingham area. Captain Hunt (who later married Lieutenant Colonel Casey's daughter) began to have problems with General Harney, the local populace, and liquor control. Finally, on April 10, 1860, Harney ordered Pickett and his company back to San Juan Island and ordered Hunt and his company to Fort Steilacoom. The detailed instructions reprinted below resulted in the removal of Harney from his command. It remains a mystery why Harney acted in apparent ignorance of Scott's agreement with Governor Douglas for "joint occupancy." It may be that General Harney considered the actions of the Territorial Government of Washington (and that of Oregon, previously), in claiming the San Juan Islands to be U.S. territory, to be "the law of the land."

Headquarters Department of Oregon,
Fort Vancouver, W.T., April 10, 1860.

Captain: You will perceive by Special Orders No. 41, of this date, a copy of which is inclosed, that the general commanding has replaced you in command of your company on San Juan Island.

For your information in this position you receive, as accompanying papers, the correspondence and instructions of Lieutenant-General Scott with reference to San Juan Island, with an extract from the orders of Rear-Admiral Baynes, commanding her Britanic Majesty's naval forces in the Pacific, to Captain George Bazalgette, of the Royal Marines, commanding a detachment of Royal Marines landed on San Juan Island by the consent of General Scott. These orders of Admiral Baynes communicate to his officer that he is placed on the island for the protection of British interests, and to form a joint military occupation with the troops of the United States.

To meet these orders of the admiral, and to remove any misconception on the part of the British authorities as to your duties, I am directed to impart to you the following explanations and requirements of the general commanding, a copy of which you will furnish Captain Bazalgette for the information of Rear-Admiral Baynes:

First. Lieutenant-General Scott has left no orders or instructions with the general commanding to grant a joint military occupation of San Juan Island with British troops; neither has any authority been delegated by the government of the United States to the general to offer or accept such occupation of that island. The offer made by General Scott, when in command here, was not accepted by Governor Douglas at the time, and consequently concluded that transaction. No arrangement has been made since to review it, within the knowledge of the general commanding.

Second. The British authorities having submitted the assurance to General Scott that no attempt would be made by them to dislodge by force the United States troops on San Juan Island, they were permitted to land troops for similar purposes to which your command was designed in the original orders conveyed to you in July last, viz., the protection of our citizens from Indians both native and foreign. In connection with this service, the general commanding takes occasion to present you to Admiral Baynes and the officers with whom you will be brought in contact, as an office possessing his highest confidence, and nothing will be omitted in maintaining a frank and generous intercourse in all matters coming within your powers to establish a practical solution of the present misunderstanding, which shall prove honorable and satisfactory to all parties, until a final settlement is attained by the governments.

Third. Under the organic act of the Congress of the United States for the establishment of the Territorial government of Washington, the first legislative assembly in 1854 passed an act including the island of San Juan as a part of Whatcom County. This act was duly submitted to Congress, and has not been disapproved; it is, therefore, the law of the land. You will be obliged, consequently, to acknowledge and respect the civil jurisdiction of Washington Territory in the discharge of your duties on San Juan, and the general commanding is satisfied that any attempt of the British commander to ignore this right of the Territory will be followed by deplorable results, out of his power to prevent or to control. The general commanding will inform the Governor of Washington Territory that you are directed to communicate with the civil officer on the island in the investigation of all cases requiring his attention. In the event of any British interests being involved, you will notify the officer placed there by Admiral Baynes to enable him to propose some arrangement satisfactory to his instructions, as well as those of the civil officer. Let it be understood in case of disagreement of these parties that no action is to be taken until the case has been referred to Admiral Baynes and the Governor of Washington Territory, respectively.

These suggestions will be acceptable to the conditions which govern the Territorial authorities of Washington, while satisfying the obligations of the military service to their own as well as the civil laws of the country, and it is fair to presume they will be adopted by Admiral Baynes, since the tenor of his instructions to Captain Bazalgette is sufficiently liberal to justify this conclusion.

I remain, Captain, very respectfully, your obedient servant.
A. Pleasanton
Captain Second Dragoons, Acting Assistant Adjutant-General

Captain George E. Pickett,
Commanding Company D, Ninth Infantry,
Fort Bellingham, Puget Sound. W.T.

When the President and his Cabinet in Washington, D.C. learned about this (Captain Hunt may have helped with a personal letter to General Scott about General Harney's action), the Secretary of War relieved Harney of his command and replaced him with Colonel George Wright on June 8, 1860. Wright seemed to

Above: **Camp Pickett, San Juan Island, 1859.**

Below: **British Royal Marines and Headquarters,
Roche Harbor, San Juan Island, 1861.**

[Both photos, Provincial Archives, Victoria, British Columbia]

have had confidence in Pickett, for he left him in command on San Juan Island and gave him considerable latitude in his actions.

Pickett took command on San Juan Island in the latter part of April, 1860, and immediately found that his major problems were no longer with the British but with the local populace, which seemed to have accumulated a considerable number of undesirable scoundrels and drunks (the same situation that Captain Hunt had faced). He later referred to San Juan Town as rowdy and roistering, and "a bedlam day and night." His first action was to get a suitable civil officer for the area. E. C. Gillette of Whatcom County was appointed Justice of the Peace and U.S. Commissioner for the island, and arrived toward the end of May. Pickett and Gillette began to crack down on the illegal liquor trade and to bring to justice the murderers and robbers of a Haida Indian who had been killed in San Juan Town. Before long, some semblance of peace and order was restored to the area.

During this period a company of British Marines commanded by a Captain Bazalgette established a camp in the northernmost part of San Juan Island, near present-day Roche Harbor, which became known as "English Camp." A cordial relationship developed between Pickett and Bazalgette and no further disputes developed between the two. Pickett was able to devote almost all of his time to cleaning up the lawlessness he had found when he returned to San Juan. But in April, 1861, shots were fired at Fort Sumter, and the Civil War began. On June 25, 1861, George Pickett resigned his commission in the United States Army and left for Virginia to become a colonel in the Confederate Army.

Thus ends the Washington Territory chapter of the George Pickett story. The "joint occupancy" situation on San Juan Island remained unresolved until 1869, when the United States and Britain agreed to turn the matter over to Kaiser Wilhelm of Germany for arbitration, and to be bound by his decision. The Kaiser established a panel of "experts" who eventually gave him a "two to one" recommendation in favor of the U.S. position. He endorsed this in 1872, "the Canal de Haro" to be the boundary, with the San Juan Islands going to the U.S. The countries agreed, and the British finally evacuated in November, 1873. On October 31, 1873, the Washington Legislature created San Juan County for the islands.

Though Pickett's efforts in Washington Territory were overshadowed by his renowned exploits during the Civil War, they were not altogether forgotten. An article dated August 7, 1875, at the time of Pickett's death and reportedly written by General George B. McClellan, a Union General who, like Pickett, had earlier been stationed in the Washington Territory reads: "It is a fact not generally known, that the movements which are referred to herein, occupation of San Juan, had their origin in the patriotic attempt on the part of General Harney, Governor Stevens, of Washington Territory, and other Democratic federal officers on the coast, with the knowledge and zealous concurrence of Captain Pickett, to force a war with Great Britain in the hopes that by this means the then warring sections of our country would unite in a foreign war, and avert the civil strife they feared they saw approaching." That such a motive for the San Juan incidents actually existed is questionable. Certainly Pickett could have opened fire on the British and started hostilities; but he did not. Instead he asked for time to consult his superior. In addition, he appears to have been rather conciliatory toward the British. Governor

Resolution

Tendering thanks to Captain Pickett, U.S.A.

Resolved, By the Legislative Assembly of the Territory of Washington that the thanks of the people of this Territory are due Captain Pickett U.S.A. for the gallant and firm discharge of his duties under the most trying circumstances with it was in command on the Island of San Juan,

Passed the House of Representatives
January 9th 1860

Speaker of the House of Representatives

Passed the Council
February 11th 1860

President of the Council

**The Territory of Washington House of Representatives'
Resolution Thanking Captain Pickett**

Stevens did not get involved, directly at least. Harney appears to have been the most bellicose, but seems to have been acting in accordance with the desires of the local territorial government, if not of Washington, D.C.

Is George Pickett worthy of the appellation "Defender of the San Juans"? He was, after all, only a captain in the Army with a small command. But in those days a captain had much more authority than one of today. Pickett, in particular, was dealing directly with representatives of a foreign government and with local civilian authorities, with only meager communications available to higher command. Pickett not only held out against the British demands, but also was instrumental in establishing law and order on San Juan Island. David Richardson, in his *Pig War Islands*, says that Pickett did a "surprisingly creditable job of restoring order and seemed more than willing to keep the peace with the British." Of Pickett, Richardson writes: "This man who stood up so valorously before overwhelming British forces at Griffin Bay would long remain the island's foremost local hero."[1]

Finally, in January of 1860, the Legislature of the Territory of Washington passed a resolution thanking Captain Pickett, U.S.A., "for the gallant and firm discharge of his duties under the most trying circumstances while he was in command on the Island of San Juan."

Colonel Ernest J.Whitaker
U.S. Army, Retired
USMA Class of 1941

---

[1]Richardson, *Pig War Islands*.

JOHN MULLAN, JR.:
ROAD BUILDER

Night after night I have laid out in the unbeaten forest or on the pathless prairies
with no bed but a few pine needles, with no pillow but my saddle, and in my
imagination heard the whistle of the engine, the whir of the machinery, the paddle
of the steam-boat wheels, as they ploughed the waters of the Sound. In my
enthusiasm I saw the country thickly populated, thousands pouring over the borders
to make homes in this far western land.

So spoke John Mullan, Jr. on April 18, 1888 to the *Tacoma Ledger*, which went on
to describe him as "a man inseparably linked with the early history of the
Northwest," "practically the first engineer of the Northern Pacific Railway," and
"the man who built the famous Mullan Road."

Born to an Irish immigrant father and a native Virginian mother in Norfolk,
Virginia on July 31, 1830, John Mullan, Jr., the eldest of 10 children, gained
admission to West Point by means of a personal visit to President James K. Polk.
Extending his hand to Mullan, President Polk said: "Well, my little man, what can
I do for you?" Mullan, who stood less than five and a half feet tall but was stocky
and well muscled, told of his wish to enter the Army by graduating from West
Point. After questioning him for some time, the President is reported to have said:
"Well, my young friend, leave your address and I will see what I can do for you."
Notice of his appointment arrived six weeks later. He graduated 15th in a class of
43 in June, 1852, and was breveted second lieutenant in the First Artillery.

The Washington Territory, formed by Congress in March, 1853, was ripe for
the unique talents of this ambitious young officer. In 1853 the only continuous
overland wagon road into the Pacific Northwest was the Oregon Trail. North of
that, travel routes were limited to what little navigable water there was, and to
game and Indian trails. The Washington Territory extended from the Columbia
River and the 46th parallel north 250 miles and westward from the crest of the
Rocky Mountains some 600 miles to the Pacific Ocean. The few settlers in the area
could be found only along the lower Columbia and the shores of Puget Sound.
Largely unexplored by white men, the territory was roamed by thousands of
Indians. Some tribes were friendly, but many bitterly resented the intrusion of the
white man.

In March, 1853 Isaac Stevens, newly appointed first Governor of the Territory
of Washington, was placed in charge of a survey for a proposed northern route
railroad extending westward from the Mississippi River to Puget Sound. Mullan
volunteered for, and was assigned to, the Stevens party. When the expedition
reached Fort Benton, Montana (about 39 miles northeast of present-day Great
Falls), Mullan was sent forward to the Bitterroot Valley to greet the Flathead Indians. En route, he was to seek the best path across the Rocky Mountains from the

Lieutenant John Mullan, Jr.

[Beverly Jaquish, artist, U.S. Department of Agriculture, Forest Service]

headwaters of the Missouri. This was a 400-mile trip, which crossed the Continental Divide at a place near the head of Prickly Pear Creek, now known as Mullan's Pass. When the Stevens main party moved west to Washington, Mullan was left at Fort Owen (vicinity of Missoula, Montana) in charge of a meteorological detachment to observe and collect data on winter conditions. Within a single year he had crossed the Continental Divide at least six times and traveled more than a thousand miles. He gathered weather data, measured elevations, talked with Indians and kept elaborate records. His engineering and weather data indicated that a railroad could cross the Rocky Mountains, and resulted in a Congressional appropriation to survey a 50-mile strip (50,000 square miles) in the area recommended by Mullan.

Mullan's final task under Stevens was to find a suitable westward route from the Bitterroot Valley to Fort Walla Walla. After examining all known or reported passes, he selected a line across the Coeur d'Alene Mountains through a pass named for his guide and interpreter, Gustav Sohon, a capable artist and gifted linguist who contributed greatly to Mullan's success.[1]

Mullan gained the confidence of Indians wintering in the Bitterroot Valley by making a practice of calling them together before each exploratory trip to explain his purpose. They, in turn, called on him to mediate in solving various problems, accepting his decisions with good humor. Governor Stevens later reported, "I received from Mullan at every opportunity, reports in regard to the Indian tribes, which were of the greatest service, and which enabled me to better comprehend their feelings. The fact that he left the valley in 1854 with the sincere regrets of all the Indians who knew or had heard of him is the best evidence of his services in connection with them."

Following the railroad surveys of 1853 and 1854, Mullan proceeded to Olympia to make his report to Governor Stevens. In January, 1855, Mullan left for Washington, D.C. carrying resolutions passed by the Legislature of the Territory of Washington recommending that Mullan continue his surveys and start building the proposed wagon road. Though Congress had appropriated funds for the project, the War Department, claiming the Congressional appropriation of $30,000 inadequate, would not authorize the work to continue at that time.

On February 25, 1855, Mullan was promoted to First Lieutenant, Second Artillery. Later that same year he received a Master of Arts degree from St. John's College in Annapolis, Maryland. He served at various Army posts from 1855 to 1857. In 1857 Governor Stevens, now Territorial Delegate from Washington Territory to the U.S. Congress, worked diligently for continuation of the road project and Mullan's appointment as Officer in Charge. The Army Topographical Engineers did not favor the appointment of Mullan, an artillery officer, to this assignment.

Back in Washington Territory, Indian uprisings were prompted partly by rumors of the military road being built through Indian lands and partly by the failure of the government to meet obligations arising from the treaties negotiated

---

[1]Sohon Pass, now called St. Regis pass, is two miles south of Interstate-90's present crossing at Lookout Pass on the Idaho-Montana border.

by Governor Stevens. The growing Indian trouble influenced the War Department to proceed with the road. Stevens's influence prevailed over the Topographical Engineers, and Mullan received his special assignment to begin the Mullan Road survey.

Mullan arrived at Fort Dalles, Oregon, on May 15, 1858, just after a coalition of tribes had badly mauled Brevet Lieutenant Colonel E. J. Steptoe's command in the Battle of Tohotonimme, near today's Rosalia, Washington. When Colonel George Wright campaigned in retaliation during August to October, Mullan served as the Colonel's topographical officer and Chief of Scouts with 33 Nez Perce Indians under his command. Mullan gained valuable knowledge of terrain for his future military road. During this period Mullan participated in the Battle of Four Lakes, the Battle of the Spokane Plains, and a skirmish along the Spokane River. On one occasion he was lucky to survive a hand-to-hand fight with a hostile Indian of powerful build, an encounter described by a fellow officer in terms befitting a John Wayne movie.

On March 18, 1859, six months after the "Wright Campaign," the War Department ordered Mullan to proceed with the military road and gave him the first $100,000 with which to do it. His command consisted of 100 soldiers for protection from any hostile Indians, 100 civilian workers, a few surveyors and engineers, a sizable herd of horses, and many wagons.

The Military Road began at the old Hudson's Bay Fort Walla Walla on the Columbia, now called Wallula (*not* the Army Fort Walla Walla near Waiilatpu, 30 miles east of Wallula, now the Veterans Hospital on the outskirts of the city of Walla Walla). The 30-mile road from the old to the new fort was part of the earlier Oregon Trail. Mullan set out from new Fort Walla Walla heading north and a bit east. He crossed the Snake River at the mouth of the Tucannon tributary, and pressed on to Spangle (on today's Highway 195), 33 miles south of Spokane. From there he proceeded to the southern edge of Lake Coeur d'Alene and on to the Coeur d'Alene Mission.[1] The Coeur d'Alene Indians were the first to oppose the road-building efforts, and caused much delay by giving false information. Mullan told some of them that Colonel Wright had ordered the road built at once, and that Mullan was to hang any obstructionists. If Mullan wouldn't do it, Wright would come and do it himself. No further acts of hindrance or sabotage were reported.

Mullan proceeded past the present mining towns of Kellogg and Wallace, Idaho, to Missoula, Montana, and, finally, to Fort Benton. The longest and most difficult stretch of road to build was the 120-mile section through the tangle of mountains between Lake Coeur d'Alene and the Clark Fork River in Montana. The terrain was heavily timbered, and the work was made still more difficult by the amount of downed dead timber that had to be cleared away. An 1863 traveler counted 69 crossings of the South Fork of the Coeur d'Alene River, most of them fords. Winter overtook Mullan in early December, 1859. Deep snow and 40-below-zero temperatures plagued his efforts. He lost most of his horses and all of his cattle; the cattle were butchered and frozen for food. Meat and flour were available, but no fruit and vegetables. Twenty-five men contracted scurvy.

---

[1]Near Cataldo, Idaho on today's Interstate-90.

Building the 624-mile Mullan Road, including surveys, took seven years and cost the Federal Government $230,000. It was primitive but was meant to be no better. It was passable for only a few months during summer and fall, because many bridges were washed out by high water every spring, and deep snows prevented winter travel. Maintenance was left up to people traveling the road. Nevertheless, the Mullan Road was a remarkable accomplishment, contributing much to opening up the Pacific Northwest. Today's Interstate-90 closely follows the Mullan Road's most difficult mountain stretches between Spokane, Washington and Deer Lodge, Montana — testimony to Mullan's choice of route.

Travel over the new road began even before completion. During the first year the road was used by an estimated 20,000 people, both settlers and Indians; 5,000 head of cattle; 6,000 horses and mules, most pulling freight wagons; 52 light wagons; and 31 heavier immigrant wagons. Mullan's 200-page report to the War Department and Congress at the completion of the road commented on the productivity of the Walla Walla area: 30 bushels of wheat, 40 of oats and barley, and 200 of potatoes per acre, as well as high yields of corn and fruit. Mullan also correctly predicted the mineral wealth of the present Coeur d'Alene mining district. He had no idea that it would come from lead, silver and zinc rather than the gold whose fantastical gleam fired the spirits of mid-19th century adventurers.

In 1859, when the road was being developed near the Coeur d'Alene Mission, one of Mullan's men discovered a little gold in a creek bed. Rather than show the sample to his fellow workers, he secretly brought it directly to Mullan, who immediately recognized it as gold. After looking at it carefully, Mullan expressed the opinion that it was worthless, but assured the man he would investigate it further. Realizing that his crew might disintegrate if the news of the gold find got out, Mullan immediately transferred the man to a different area. In his report to Congress he recognized this as one of the major crises of his road-building project.

After completing the road in 1862, Mullan resigned his Army commission as a captain — although the Civil War was in progress — and purchased 360 acres of Walla Walla land. He invited three of his brothers to join him on the farm. But disputes among the brothers resulted in Mullan's leaving the land to them and traveling to Washington, D.C. to complete his reports. While in the East he married Rebecca Williamson of Baltimore in 1863. They had five children, two of whom died in infancy; two daughters and a son survived.

Mullan next obtained a four-year contract to carry the mail from Chico, California to Ruby City, Idaho, and attempted to establish an express business. Within a year he was forced out of business by competition. He then settled in San Francisco, where he began a successful law practice. In 1865 he published *Miners' and Travelers' Guide to Oregon, Washington, Idaho, Montana, Wyoming, and Colorado via The Missouri and Columbia Rivers*. In 1878 he moved to Washington, D.C. and there continued his legal work until health forced his retirement. He died December 28, 1909, at the age of 79.

Colonel Wayne H. Elliott
U.S. Army, Retired
USMA Class of 1952

Appendix

CONTRIBUTING AUTHORS

Bradley, Robert L., USMA Class of 1949, was born in Augusta, Georgia, and entered West Point on a Presidential appointment. An Armor officer, he served in command and staff positions in the United States, Europe, and Vietnam. His decorations include three awards of the Legion of Merit and two foreign medals. Having been an instructor at the U.S. Military Academy and at the Command and General Staff College, he has continued teaching since his retirement, and is an adjunct faculty member of Pierce College, near Fort Lewis. He settled in the town of Steilacoom, Washington, served on its Planning Commission, and was elected to the Town Council. A member of the local Historical Association, he has contributed articles to its *Quarterly* and its Centennial book, *Town on the Sound: Stories of Steilacoom* — both publications co-edited by his wife, Bette. He is a member of the Board of Directors of the Friends of the Fort Lewis Military Museum and co-editor of its periodical *The Red Shield Banner*, to which he contributes regularly.

Cole, Thomas F., USMA Class of 1952, was born in Los Angeles, California. Commissioned in Armor, he fought as a platoon leader in the Korean War and as an armored cavalry squadron commander in the Vietnam War. His other assignments have included another tour in Korea, a tour in Japan, two tours in Germany, two tours at the USMA, service in the Office of the Army Chief of Staff and on the Joint Chiefs of Staff, command of Europe's Combined Arms Training Center and the National Training Center at Fort Irwin, command of the Army's largest heavy brigade, and service as Deputy Commander of the 6th U.S. Army. His decorations include the Distinguished Service Medal, three awards of the Legion of Merit, and the Bronze Star Medal for Valor. Major General Cole (U.S. Army, Retired) lives in Olympia, Washington, is a consultant for Titan Corporation, chairs the Fort Lewis Retiree Council, and serves on the Board of Trustees of the NMMI Foundation.

Elliott, Wayne H., USMA Class of 1952, was raised in Coeur d'Alene, Idaho. He commanded field artillery units in both the Korean and Vietnam conflicts. Other military assignments have included the Department of the Army staff in the Pentagon, operational testing of military equipment and employment concepts, and a tour as instructor of military history at West Point. Colonel Elliott (U.S. Army, Retired) lives in Tacoma, Washington, where he works as a financial analyst.

Fenili, Vasco, USMA Class of January, 1943, was born in Illinois and raised in New Jersey. Commissioned in Cavalry, he was first assigned to the Tank Destroyer Battalion, with which he served through the Central Europe and Rhineland campaigns of World War II. He was an Intelligence Staff Officer in 7th Army Headquarters during the Occupation of Germany, and later served several times in

Intelligence at the national level. Other assignments include military school and military college instructor, and commander of armor units in Korea and Germany. Brigadier General Fenili (U.S. Army, Retired) lives in Lakewood, Washington, where he serves the community as a volunteer in local, state, and national efforts as diverse as the Chamber of Commerce, museum management, social and health services, and yard and garden clubs.

Hemphill, John A., USMA Class of 1951, was born and raised in Boise, Idaho. A parachute- and Ranger-trained infantryman, he served in the Korean and Vietnam conflicts as a combat unit commander. Other military assignments included the Pentagon, unified command headquarters, operational testing, and Reserve Component training. His military decorations include the Distinguished Service Cross, three awards of the Purple Heart, both the Department of Defense and the Army Distinguished Service Medals, two awards of the Silver Star, the Defense Superior Medal, four awards of the Legion of Merit, 30 awards of other United States decorations, and six foreign decorations. Major General Hemphill (U.S. Army, Retired) lives in Steilacoom, a historical Washington town, supports the community as President of the Steilacoom Chamber of Commerce, and helps put on the town's annual Fourth of July fireworks salute to the nation.

Howze, Charles N., USMA Class of 1931, was born in Marion, Alabama. Initially serving in the Army ground forces, he was detailed into the Army Air Corps during the air arm build-up in the late 1930s, and completed his 30-year military career with the U. S. Air Force in staff and command assignments. He is a graduate of the National War College and the Air War College. In World War II, he served with the 9th Air Force in Europe, followed by assignment as the Department of the Air Force's Chief of Logistics Plans in the Pentagon. Other assignments included: Commander, Air Logistics Wing, Korea during the Korean War; and Commander, Air Depot, Japan. His decorations include the Legion of Merit, two awards of the Bronze Star, four awards of the Commendation Medal, the French Croix de Guerre, and the Luxembourg Croix de Guerre. Colonel Howze (U.S. Air Force, Retired) lived in Seattle, participated in numerous volunteer activities, and served as secretary to the West Point Society of Puget Sound. He died on December 22, 1991.

Matter, Robert A., USMA Class of 1939, was born and raised in Pennsylvania, from where he won an appointment to West Point. Commissioned in the Infantry, he commanded all types of infantry units from platoon through regiment. Other assignments included Director of Intelligence, Headquarters Alaskan Department during World War II; G-2, USMC Troop Training Unit, Amphibious Forces, Pacific Fleet; G-4 Section, Headquarters Eighth Army during the Korean War; 10th Special Forces Group Plans Chief, Europe; Civil Affairs Officer, Headquarters Seventh Army, Europe; G-3 Section, Headquarters Sixth Army, where his responsibilities included general staff supervision of troop participation in atomic shots at the Nevada Test Site; Commander, U.S. Military Group (Army and Air Force Missions) El Salvador; and Professor of Military Science, Seattle University. He is a graduate of the Command and General Staff College Command and Special Weapons Courses, the Infantry School, and the Army Language School (Spanish). His decorations include two Legions of Merit and the Salvadoran Medal of Merit. After retirement from the Army, he earned an MA degree in history at Seattle University and a Ph.D. in history at the University of Washington, where he was a Woodrow Wilson Dissertation Fellow. He subsequently taught history at Green River Community College, Seattle University, and aboard U.S. Navy vessels, as well as at remote Air Force and Coast Guard stations in Alaska for Chapman College, retiring as an Associate Professor. He has written several historical articles, and his doctoral thesis on *Pre-Seminole Florida* recently was published as one of 31 outstanding dissertations on North American Indians. He is a member of the Governor of Florida's Spanish Mission Trail Committee to help plan that state's commemoration of the 1992 Columbian Quincentennial. Colonel Matter has resided in Seattle since 1963.

Smith, C. Coburn, USMA Class of 1931, was born in the Philippine Islands. He entered the U.S. Military Academy through the California National Guard, graduating with the class of 1931. During World War II he served in North Africa and Italy on the 5th Army staff. In the Korean War he commanded Division and Corps artillery, with a short stint on the 8th Army staff. After two years on the Army War College faculty, he went to Germany as Commanding General of the 8th Division Artillery, and later VII Corps Artillery. His final tour was as U.S. Army Attaché to France. He now resides in Issaquah, Washington, and is Treasurer of the West Point Society of Puget Sound.

Sonstelie, Richard R., USMA Class of 1966, is the President of Puget Sound Power & Light Company, headquartered in Bellevue, Washington. A native of Ottawa, Canada, Sonstelie served with the U.S. Army Corps of Engineers, saw combat as a company commander in Vietnam, and later served as a project manager at Los Alamos Scientific Laboratories, New Mexico. Sonstelie holds master's degree in nuclear engineering from Massachusetts Institute of Technology, and business administration from Harvard. In 1987 he was appointed Civilian Aide to the Secretary of the Army for the State of Washington.

Whitaker, Ernest J., USMA Class of 1941, was born in September, 1916, at Norfolk, Virginia. Appointed to West Point from Pennsylvania in 1937, he was graduated in 1941 as a second lieutenant of Field Artillery. During the Second World War he served in Europe during 1943-45 with Armored Field Artillery units, and won two Bronze Stars. In 1951-52, he served in the Korean War on the staff of the 24th Division Artillery. He was Deputy Chief of the Army-Air Force Japan and Korea Exchange System in 1953-54, winning the Legion of Merit Medal. Colonel Whitaker's other assignments have included two tours on the Department of the Army's General Staff (1948-50 and 1955-58); and Program and Budget Manager for the Continental Army Command (1963-65), which won him his second Legion of Merit Medal. He holds an MBA degree from Harvard University, awarded in 1948. Retiring from the Army in 1965, he took up residence on Mercer Island,

Washington, where he still lives. For 15 years, he taught business administration at the Seattle Community Colleges. He and his wife Mary Kay have six sons and nine grandchildren.

Worthington, Fayette L., USMA Class of 1945, was born in Fort Reno, Oklahoma, and entered the military service from Texas. He was commissioned in the Corps of Engineers. As a lieutenant he served in the Seattle Engineer District, where he worked on the construction of the Veterans Administration Hospital on Beacon Hill, and the early phase of Chief Joseph Dam on the Columbia River. He served repeatedly in construction planning and in command of engineer combat units. Other military assignments included the War Plans Division of the Army Staff, Engineer officer assignments, and Post Engineer of Fort Lewis, Washington. He served 10 and a half years overseas, including duty in the Philippine Islands, Japan, France, Germany, and two tours in Vietnam. He holds Master's degrees from both Texas A&M and George Washington University, and is a graduate of the Army War College. Colonel Worthington's military decorations include three awards of the Army Commendation Medal, five awards of the Legion of Merit, and other United States and foreign decorations. He retired in 1975 and lives with his wife, Yole, in Lakewood, near Tacoma, Washington.

Cumbow, Robert C., Editor, has been a teacher, a corporate communications manager, and a free lance writer. He edited *A Century of Service*, a history of the Puget Sound Power & Light Company, and is the author of *Pardon Me, Roy & Other Groaners*, *Once Upon a Time: The Films of Sergio Leone*, and *Order in the Universe: The Films of John Carpenter*. In 1991 he graduated from the University of Puget Sound School of Law and is now an associate with the Seattle law firm Perkins Coie.

BIBLIOGRAPHY

WEST POINTERS AND EARLY WASHINGTON

THE SETTING: A Decade of Washington Territory, 1853-1862

Archives

United States Military Academy Archives, West Point, New York.

"Cullum Files," Special Collections Division, United States Military Academy Library, West Point, New York.

Books

Annual Reports of the Association of Graduates. United States Military Academy Archives.West Point, New York.

Bennett, R. A. *A Small World of Our Own.* Walla Walla, Washington: Pioneer Press Books, 1985.

Bonney, W. P. *History of Pierce County, Washington.* Vol. 1 Chicago: Pioneer Historical Publishing Company, 1927.

Brown, F. R. *History of the Ninth U.S. Infantry, 1799-1909.* Chicago: R.R. Donnellely & Sons Company, 1909.

Brown, W. C. *The Indian Side of the Story.* Spokane: C.W. Hill Publishing Company, 1961.

Cross, F. E. and Parkin, C. M., Jr. *Captain Grey in the Pacific Northwest.* Second edition. Bend, Oregon: Maverick Publications, 1987. (Originally published in 1981 as *Sea Venture: Captain Grey's Voyages of discovery 1787-1793,* by Valkyrie Publishing House, Inc.)

Cullum, G. W. *Biographical Register of the Officers and Graduates of the United States Military Academy at West Point, N. Y. From Its Establishment in 1802 to 1890.* Vols. I and II. Third edition. Boston and New York: Houghton, Mifflin and Company; Cambridge, Massachusetts: The Riverside Press, 1891.

Dawson , W. *The War That Was Never Fought.* New York: Auerbach Publishers, Inc., 1971.

Eckron, J. A. *Remembered Drums: A History of the Puget Sound Indian War.* Walla Walla, Washington: Pioneer Press Books, 1989.

Fuller, G.W. *A History of the Pacific Northwest.* Second edition revised. New York: Alfred A. Knoff, 1947.

Glassley, R. H. *Pacific Northwest Indian Wars.* Portland, Oregon: Binfords & Mort, Publishers, 1953.

Guie, H. Dean. *Bugles In the Valley, Garnett's Fort Simcoe.* Revised edition. Portland, Oregon: Glass-Dahlstrom, Printers, 1977.

Herr, J. K. and Wallace, E. S. *The Story of the U.S. Cavalry, 1775-1942*. Boston: Little, Brown & Co., 1953.

History of the Pacific Northwest: Oregon and Washington. Volume II. Portland, Oregon: North Pacific History Company, 1889.

Hussey, J. A. *The History of Fort Vancouver and Its Physical Structure*. Portland, Oregon: Abbott, Kerns & Bell Company, 1957.

Keyes, E. D. *Fighting Indians In Washington Territory*. Fairfield, Washington: Ye Galleon Press, 1988.

Kip, Lawrence. *Army Life of the Pacific*. New York: Redfield, 1859. (Reprinted in 1914 by William Abbatt, New York.)

Knuth, P. *Picturesque Frontier: The Army's Fort Dalles*. Second edition. Portland, Oregon: Oregon Historical Society Press, 1987.

Murray, K. A. *The Pig War*. Tacoma: Washington State Historical Society, 1988.

Nicandri, D. L. *Northwest Chiefs: Gustav Sohon's Views of the 1855 Stevens Treaty Councils*. Tacoma, Washington: Washington State Historical Society, 1986.

Powell, W. H. *List of Officers of the Army of the United States from 1779 to 1900*. New York: L. R. Homersley & Company, 1900.

_____ *A History of the Organization and Movements of the Fourth Regiment of Infantry, United States Army from May 30, 1796 to December 31, 1870, Together with a Record of the Military Services of All Officers Who Any Time Belonged to the Regiment*. Washington, D.C.: McGill & Witherow, 1871.

Register of Graduates and Former Cadets of the United States Military Academy. (Annual.) The Association of Graduates, United States Military Academy. West Point, New York.

Richards, Kent D. *Isaac Stevens: Young Man in a Hurry*. Provo, Utah: Brigham Young University Press, 1979.

Richardson, D. B. *Pig War Islands*. Eastwood, Washington: Orcas Publishing Company, 1971.

Ruby, R. H. and Brown, J. A. *A Guide to the Indian Tribes of the Pacific Northwest*. Norman, Oklahoma: University of Oklahoma Press, 1986.

Schlicke, C. P. *General George Wright: Guardian of the Pacific Northwest*. Norman, Oklahoma: University of Oklahoma Press, 1988.

Schwantes, C., Morrissey, K., Nicandri, D. and Strasser, S. *Washington: Images of a State's Heritage*. Spokane: Melior Publications, 1988.

Utley, R. H. *Frontiersmen in Blue: The United States Army and the Indian, 1848-1865*. New York: Macmillan Publishing Company, Inc., 1973.

Watt, R. F. *Four Wagons West, The Story of Seattle*. Portland, Oregon: Binford & Mort, Publishers, 1931.

Documents

Joint Task Force of the Governor's Advisory Council on Urban Affairs and the Governor's Indians Advisory Committee. *Are You Listening Neighbor?: Report of the Indian Task Force.* Olympia, Washington: State of Washington, 1971.

Nez Perce Country: A Handbook for Nez Perce National Historical Park Idaho. Washington, D.C.: National Park Service, U.S. Department of the Interior, 1983.

Washington National Guard.*The Official History of the Washington National Guard*, in 7 volumes, Camp Murray, Washington: Headquarters Washington National Guard, 1961. (Pamphlet ARNG 870-1-Series/ANG 210-1-series.)

Periodicals

Boxberger, D. L. and Taylor, H. C., Jr. "Treaty or Non-Treaty Status." *Columbia.* Fall, 1991, pp. 40-45.

Overmyer, P. H. "George B. McClellan and the Pacific Northwest." *The Pacific Northwest Quarterly.* Volume XXXII, Number 1, January, 1941.

BENJAMIN L. E. BONNEVILLE:

Cullum, G. W. *Biographical Register of the Officers and Graduates of the United States Military Academy at West Point, N. Y. From Its Establishment in 1802 to 1890.* Vol. I. Third edition. Boston and New York: Houghton, Mifflin and Company; Cambridge: The Riverside Press, 1891.

Fuller, G. W. *A History of the Pacific Northwest.* Second edition revised. New York: Alfred A. Knoff, 1947.

Irving, Washington. *The Rocky Mountains; or, Scenes, Incidents and Adventures in the Far West; Digested from the Journal of Captain B. L. E. Bonneville of the Army of the United States, and Illustrated from Various Other Sources..* Philadelphia: Carey, Lee & Blanchard, 1837. (Reprinted many times by various publishers.) (Reprinted as *The Adventures of Captain Bonneville with illustraions by Robert A. Reynolds*, Portland, Oregon: Binfords & Mort Publishers, 1957.)

Johnson, Allen, ed. *Dictionary of American Biography*, Volume I. New York: Charles Scribner's Sons, 1957.

ISAAC INGALLS STEVENS:

Buerge, David M. "Big Little Man: Isaac Stevens (1818-1861)," *Washingtonians: A Biographical Portrait of the State*, pp. 73-95. Edited by David Brewster and David M. Buerge, with an Introduction by Roger Sale. Seattle: Sasquatch Books, 1988.

Catton, Bruce. *The Centennial History of the Civil War.* 3 vols. Volume 2, *Terrible Swift Sword*; Volume 3, *Never Call Retreat.* Garden City, New York: Doubleday & Comapny, Inc., 1963, 1965.

"Cullum Files." Special Collections Division, United States Military Academy Library. West Point, New York.

Cullum, G. W. *Biographical Register of the Officers and Graduates of the United States Military Academy at West Point, N. Y. From Its Establishment in 1802 to 1890.* Vol. I. Third edition. Boston and New York: Houghton, Mifflin and Company; Cambridge: The Riverside Press, 1891.

Doty, James. *Journal of Operations of Governor Isaac I. Stevens of Washington in 1855.* Edited by Edward J. Kowrach. Fairfield, Washington: Ye Galleon Press, 1978.

Freeman, Douglas Southall. *R. E. Lee: A Biography.* 4 vols. Volume 1. New York: Charles Scribner's Sons, 1943.

_____. *Lee's Lieutenants: A Study in Command.* 3 vols. Volume II: *Cedar Mountain to Chancellorsville.* New York: Charles Scribner's Sons, 1943.

Fuller, George W. *A History of the Pacific Northwest.* Second edition revised. New York: Alfred A. Knoff, 1947.

Guie, H. Dean. *Bugles in the Valley: Garnett's Fort Simcoe.* Yakima, Washington: Republic Press, 1956.

Hazard, Joseph T. *Companion of Adventure: A Biography of Isaac Ingalls Stevens, First Governor of Washington Territory* Portland, Oregon: Binfords and Mort, 1952.

McClellan, George B. *McClellan's Own Story: The War for the Union.* New York: Charles L. Webster & Company, 1887.

Nicandri, David L. *Northwest Chiefs: Gustav Sohon's Views of the 1855 Stevens Treaty Councils.* Tacoma: Washington State Historical Society, 1986.

Register of Graduates and Former Cadets of the United States Military Academy. West Point, New York: Association of Graduates, United States Military Academy, 1990.

Richards, Kent D. *Isaac Stevens: Young Man in a Hurry.* Provo, Utah: Brigham Young University Press, 1979.

Schlicke, Carl P. *General George Wright: Guardian of the Pacific Coast.* Norman, Oklahoma and London: University of Oklahoma Press, 1988.

Stevens, Hazard. *The Life of General Isaac Ingalls Stevens.* 2 vols. Boston and New York: Houghton, Mifflin and Company; Cambridge, Massachusetts: The Riverside Press. Vol. I, 1900; Vol. II, 1901.

Stevens, Isaac Ingalls. Miscellaneous correspondence, reports, journals, writings, directives, and speeches, 1835-1862. Pacific Northwest Collection, Special Collections and Preservation Division, Allen Library, University of Washington.

Williams, Kenneth P. *Lincoln Finds a General: A Military Study of the Civil War.* 5 vols. Volume 1. New York: The Macmillan Company, 1950.

WILLIAM A. SLAUGHTER:

Bonney, W. P. *History of Pierce County, Washington*. Vol. I. Chicago: Pioneer Historical Publishing Company, 1927.

Cullum, G. W. *Biographical Register of the Officers and Graduates of the United States Military Academy at West Point, N. Y. From Its Establishment in 1802 to 1890*. Vol. II. Third edition. Boston and New York: Houghton, Mifflin and Company; Cambridge: The Riverside Press, 1891.

Eckron, J. A. *Remembered Drums: A History of the Puget Sound Indian War*. Walla Walla, Washington: Pioneer Press Books, 1989.

Richards, Kent D. *Isaac I. Stevens: Young Man in a Hurry*. Provo, Utah: Brigham Young University Press, 1979.

Spreen, Christopher A. *History of Steilacoom Lodge #2, F & AM 1854-1952*. Steilacoom, Wash.: Steilacoom Masonic Lodge, 1952.

AUGUST V. KAUTZ:

Cullum, G. W. *Biographical Register of the Officers and Graduates of the United States Military Academy at West Point, N. Y. From Its Establishment in 1802 to 1890*. Vol. II. Third edition. Boston and New York: Houghton, Mifflin and Company; Cambridge: The Riverside Press, 1891.

Kautz, August V. *Nothing Worthy of Note Transpired Today: The Northwest Journals of August V. Kautz*. Edited by Gary Fuller Reese. Tacoma: Tacoma Public Library, 1978.

Malone, Dumas, ed. *Dictionary of American Biography*, Volume I. New York: Charles Scribner's Sons, 1961.

Reese, Gary Fuller. *A Documentary History of Fort Steilacoom, Washington*. Tacoma: Tacoma Public Library, 1978.

Wallace, Andrew. *General August V. Kautz and the Southwestern Frontier*. Tucson: published by the author, 1967. (A copy is held by the Northwest Room, Tacoma Public Library.)

SILAS CASEY:

Cullum, G. W. *Biographical Register of the Officers and Graduates of the United States Military Academy at West Point, N. Y. From Its Establishment in 1802 to 1890*. Vol. I. Third edition. Boston and New York: Houghton, Mifflin and Company; Cambridge: The Riverside Press, 1891.

Curtis, J., Watson, A., and Bradley, B. *Town on the Sound: Stories of Steilacoom*. Steilacoom, Washington: Steilacoom Historical Museum Association, 1988.

Emmons, D. G. *Leschi of the Nisquallies*. Minneapolis: T. S. Dennison and Company, 1965.

Glassley, R. H. *Pacific Northwest Indian Wars*. Portland, Oregon: Binfords & Mort, Publishers, 1953.

Kautz, August V. *Nothing Worthy of Note Transpired Today: The Northwest Journals of August V. Kautz*. Edited by Gary Fuller Reese. Tacoma: Tacoma Public Library, 1978.

Morgan, M. *Puget's Sound: A Narrative of Early Tacoma and the Southern Sound*. Seattle: University of Washington Press, 1979.

Richards, K. D. "Isaac I. Stevens and Federal Military Power in Washington Territory." In Edwards, G. T. and Schwantes, C. A., editors, *Experiences in a Promised Land: Essays in Pacific Northwest History*. Seattle: University of Washington Press, 1986.

Schlicke, Carl P. *General George Wright: Guardian of the Pacific Coast*. Norman and London: University of Oklahoma Press, 1988.

Woodward, W. *Military Influences on Washington History*: Proceedings of a Conference Held at Camp Murray, Tacoma, March 29-31, 1984. Camp Murray, Washington: Headquarters, Washington National Guard, 1984.

GEORGE WRIGHT:

Army War College, The. *Indian Battles and Skirmishes on the Indian Frontier, 1790-1898*. (Tabulation of actions and casualties.)

Case, Mathew. *Northwest Frontier*. Bothell, Washington: BCS Educational Aids, 1982.

Cullum, G. W. *Biographical Register of the Officers and Graduates of the United States Military Academy at West Point, N. Y. From Its Establishment in 1802 to 1890*. Vol. I. Third edition. Boston and New York: Houghton, Mifflin and Company; Cambridge: The Riverside Press, 1891.

Doerksen, H. R. *The Columbia Basin Compact Issues Review*. Pullman, Washington: Pacific Northwest Regional Commission, 1975.

Dryden, Cecil. *Dryden's History of Washington*. Portland, Oregon: Binfords & Mort Publishers, 1968.

Fuller, G. W. *A History of the Pacific Northwest*. Second edition revised. New York: Alfred A. Knoff, 1947.

Glassley, R. H. *Indian Wars of the Pacific Northwest*. Portland, Oregon: Binfords & Mort, 1972.

Guie, H. Dean. *Bugles in the Valley*. Yakima, Washington: Republic Press, 1956.

Hunt, Herbert, and Kaylor, Floyd C. *Washington — West of the Cascades*. Vol. I. Denver: Clarke Publishing Co., 1917.

Keyes, E. D. *Fighting Indians In Washington Territory*. Fairfield, Washington: Ye Galleon Press, 1988.

Kip, Lawrence. *Army Life of the Pacific*. New York: Redfield, 1859. (Reprinted in 1914 by William Abbatt, New York.)

Schlicke, Carl P. *General George Wright: Guardian of the Pacific Coast*. Norman and London: University of Oklahoma Press, 1988.

Tannant, Elizabeth and Esther Reed. *Indian Battles in the Inland Empire*. Spokane, 1914.

EDWARD STEPTOE:

Bennett, R. A. *Walla Walla — Portrait of a Western Town (1804-1899)*. Walla Walla, Washington: Pioneer Press, 1980.

Converse, G. L. *A Military History of the Columbia Valley*. Walla Walla, Washington: Pioneer Press, 1989.

Cullum, G. W. *Biographical Register of the Officers and Graduates of the United States Military Academy at West Point, N. Y. From Its Establishment in 1802 to 1890*. Vol. I. Third edition. Boston and New York: Houghton, Mifflin and Company; Cambridge: The Riverside Press, 1891.

Glassley, R. H. *Indian Wars of the Pacific Northwest*. Portland, Oregon: Binfords & Mort, 1972.

Guie, H. Dean. *Bugles in the Valley*. Yakima, Washington: Republic Press, 1956.

Manring, B. F. *Conquest of the Coeur d'Alenes, Spokanes and Palouses*. Fairfield, Washington: Ye Galleon Press, 1975 (reprint; originally published by John Graham Co. in 1912).

GEORGE EDWARD PICKETT:

Brown, F. R. *History of the Ninth U.S. Infantry, 1799-1909*. Chicago: R. R. Donnelly & Sons Co., 1909.

Cullum, G. W. *Biographical Register of the Officers and Graduates of the United States Military Academy at West Point, N. Y. From Its Establishment in 1802 to 1890*. Vol. II. Third edition. Boston and New York: Houghton, Mifflin and Company; Cambridge: The Riverside Press, 1891.

Dryden, Cecil. *History of Washington*. Portland, Oregon: Binfords and Mort, 1968.

Freeman, Douglas Southall. *Lee's Lieutenants*, Vols. I, II, and III. New York: Charles Scribner's Sons, 1945.

Pickett, LaSalle Corbell (Mrs. George E. Pickett). *Pickett and His Men*. Philadelphia: J. B. Lippincott & Co., 1913.

Richardson, David. *Pig War Islands*. Eastwood, Washington: Orcas Publishing Co., 1971.

Schlicke, Carl P. *General George Wright: Guardian of the Pacific Coast*. Norman and London: University of Oklahoma Press, 1988.

JOHN MULLAN, JR.:

American Heritage Pictorial Atlas of United States History. New York: American Heritage Publishing Company, Inc., 1960.

Coleman, L. C. and Rieman, L. *Captain John Mullan: His Life. Building the Mullan Road; As It Is Today and Interesting Tales of Occurrence Along the Road*. Compiled by B. C. Payette. Montreal: Private printing for Payette Radio, Ltd. (A copy is held by the Northwest Room, Tacoma Public Library.)

Cullum, G. W. *Biographical Register of the Officers and Graduates of the United States Military Academy at West Point, N. Y. From Its Establishment in 1802 to 1890*. Vol. II. Third edition.

Boston and New York: Houghton, Mifflin and Company; Cambridge: The Riverside Press, 1891.

Erickson, H. "Mullan's 1862 Interstate Road." *The Franklin Flyer*. Volume 19, Number 1, April, 1986. Pasco, Washington: The Franklin County Historical Society, 1986.

Jackson, W. Turrentine. *Wagon Roads West: A Study of Federal Road Surveys and Construction of the Trans-Mississippi West*. Berkeley: University of California Press, 1952.

Malone, Dumas, ed. *Dictionary of American Biography*, Volume I. New York: Charles Scribner's Sons, 1961.

INDEX

Bolon, Andrew Jackson ("A. J.")   40, 109n, 117, 127
Bonneville, Benjamin, Louis Eulalie   3, 11, 18, 22-23, 28, 34, 36, 80, **84-91**, 98, 142
Bonneville Dam   85, 91
Bonneville, Nicholas de   85
Bonneville Power Administration   85, 91
"Bostons"   18, 26, 28, 32, 36, 40, 58n
Breckinridge, John C.   121-22
Brevet ranks, explained   20, 168n
Bridger, Jim   87
British Columbia   74-75, 187, 193
Brontes, The   49
Brother Jonathan (steamship)   163
Brown, J. Ross   172
Brulé Sioux Tribe   69
Buchanan, James   19, 69n, 73-75, 122, 184, 192
Buckley, Washington   45
Buckstead, John Wendell   6
Buena Vista, Battle of   47, 110n
Bull Run (Manassas), Battles of   122, 123, 123n, 163
Bush, George W.   21

Cadet Dialectic Society   94
Cadotte's Pass   25, 97
California   15, 17, 18, 22, 23, 26, 28, 34, 46, 48, 51, 61, 64, 66, 68, 69, 73n, 76, 77, 77n, 79, 86, 87, 91, 98, 126, 142, 143, 144, 150, 151-52, 162, 163, 173, 186, 203
California, Department of   69, 186
California, District of   163
camas   169, 176
Camp Bonneville   91
Camp Chehalis   75, 77, 134
Camp Colville   70
Camp Drum   22-23, 80
Camp Montgomery   129
Camp Pickett   193, 195
Camp Semiahmoo   134
Camp Stevens   36
Camp Vancouver   22
Camp Washington   27
Cape Flattery   32-33
Cape Horn   22, 23, 126
Cascade Indians   53-54, 144, 146
Cascade Range   9, 11, 12, 17, 19, 25, 27, 33, 36, 38, 40, 47, 49, 51, 53, 59, 97, 98, 100-01, 104, 104n, 106, 110n, 111, 111n, 113, 115, 127, 133, 135, 137, 138, 143, 149, 169
Cascades Massacre   53-54, 144-46, 169
Casey, Silas   11, 48, 50-52, 54, 59, 73-74, 112, **135-38**, 143-44, 183, 185, 190, 192-93
Cataldo, Idaho   202n

Jefferson Barracks, Missouri   134, 139, 141
Jefferson Davis, The   45n, 71
Jefferson, Thomas   17, 183
John Day River   70, 91
John Handcock, The   45n
"Joint Occupancy"   184
Joseph, Chief   16, 18, 38, 38n, 57
Joseph, Chief (younger)   38n
Joset, Father Joseph   62, 151, 159, 165, 180
Judith River   108
Julia, The   71

Kalispel Tribe   40, 70
Kamiakin   15, 26, 28, 36, 38-45, 52-55, 57, 62, 64, 68n, 70, 107n, 147-51, 156, 158-60
Kautz, August Valentine   11, 46, 51, 59, 75, **131-34**, 138
Kearny, Philip   123
Kellogg, Idaho   202
Kettle (Colville) Tribe   48, 55, 57, 70, 109
Kettle Falls   66
Keyes, Erasmus D.   47, 154, 154n, 155, 157, 158-59, 160, 164, 165
"King George Men"   18, 26, 28, 32, 58n
Kittitas Valley   147
Klickitat River   41
Klickitat Tribe   32, 38, 53, 144, 146, 169
Kutenai Tribe   40, 107-08

Lafayette, Marquis de   85
Land Donation Act of 1850   29, 103-04, 117
Lander, Judge Edward   99n, 111n
Lane, Joseph   90
Lapwai   15, 48
Larnard, Charles H.   28
Latah Creek   159
Lawyer, Chief   15-16, 36-39, 38n, 48, 55, 57, 63, 80, 107, 161, 172
Leavenworth, Henry   139
Lee, Robert E.   95, 123n, 181, 181n
Leonard, Zenas   87n
Leschi   32, 45, 49, 49n, 50n, 59-60, 117n, 129, 138
Lewis and Clark Expedition   17, 80, 98, 109, 183
Lewis, Meriwether   17, 36, 80, 98, 109, 183
Liche, William   161
Lincoln, Abraham   76, 95n, 122-24, 134, 181
Longmire, James   32, 45, 52
Longstreet, James   181, 181n, 183, 185
Looking Glass, Chief   38, 57, 161

Treaty of 1846 (Treaty of Washington)   19, 23, 71, 73, 75, 100, 184, 185, 192
   100, 184, 185, 192
Treaty of Guadalupe Hidalgo 126
"Treaty of Olympia"   33, 104n
Treaty of Walla Walla   172
Treaty of Washington (Treaty of 1846)   19, 23, 71, 73, 75, 100, 184, 185, 192
Tribune (frigate)   188-92
Troy, New York   141
Tucannon River   67, 67n, 152, 202
Twana Tribe   32
Tyler, John   19, 141
Tyler, Robert O.   155, 155n, 157

U.S. Army Engineers   20, 24, 95, 95n
U.S.-Canada Border Commission   134
U.S. Coast and Geodetic Survey   95n
U.S. Marines   49-50
U.S. Navy   49, 113
U.S.S. Ohio   126
"Ultimate Map"   18-19
Umatilla Agency   76
Umatilla Tribe   37, 39, 56-57, 107
Umpaqua River   17
Union Academy, Olympia   186
Union Army   66n, 67-68n, 74n, 95n, 123, 123n, 125, 196
Union Pacific Railroad   98
United States Coast Survey   24, 95, 95n, 96
Utley, Robert M.   20

Van Buren, Martin   18
Vancleave, J. S.   173
Vancouver Central Park   91
Vancouver Island   14, 19, 27, 32, 71, 99, 183-87, 192
Vera Cruz, Battle of   88, 95, 141
Victoria, Vancouver Island   27, 73, 75, 99, 111, 185-87, 191
Vincent, Chief   159

Waiilatpu 202
Waite, Edward 163
Walker, Joseph Reddeford   85-88, 87n, 91
Walla Walla Council, First   15, 16, 36-40, 38n, 48, 106, 107, 107n, 109n
Walla Walla Council, Second   55-58, 59, 107, 107n, 113-15, 169-70
Walla Walla County   173
Walla Walla River   15-17, 19, 21, 24, 36, 43, 48, 52-57, 61, 87, 110, 113, 115, 143, 144,
   149, 150, 160, 166, 167, 169, 170

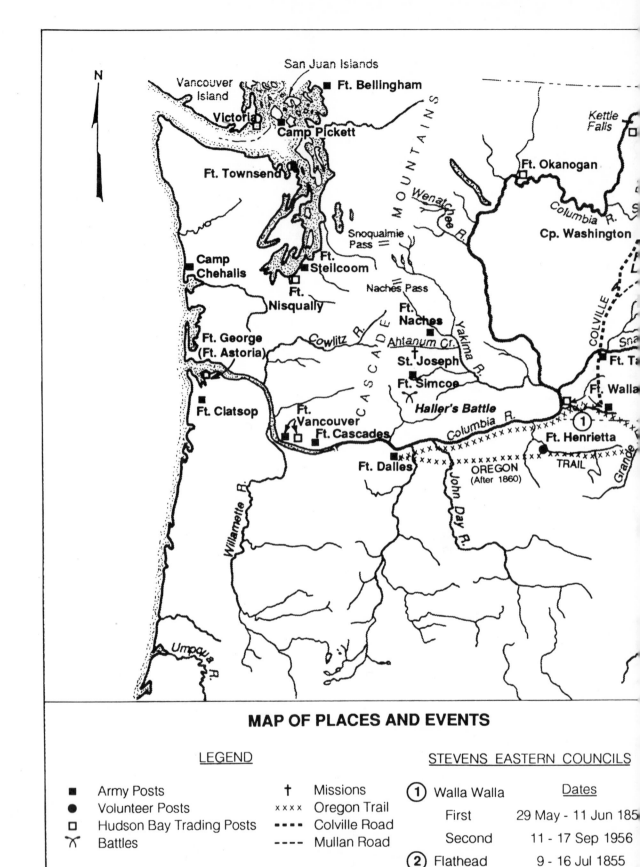

MAP OF PLACES AND EVENTS

LEGEND

- ■ Army Posts
- ● Volunteer Posts
- □ Hudson Bay Trading Posts
- ⋊ Battles
- † Missions
- xxxx Oregon Trail
- ---- Colville Road
- ---- Mullan Road

0	60	120

Scale in Miles

STEVENS EASTERN COUNCILS

		Dates
①	Walla Walla	
	First	29 May - 11 Jun 185
	Second	11 - 17 Sep 1956
②	Flathead	9 - 16 Jul 1855
③	Blackfoot	16 - 18 Oct 1855
④	Spokane	4 - 5 Dec 1855